TURNING WITHIN

Reclaiming Your

Soul from Shadow

Steven Twohig, Sr.

TURNING WITHIN
Soul from Shadow

COPYRIGHT © 2024 by Steven Twohig, Sr.

Cover Art by Klassic Designs of 99Designs, LLC

Published by: Mastering Change, LLC

Contact Information: steven@MasteringChange.com
WEBSITE: MasteringChange.com

Publishing History
Print Book ISBN- 979-8-9897122-0-5
Digital ISBN- 979-8-9897122-1-2
Library of Congress 2024910596

Contents

Contents

Poem:

Time Was When the Wood Floor Talked

I am living proof that once you have experienced the oaken wood floor
come alive in technicolor and begin talking with you,
life as you know it changes, nothing can ever be the same again.
In the curves and bends of infinity wrapping its figure-eight self
around itself,
have I not already experienced this rebirthing of recall?
Am I not meant to be here now awaiting the cycle of repetition,
to return to this sacred spot, to find anew the mystery teachers
who have steeped themselves in the medicine not sought or taught in
the West?
Listen with me now, the wood floor is speaking, to me, to you, listen.

—Paul Goldman

Dedication

For my children. May this book help walk you out of the generational shadows I unconsciously handed over to you. May this book help you find your own path, your own axis mundi, and your own unfolding. This book was written for you. For all of my teachers, those who shared their work with me and those who helped me understand my own, may this book continue the conversation you and I have been blessed to participate in. For the weary seeker, take a seat, sit down, and take a load off. May you find light in the darkest of places.

Preface

Turning Within is written to support the transitional moments of everyone's life. It's constructed to help you gain insights into the most important parts of you. This content is developed to usher you through the core of your resistance, which at some point in your life's journey *must* be navigated in the dark nights of your soul. This book is your navigator's manual. Welcome to the journey!

I've practiced a form of life enhancement called *Shadow Work* for twenty-three years. In this book, I present to you the benefits of my gathered wisdom. Your journey begins with understanding *meaning*. Without that understanding, there can be no emotional engagement in life. Without meaning, life is nothing but a muddle.

The work you are about to embark on is deeply rooted in my extensive experience and the transformative journeys I have facilitated for countless individuals. This practice has the power to profoundly influence various dimensions of your existence. It touches the very essence of your self-identification.

Shadow Work is instrumental in enhancing emotional intelligence, fostering healthier relationships, catalyzing professional and personal growth, navigating life transitions with grace, and it is critical in the realms of creativity and spiritual exploration. *Meaning* is the subjective interpretation that emerges from the interaction between our external world and internal mental states of emotion, cognition, and context.

It's time for you to take control of the meaning you've made—yes, you create your meaning from your external world and your internal mental states. Your *genius* is the unique expression of the universe that can only come through you. Understanding that *you* make meaning offers you the opportunity to no longer be controlled by that meaning. When you take control, you become open to everything becoming a miracle.

The process, *Closing the Circuit*, presented in this book, is practiced, tweaked, refined, and enhanced through integration groups maintained by a community of committed Shadow Guides and practitioners. Our circle—a gathering of guides and practitioners—is a "container," a sacred, safe space of energy, which becomes a cauldron brimming with healing and insights. We offer these containers to deepen our practice and support the revealing of the innate genius of the human spirit, which lives in each of us.

The seekers who have come, and continue to participate in these circles, are gift-givers. Everyone in the circle may learn from the work of another, as well as, their own. Each of us comes to the circle as an equal. The "teacher" comes through the person who presents their work in the container. We become a tribe, sharing in our work while holding space for one another and witnessing the work done by others.

The space held by this container is the soil by which this book took root. I have written this book while standing on the shoulders of this tribe. The tribe is standing with many other tribes doing this powerful work. After all, I believe some wounds heal best within a community. This is the reason this book exists—to support the community of seekers in their Shadow Work.

And you need to know, this book isn't meant to be read—it's meant to be experienced.

A final note: As a Shadow Guide, the very nature of my practice requires confidentiality. Therefore, trusting your guide is paramount because when doing this work, you operate in the dark where monsters dwell. My promise is never to knowingly betray your trust. However, I also understand the power of story (more on that later) and its value in helping each of us feel we aren't alone in our struggle. Stories are the most effective and sometimes the only way to convey a message. Throughout the book, I sought to balance the need to share my clients' stories with you, the reader, with my vow of confidentiality to my clients, students, brothers, and sisters—ultimately, they are my teachers.

Thank you to those who have permitted me to step, as best I am able, where you have stepped. Through your work, I strive to light-up the work in others through going back to our time together and remembering those threshold-moments.

I thank you.

Steven Twohig, Sr

P.S. This book isn't meant to be read—it's meant to be experienced.

Excerpts From Your Journey
Through *Turning Within*

"Being born isn't living. Being born is the invitation to live."

"This is your opportunity to be you, which is only possible with light and dark mixed and mastered."

"Shadow presents itself in "the now" as an echo of the past."

"You can't have a relationship with anything else but through your initial relationship with yourself."

"The more faith you put in trusting the process, the more insights this process will reveal to you."

"The identity you created... flows through your life, connecting all you hold sacred."

"Change your identity, change your life."

"The impact is geometric, not linear."

Remember
this book isn't meant to be read; it's meant to be experienced.

Chapter 1
Welcome!

If you are reading this book, you are being presented with an opportunity. I need you to know I will continue to remind you, from this point forward, this book isn't meant to be read—it's meant to be experienced.

Whether by happenstance or suggested by a loved one, you have stumbled onto a doorway. For those who are here for something other than the opportunity to create a practice of Shadow Work, you'll still find this book entertaining and worth the read.

However, for those of you seeking something more, you have found the entry point—the first portal. It's the wink and nod from the universe, the white rabbit worth chasing, the beginning of a lifelong journey.

For those of you who may be farther down the path, this book offers you a deeper dive into your journey. Within you there sits something beyond the ordinary, something beneath the surface. This book is the portal to that part of you.

The first door you will open is the one offering the foundational understanding of meaning.

Meaning is the value an individual borrows or gives to life. It is this creation that becomes the very building blocks of your experience.

- *Emotional meaning relates to the value or importance we attach to different experiences.*
- *Cognitive meaning involves the interpretation and understanding we derive from these experiences.*
- *Contextual meaning is influenced by our cultural, social, and personal backgrounds.*

Consider how the mind is like emerging extended-reality (XR) glasses technology and it gives a person an augmented reality, which they aren't aware is present.

This mind-system has highly advanced Artificial Intelligence (AI) programmed to constantly scan for danger. This part of the mind has been infected with a virus which inflates the risk individuals experience. This mind-virus needs to be purged from the system of all our minds, otherwise our society will remain hobbled and mired in suffering.

This journey of Turning Within will wind you downward into the deep recesses of the dark forest within you. The overgrown meaning you've created over a lifetime of programming is where you track shadows of monsters and demons plaguing you. Unchecked, you are in the clutches of a modern-day possession *and* it's your own creation.

When embracing your journey, it will take you through the forest and across the vistas of your mind. You will travel to peaks of mountains you've forgotten you dwelled. You will travel along shores and flow with the current. You will visit the sacred, living within you now. The identity you created are sacred moments held together by whispers, for love never shouts, demands, or seeks to take the spotlight. It flows through your life, connecting all you hold sacred.

This book strives to show you the path of "unlearning" to support you in a safe place to unpack your issues and then heal. The Welsh have a word, *"Cwtch"* (pronounced *'kutch,'* to rhyme with 'butch'). It's their word for a cuddle or hug, but even more, it's a feeling of safe space, of home. By learning to hold space for yourself, you unlock possibilities of growth and discovery that are kept from your conscious awareness. I hope this unlearning sparks a practice for you which you will carry for the rest of your life—and my hope is you will create your "*Cwtch*."

Why this book

The mind is designed to create meaning. It creates meaning by creating layers and layers of story. All day and night, your mind asks, "What does this mean?" That question widens into, "What does I, this, that, and all of this relating to that, actually mean?"

Over and over again, you are studying existence. You are magnetized and hypnotized by it. Your narrative is overrun by it. But mostly, you have numbed yourself and became unconscious of it. That unconsciousness has become your undoing.

You are so attached to creating meaning and living out of the story that your mind continues the process even while you're asleep. You're a compella-tion of the stories you tell yourself.

Each of us is a unique, unduplicatable light signature. Your insight, perspective, and distinctive way of moving through time and space shall never exist again. In the architecture of your being, you yearn for your genius to come forward.

You can grab onto a thought and design a strategy to make your thought "real," acting on a strategy to manifest an idea into a tangible thing. Humans are the only animal to understand the concept of *thoughts become things*. Another way to say it is—thoughts are "realized."

I believe manifesting *thoughts to things* is fundamental to our core design, our true purpose, our ability to make our dreams real. This book aims to guide you to locating and learning to cultivate your genius. It begins with the mind.

The processing capacity of the conscious mind has been estimated at only *forty to fifty bits per second*. Neurons are collectively the "attentional filter." But how does it present those forty to fifty bits?

Yet, the human mind is projected to be able to process eleven million. The mind, using a simulation system, decides what comes through, how, and what receives attention and focus. This advanced process, honed over countless eons, is how we operate in such a fast-paced world. Without it, we'd be dead. We'd have no filter to protect us, no common sense, which could result in anyone of us walking out in front of an oncoming bus. However, the fact that the mind processes doesn't guarantee its simulation system displays accurately. Without tuning it, it becomes trapped in loops of suffering.

The challenge for most of us is understanding our mind's programming, how to maintain the system, and to grasp where it exists. Without tuning, we are trapped in loops of suffering, a simulation, which blinds us to our reality. Our system has been hijacked by over 3.5-million years of programming— programing for our survival. It reaches all the way back to the extinction of the Australopithecus africanus.

In our current state, it's suggested we suffer from twenty-four Cognitive Biases, such as attack thoughts, awfulizing, negative bias, and confirmation bias. The Biases are designed to simulate a worst-case scenario of what could, is, or did happen. All of the biases are naturally designed to keep us safe in the world. All are shortcuts. All are done with literally little to no thought on our part.

Our world is under a plague—a virus of the mind. You can sense it in the air. You hear it in the music. You see it in the eyes of people you meet. This mind-virus has spread into all corners of the globe. An impending doom, an Armageddon moment, lodged like a wedge in people's lives through unmaintained *meaning* we've created in a world, which is both asleep *and* on fire.

I sometimes wonder what it would be like to be blindfolded on a game show and told to reach into a bag filled with spiders—I detest spiders. But I must reach into the bag anyway. Or I'm blindfolded in a room with razor-sharp knives at every turn. Then, I imagine moving through the room, anticipating each painful jabbed, stab, or slice.

Imagine what's happening inside you as you face this risk.

- What pain do you anticipate avoiding in your life?
- What is the cycle of suffering you experience over and over?
- What is the life you resist living?

Now is the time to take off the blindfold.

In our current times, going through trauma is not rare. A random quote on the internet suggests approximately six-of-every-ten men and five-of-every-ten women experience at least one trauma in their lifetime. But Peter Levine, the developer of Somatic Experiencing®, a naturalistic with a neurobiological approach to healing trauma, suggests trauma is part of life. The birthing process itself is a traumatic act. Stanislav Grof, the founder of holotropic breathwork, an innovative form of experiential psychotherapy used worldwide, built a large body of work on the "Four Matrices of Birth," which he calls the first trauma.

Most of the world's population simply manages the circumstances of their lives rather than building their ideal world. The circumstance we manage is what author and rabbi Marc Gafne calls "The False Self."

As humans, we are programmed to operate at a specific frequency and will do *anything* to stay at that frequency, even when our mind is plotting our demise. We lie to ourselves, thinking we're navigating our life. However, *the meaning we make becomes the meaning we reinforce.* This is our False Self.

I have often heard someone express their feeling of "just getting by." They're operating from their False Self, staying in the frequency they know, that zone where they've made meaning, where their mind is survival-rooted. It's a place where pain rules their day.

That is the initial reason I came to Shadow Work. The pain had to stop—or I wouldn't survive. I was trapped in a basement I couldn't see—a prison with no walls. After multiple suicide attempts, being trapped in addiction, and failing at every level, I needed to learn to reprogram the years and years of faulty code. My mind had had enough.

I was introduced to my Shadow on April 14, 2000, introduced to a part of myself which was unconsciously always on the run. In doing Shadow Work, whenever I felt triggered, I learned an awareness about my feelings. Feelings became threads that allowed me to see my programing. In turn, programing provided a visual of how the mind structures my experience of reality. Yet, some of the layers of my programmed code were more painful than what my conscious mind could process.

There is a greater danger which accompanies being stuck on a reaction, such as my reaction to feeling trapped in a basement. My assumption of tomorrow being the same as yesterday, caused me to make decisions based on old information. I needed to understand how holding on to the past gave yesterday power over today. However, nothing truly stays the same.

The velocity of change in our world continues to speed up. Change that typically happened in a hundred years has been condensed to within ten years. Velocity has amped up, and what used to happen about every ten years is now an annual occurrence. The world is faster, deeper, and more connected through technology and information than ever in our known history.

Both individually and globally, we are faced with increasing circumstances to manage. This draws more and more of our focus to the outside world and reduces our time to work on what's going on inside of us.

Today, an added twist takes our challenges to a new level. We exist in a virtual world, creators all around us. Change is speeding up even more. The velocity of the advancement of AI will highlight our one human super-power—the ability to create and navigate meaning.

Now, a new reality is awaiting you. Your automated—the mind puts meaning on autopilot— decisions derived from your False Self won't cut it any longer. You're on the verge of something remarkable.

Beware, the information you'll discover while going through this book isn't necessarily going to feel good at times. If you're like any of the tens of thousands of people I've worked with, you have a gnawing feeling there is more to see right in front of you, but you keep experiencing the same loops of suffering. Therefore, you must find a way to get clear on *how* you're blind. The time has come for you to evolve your thinking around how you maintain the software that is your mind.

Your journey starts with you looking in the one place you are least willing to go. This book is your roadmap.

Chapter 2

Packing for the Journey Begins

Finding the Boogie-Man Process

I remember, during my childhood, being fear-stricken about the "Boogie Man." My mind would get the best of me. My mental simulation would overtake my rational thoughts, resulting in me burrowing under the blanket to hide. I believed if the Boogie Man couldn't see me, then I'd be safe. Have you had a similar experience?

The Experiential Adventure: Remember, this book is not just a read, but an experiential adventure diving into your consciousness. Are you ready to face the demons lurking in your Shadows?

Recalling Childhood Fears: Close your eyes and take a deep breath. Can you remember a time from your childhood when you were lying in bed, afraid of the dark or the Boogie Man?

The Blanket Shield: Did you ever hide under a blanket, thinking you'd be safe if the Boogie Man couldn't see you? Was there a time when you let your mind get the best of you? Remember how your mind plays games with you?

Self-Deception Check: If you find it hard to admit to these fears, then ask yourself—If you're lying to yourself about this, what else might you be lying to yourself about?

Locating the Feeling: Can you identify *where* in your body you carry that old feeling of fear? Take a moment, take a pause, and locate where it resides.

Reclaiming Light: As you venture through this book, you'll have the opportunity to confront your fears and reclaim the light stolen from you. How does that possibility make you feel?

Commitment to the Journey: Are you committed to taking this journey, knowing it will require you to face fears more substantially activated in your life than you may currently be aware?

Moving forward, take your time with each question. Engage fully with the experience it offers. This is the first step in a journey deep into your understanding of yourself and the world around you.

The Next Step is only 2mm Away

Look at your life experience subjectively, examining what you think, believe, feel based on your personal opinions rather than facts. Where does the symbol of the Boogie Man, aka fear, live in your life story today? Are you able to identify the space where your mind fixates and magnifies the fear? Is it your financial situation? Is it regarding your relationships? Is it dread of death? What's your grown-up version of the Boogie Man?

Now, notice what you created as your blanket of protection. Top of Form

Like Alice in Lewis Carroll's *Alice in Wonderland*, your journey appears and takes you through your looking glass.

- You'll learn basic concepts to serve and support your ongoing practice of Shadow Work. It matters not whether you're a newbie or advanced in this work.
- You'll connect with sacred and profane identities you've kept from your conscious awareness.
- You'll learn maintenance of your sacred looking-glass, your navigation equipment. Along the way, you'll dive into the depths of your human emotion.

This book is written to remind you of things, concepts, ideas you have known for so long, however, you have forgotten you knew them.

As you remember, you'll wake up. Waking up only requires you to shine a light in a few key areas. Know this: **The problem isn't the Boogie Man. It's the blanket still pulled over your head.**

It's time for you to awaken to your true self. It's time to pull back the blanket. It's time to take your power back.

How to read this book: You have to be there

We will be using well-known and worn maps of human experience, which I have curated over twenty-two years of research into how deep-change happens. I have spent years in dark holes copying sacred scrolls and rediscovering the lost knowledge stripped from us. This knowing sits across the bridge of your personal mythology. The gateway to change is what is being presented to you. Yet, how you traverse the landscape, once crossing through the gateway, can't be taught. It must be experienced.

One of the many teachers I was blessed with was my Uncle Dave. He taught me how to swim. How to move my body in the water. How to breathe—with my head in and out of the water. He also taught me the value of the statement, "You kinda of have to be there."

Uncle Dave was an ex-Marine and one of my true heroes. He had open-heart surgery after getting stabbed in a bar fight with two men. He was "Oorah" tough. I was lucky to have him in my life, though his teaching style was abrupt, clear, to the point.

I still recall the specific day I learned to swim. The memory takes me right back there. Uncle Dave had me lie down on the couch to practice swimming, moving my arms and legs. He laughed when I got tangled up. The dark brown couch cushions were a poor substitute for water, which was what I was about to conquer.

"Close enough," he snickered.

"No, no, it isn't! NOT EVEN CLOSE!" I pleaded, "Don't make me go." In my mind, I had zero chance of surviving the experience.

Then he took me to a lake in my hometown, rowed out to the middle, threw me in.

In that moment, I knew I could swim.

Some things can't be learned. They must be experienced.

This will be the first and only time I recommend the *how* first. Usually, *how* is the terrorist sabotaging your dreams at night. With this book, the *how* will lead you to a portal I have developed over twenty-three years of working in the human-development field. My focused study and purpose were to learn to create and hold space for people to change. That's what I offer you with this book. It's a portal to be opened and leveraged repeatedly—anywhere, anytime—to transport you to real change—transformation at the highest and most profound level of your existence.

But I cannot take this journey for you. In the words of Uncle Dave, "You kinda of have to be there." Thus, I am sending you these words as guideposts for your journey.

How does the portal open? You bring your energy, your raw, powerful, and unique energy. Then, once you've charged the portal, it's up to you to step through it.

You will do your own work. This is how it has always been. Whatever struggle you have brought through the portal with you, I believe this book will help light up the doorway for you to step through the struggle and begin a journey to true healing.

This is the tricky part; it will likely hurt.

The Western mind has been programmed to avoid pain at all costs, even unconsciously avoiding areas where change is ready to happen. You will be lighting up the frames of conceptual meaning and holograms that have left you trapped in a simulated hell of your unconscious design. Let your tears be the cleansing purge that bring flowers to bloom.

Lighting up the frame requires more of you than just thinking "about" things. You will need to remember them.

Once again, you will need to remember them.

You will need to jump in the water and swim in them.

Jump in and swim.

That means you allow yourself to go into the subjective experience of your suffering, which is the very thing you have been unconsciously programmed to avoid all of your life. It's the difference between the first-person and third-person experience. In first-person, you're sharing your experience as the narrator of the story. In third person, your story is told to others through characters, and you, as the narrator are not seen, you're not directly speaking your experience.

People often find me when they're seeking a solution to their pain. They're weary of disappointing encounters, claiming to have the key to end their suffering. They have taken all the workshops, read countless books, and remain feeling as though they are slowly bleeding out.

This is because they are *reading* about change. You must walk through the portal and take the journey.

You are the key to changing you.

Turning Within will guide you to yourself. If you're looking for another book to teach you something, you've picked the wrong book. If you're reading this book, it offers the path to the gateway to your answers. The only way you will find them is to take the journey. This book isn't meant to be read—it's meant to be experienced.

Let Me Stress: The only way out is through.

And again, as Uncle Dave said, "You kind of have to be there."

It's time to stop avoiding and start standing your ground. In doing so, you will take a trip beyond the container you identify as you. The time has come. *Feel* what it feels like to be at the beginning of this exciting and dangerous journey.

One note of caution before we continue.

Caution When Practicing Turning Within

Embarking on the journey of Shadow Work is a transformative and deeply personal experience. It's a pathway to profound insights, healing, and a more meaningful life. However, it's essential to approach this work with caution and awareness. As Carl Jung once said, "One does not become enlightened by imagining figures of light, but by making the darkness conscious."

The mind is a complex and intricate landscape, and while it may not give us more than we can handle, it sometimes places more trust in us than we place in ourselves. This can make the process of Shadow Work both challenging and disorienting. It's crucial to remember that Shadow Work is a marathon, not a sprint. The initial stages can be dramatic and impactful, but the fundamental transformation comes from consistent, long-term practice.

Clinical and forensic psychologist Dr. Stephen A. Diamond, warns, "Becoming conscious of these dark aspects can be a painful and horrific process." This underscores the importance of pacing yourself and seeking professional guidance when necessary. Another expert, Dr. Robert Augustus Masters, adds, "If Shadow Work is done prematurely—without adequate preparation, understanding, maturity, and ego strength—it can backfire, fostering further dissociation, re-traumatization, and harm."

Turning Within will challenge you. It can be difficult on a good day. Your mind wants to stay on automation. Shadow Work, therefore, requires form, focus, and patience. As a result, seeking support is vital. Whether it's a certified guide or a community of like-minded individuals, having external support provides a safety net when the work pushes you hard into overwhelm. Professionals and communities offer additional perspectives, coping strategies, and resources to help you navigate the complexities of your inner world.

Moreover, Shadow Work cannot replace professional medical advice and treatment if you're dealing with mental health issues, trauma, or other significant challenges.

Shadow Work has been proven, when paired with any human development technology, both traditional and non-traditional, to create a powerful entourage effect of support. Yes, even the bravest heroes need allies. Therefore, precautions safeguard your mental and emotional well-being and set the stage for a more meaningful and effective practice. Noticing how you engage in this new way can give you massive insights into how you operate under the crust of the 120 bits of data you think you are.

Your journey into the Shadow is courageous. So, as you Turn Within, do so with caution.

Respect the process and keep an open heart.

Trust in the process.

And the journey begins.

Chapter 3

Let's Talk About Change

The Circle, The Square, and The Triangle

Once upon a time, there lived a square. She lived in a box, drove a box, and even worked on a box. She found herself yearning as all living beings do. She felt as though there must be something more. Life seemed paper thin. Her edges were becoming worn and sore from constantly bumping up against life.

One day, she came upon a magic mirror. Looking at herself for the first time, she became aware of how her edges defined her. She was disgusted by the way life had treated her edges. As a square, she felt triggered all the time, her edges always catching on everything. She experienced life as though it were flat. Nothing had any flavor. She searched desperately to end this feeling, unable to live such a sharp existence. She searched every corner of her existence and couldn't find what she needed to take the edge off.

One day, she saw a group of triangles. She felt they moved about the world with a sense of balance. Because they had fewer edges, she thought, "Surely a triangle is better; look at their balance." She marveled at the thought of having fewer edges to run into things. She would hide one less area of her life from the world. "This is what I must become."

So, she toiled day and night, changing herself to the very core. She ate what triangle people ate (slices of pizza, slices of pie, slices from a wedge of cheese) and went where the triangle people went—visiting the Louvre in Paris. The pyramids of Egypt left her in awe.

Soon, after enough pain and enough work, she looked in the magic mirror and noticed she had changed into a triangle, having shoved a corner down so far, she finally had only three sides. Everyone called it a miracle.

Immediately, she experienced even more sadness and still felt edgy inside. "How do I get rid of this edginess inside of me?" she anguished. Would she ever find peace? "No matter how many corners I have, they always leave me feeling like I don't fit in."

Wandering along, she then noticed something she never thought possible. She saw the circle people. "There it is," she cried. "There is my answer. I shall remove all my edges. There will be no end and no beginning for me." The problem, she realized, was her sharpness. "I need to hide all my edges. I SHALL BE SO SPIRITUAL! I WILL BECOME ONE WITH GOD!"

She got to work, cutting out anything with edges from her life, and moved into a geo-dome. For the first time, she loved how she aligned with Mother Earth. Her search carried her deeper and deeper into the meaning of a circle. She kept coming back to herself, becoming spiritual. Finally, she had no corners for anyone to bump into and began to roll through life with relative ease.

However, she felt so ashamed each time someone saw her sore, worn corners, especially those moments where her corners would spring out. Those corners caught onto everything, causing herself and everyone around her pain. She reached her breaking point due to her inability to contain them.

She finally came to the magic mirror and again became distraught—she still felt empty inside. Her life was hollow. She gasped. She had blamed her edges for the empty feeling in her soul. Beyond the hollowness, she now also felt the flatness of her existence. This chilled her to her core.

Chasing something you believe will make you feel better, getting it, and then realizing nothing changed made her feel worse. "This is dreadful." she thought.

While sitting and munching on a doughnut, she noticed a square beside her on the bench, wearing the goofiest smile. It was as though he didn't have a care in the world.

"Why do you smile so, dear Square? Life is pointless! I have worked to remove all that catches on me in this world and still feel terrible inside."

Square stroked his chin in contemplation. "Would you like to know why you suffer? Would you like to know the nature of your pain?" he offered.

Circle noticed how he radiated happiness. "How," she pleaded. "How do you look as though you don't have a care in this world?"

Square smiled. "You miss the point completely," he quipped. "You think if you change your external self, you will feel enough, whole, as though your physical identity is the very problem. You have spent your life trying to become something other than yourself. This is not the true nature of transformation. Would you trust me with your mirror for a moment so I may show you the truth?"

She resisted giving up the mirror. Although it had brought her nothing but pain, the mirror showed her more than she could see on her own. Reluctantly, she handed Square the mirror. "How much worse can it get?" she thought.

Square took ownership of the mirror with certainty and confidence. Square's skills impressed Circle with the sense that Square had held this mirror before, holding it with a sacred reverence for what it could convey. He gazed into the mirror.

Circle noticed how he looked at himself with compassion and understanding. And there was something more, something greater, something deeper—it was love. Something she had never felt for herself.

He then spun the mirror to face her.

"What do you see?" he asked.

"I see someone who is ugly, hollow, flat. I am a failure. I spent my entire life becoming something I am not. I go through life hiding my edges from the world. This is the closest I have gotten to feeling okay. And, in the end, it makes me feel worse." She tried to look away, but Square held firm.

"Show me?" Square asked.

"Please, no," Circle pleaded. "It hurts!"

"Yes, but isn't it true your suffering is always there? No matter whether edges show or not?"

"Oh god, yes! It hurts so bad." Circle's pain began to intensify.

"Follow that thread." He pointed to the space inside of her, something she had never seen. "The way out is through. It is the only way."

At first, Circle's pain intensified, but after a second… Circle let go. She opened to her suffering. Then felt something different. Grief brought something to the surface. Something new. Something she had no words to describe. It existed beyond anything she had words for. "What am I seeing?"

"Depth," replied Square.

She glanced at him and saw he was no longer square. He'd transformed into a cube.

"You see," Cube revealed, "Your suffering is only a vehicle; it opens you to see the parts of you which you have kept hidden from yourself. You suffer because you are making *this* plane the whole of your experience. By opening yourself up to where you have suffered, you become conscious of the depth of who you are. The nature of transformation isn't for a square to become a triangle and then eventually a circle. It's about the square becoming the cube, a triangle transforming into a pyramid, and a circle growing into a sphere. You step past the material world and are no longer trapped in a flat existence."

Circle again gazed into the sacred mirror.

"With compassion," Cube instructed.

Softening her gaze, the brilliance of who she was revealed itself to her. She was so much more than she had ever imagined. She sobbed with healing waves of gratitude.

"Yes." Cube nodded. "Isn't it beautiful?"

Suddenly, she transformed into a sphere, and then a globe, transforming into Mother Earth.

This is Change

By choosing to do your work, you do the work for the whole planet.

Let's begin. Right now, as you read these words, you hear a voice in your head speaking them. However, the voice is in your head. Right now, speak and say, "Hello."

Hear that? That's not my voice, it's a thought generated by your mind.

Now, hold your breath for a second.

Hold it.

Now, breathe again.

What just happened?

What happened with that breath work? You took control of your breath. Like your breath, the mind can be controlled, even directed. But once you stop paying attention to your breath, what happens? It goes back to automatic pilot. You breathe again. In the mind, when you remove your focus, it begins to chatter again.

Now notice how much more sits in your mind than just your focus on this book. Notice all the worries and backstories. Notice all the layers and layers of thought your mind is producing.

All those semi-conscious thoughts, running in the background, are painting your life experience at a deeper level than you understand. Shadow is the result of your conscious mind rejecting the meaning you cling to in order to make sense of your reality. We call that meaning a "construct." You possess constructs that were unconsciously created and mindlessly strengthened over a lifetime of miseducation.

You have the ability to re-write all of that coding.

If you didn't go through the breath exercise above, please, go back and go through it now. Don't just read it. It's there because it's important. This book contains layers of insights that can't be taught—it must be earned through your work.

Now, please take a moment to answer the questions below. No need to write down the questions and answers unless you feel called to do so. Here, this is setting the stage for the work you are about to do.

Your Call to Adventure: Questions to Ponder

We are looking for nothing short of a metanoia—a profound, usually spiritual, transformation.

In classical Greek, *metanoia* (met*a*noi*a) is to change one's mind, to expand it in such a way as to have a new perspective on oneself or the world. When personified, Metanoia was a figure of unclear description who accompanied Kairos, the god of Opportunity, and ultimately inspired human individuals to make deep changes in their normal consciousness modes; a feeling of personal regret would provide the emotional catalyst to approach life with a substantially different perspective.

The lesson is in the telling, the living through an experience. You then delve into the decided place you've created through knowing what you want and knowing what you don't want. Yet, when you willingly to change your mind, you become open to the opportunities you had previously relinquished. Those opportunities were part of the strategic trade-off from your previous mindset.

Every strategy has a trade-off. When you no longer live the old way of life, you unlock opportunities that would have appeared unreachable or, more likely, invisible.

What looks like chaos to the fly is in perfect order to the spider. It's time you stopped thinking like only a fly and begin to understand how you are also the spider. When you expand who you are beyond either the fly or the spider, it is easier to return avoid traps which previously ensnared you.

As you embark on this transformative journey through the pages of this book, it's crucial to start with a moment of introspection with your first Shadow process. As with anything, intention matters. Setting the intention now, through a sacred confirmation, offers you the positive possibility to have a fantastic journey.

A Shadow process is like a voucher to initiate a perspective or insight. The processes have prompts or questions. Just like your favorite AI, your mind is designed to answer prompts. These are your keys to activating this material in your 3D world. The process will help you tune into your current state of mind and prepare you for the deep work ahead. It's a sacred confirmation of where you are when you start and then bookended with assessing how you feel at the backend.

Take time to ponder and jot down your thoughts. Your answers may change each time you revisit this book, and that's okay. It's all part of the process.

What do you hope to gain by reading through this book?

What would life be like if the change you intended this book to support happened?

What are you here seeking now?

(Your goals may evolve each time you read this book.)

What is the story that steals your joy?

This query aims to make you aware of the narratives you've unconsciously adopted which might block your experience of joy.

What would your life be like if that story wasn't true?

Consider creating a new story where your joy isn't blocked and "see" what your life would look like.

What keeps you from showing up with love?

Love is a powerful force, yet we often find barriers, keeping us from fully experiencing it. What are those barriers for you? What keeps you from showing up filled with enough love to offer to others?

What is that one change you've been postponing?

Change is the essence of growth, yet we often delay it. What's holding you back?

What are you resisting dealing with in your life?

Resistance often indicates areas where growth is needed but feared. What are you avoiding?

What do you believe is the cost from your current perspective?

What are the fears you dare not speak?

In this book, you will take a hard look and must be willing to speak the fears, once typically too hard to hear. Often, our deepest fears are the gatekeepers to our most significant transformations.

What roles have you been playing in your life's drama?

This question will prepare you for the concept of "constructs" you'll encounter more in-depth later in the book.

If you were playing a role in a movie, in the context of the work you are currently doing, which character role would you be fulfilling? The victim, the fool, the agent of change? What role do you typecast yourself?

What has been your emotional home?

The quality of your life directly reflects the quality of the emotions you experience. What is the predominant "emotional home" you live in?

How do you react when faced with the unknown?

Your answer will offer a glimpse into how you might approach the thing you most fear. You're already taking the first steps on your Hero's Journey by pondering these questions. Keep these answers close. You'll want to revisit them as you delve deeper into the transformative power of Shadow Work.

Now, join me on a tour of my constructs and my Shadow.

Chapter 4

My Journey

"The size of the couch, I can remember that." I nod with hazy recollection. "It stood up to about here." I touch somewhere between my chest and shoulder.

My gaze lightens further as my guide prompts me to go deeper. "Remember this one time when…"

My mind takes me back. I remember tracing a pattern on a brown couch. My 3-year-old hand rubbed a Velcro-like surface, feeling the roughness.

I load the hologram of that memory. In other words, I pull up that moment through a specific construct of probing and sorting and experiencing the moment. The associations bring me into the face of my work. I recall the moment. My father had walked out of his bedroom wearing a leather biker jacket and holding his motorcycle keys. He appeared excited that I was there. I remember that made me happy.

"Well, partner," my father said, walking into the living area. "Come over here and give me a hug goodbye."

The hug, I recall, being very intentional. He even complimented me. I remember that childhood hug. My kids carry that hug. My wife… *Cwtch*. I recall my three-year old mind thinking maybe I was ok. As if I was already searching for something safe.

We lived in a basement apartment in Omaha, Nebraska. The weather shone with light and color typical for early fall. Everything in my memory has deep blue overtones, like overexposed film. That IS the feeling. Exposed.

I recalled the sharp cold air and how it prickled my skin when I stepped outside. There was his motorcycle, black on the tank. But then my mind goes dark, a hard dark, darkness as thick as cement.

That was as far in as my mind would allow me go in that moment. But just because I don't remember more didn't mean I wasn't living out the results of those hidden moments.

My Boogie-Mom

My mind resists recalling my three-year-old self. My stepmother physically tortured me. For the longest time, and for the most part, my memories failed to surface. I've been told the woman starved and beat me and my sister. Then, because I had the look of my mother, my stepmother locked me in the basement. Dad never knew because we were scared into silence.

At age three, for children, mom and dad are GOD. Our parents are the channels to our everything. Remember what three years old feels like? Love is currency at that age. It's preverbal. Experts suggest this is "pre-recall." But it's not pre-feeling.

Torture, a feeling that intense, does things to the mind. The bigger question is why would the mind recall such a painful experience?

Eventually, Mom got us out of my stepmother's clutches. The time of torture lasted weeks to many months, though the impact of that torture has remained monumental in my life. My child-thinking mind chose silence rather than to say anything.

When my father learned of the torture, he blamed himself, crawled into a bottle, and never came out.

Fast-forward to my adulthood, and I'm no longer in the basement. Yet, the fear of being trapped became a radar through which I navigated and made meaning out of my life. It smothered me, it broke me, it addicted me, halting my ability to move forward. At times, the impact of the torture can still completely overwhelm me. My mind knows the structure of the fear of being trapped from my childhood, and I can get triggered.

Some people misunderstand what it means to be triggered. What I've come to understand through my work, both my personal work and my work with countless others, is how a thought automates or operates automatically. Especially thoughts built on survival from an early age. Feelings are running within us, and if we don't want to feel their presence, we ignore them. Many times, thoughts are like the refrigerator humming in the background that your mind edits out. Other times, thoughts are a freight train—whistle blowing, engine roaring—bearing down on you. **That** is being triggered.

A three-year old who fears being trapped appears different from an adult who has created highly advanced strategies to avoid getting trapped. The more the feelings run, the more the mind creates complex schemes to avoid them.

The mind drives everything to automate.

The Shadow clutches to every hook, anchor, and trigger it finds. This is a natural byproduct of a mind-system trying to anticipate what can go wrong in a world where anything can happen.

The challenge presented arises because the mind is much more powerful than we know. We wholly and unconsciously become trapped within constructs built to keep us safe. An image, the False Self, attended to—actions we take to reinforce a wound—becomes imprinted on the augmented reality we call our imagination—a ghost in the system.

Some part of the adult-me came "online" and said, "I got you, buddy, you'll never get stuck in the basement again. I'll keep a look out!"

Then, my risk manager came "online" and started predicting, searching, and anticipating. He started watching for ways I could get trapped.

This unconscious process became etched on the glasses I saw the world through.

So, although I'm no longer in the basement, some lost wordless part of me, for years, continued to reside there (and occasionally still does). Some experiences/memories/ are captured in the looking glass so deep it can take a lifetime of therapy to understand. Each of my interactions, from that moment forward, had this Shadow cast on it. From then on, I always moved towards, or away from, the feeling of being trapped. I spent decades trying to discover the reasons I couldn't break free—constantly navigating my life with a sense of certainty of being trapped at any moment.

You'll soon learn, the mind will take pink and make it red. Because the mind craves patterns. Patterns I started to watch for involved me being trapped. THERE IT WAS. My journey had brought me to the hell I'd been carrying around and unconsciously creating all this time. That part of me had become a victim-identity. I learned to survive through it.

The mind automates identity. Automation is unconscious. Now my mind sends me unconscious signals of pain: What could go wrong?

The mind automates anything it deems helpful for survival. Now, though circumstances constantly change, the underlying sense of impending doom caused by a victim-identity programming remains constant.

How We Plot a Course Through Life

Isn't it true you constantly run "what-if" scenarios in your head? Go ahead and check, I'll wait.

Just as a ship's captain uses a ruler, scale, and dividers to measure the distance to potential hazards and then plots a course accordingly, the mind uses tools to navigate life and anticipate future threats.

- Your mind's "ruler" is its way of measuring the emotional distance between safety and danger.
- The "scale" represents the mind's perception of the severity of the trauma, adjusting it to fit the current context.
- The "dividers" symbolize the mind's ability to partition experiences, marking off safe and dangerous zones based on past traumas.

In every moment, the mind is making meaning. That meaning is an imprint of its emotional and psychological state. When trauma erupts, the grooves of the imprint tend to deepen. These imprints serve as reference points, and your mind uses them to navigate the way a ship's captain uses nautical tools.

As you maneuver in life, your hijacked mind constantly uses these tools to anticipate similar dangers, adjusting the scale of the threat based on your current ability to cope.

For example, the trauma from being trapped in a basement as a child may have felt like being stuck in a storm in the middle of the ocean. The risk scale adjusts as you age and develop more coping skills. As an adult, a storm in the middle of an ocean might be signified by a relationship wreck or a financial tsunami. The impending doom—the Shadow hanging over you—may feel just as painful and overwhelming and impossible as the original trauma, which results in new concerns regarding your ability to navigate the seas of life.

Stop for a moment and ask yourself, **"How** (not if) **do you plot your own demise?"**

This is one way Shadow overwhelm us. It uses measurement tools—our emotional ruler, scale, and dividers—to keep us in a perpetual state of vigilance, always anticipating the next significant threat. And because this system of the mind isn't taught discernment, it leads us into a self-fulfilling prophecy where we manifest the very danger we're trying to avoid.

Having a trapped Shadow produces interesting byproducts. In life, we tend to create the thing we most fear. Identity is the most potent force of the human condition. We will do nearly everything to stay consistent and persistent with the rules and labels we use to identify ourselves.

As a result, I could never get too far away from feeling trapped for fear of forgetting or unconsciously ending up there again. Like a sailor using the coast to navigate the shoreline, I unconsciously tethered my life to the experience of imprisonment. Without additional knowledge to navigate meaning I'd made from my experiences, staying next to the shore feels paramount for survival.

As humans, we prefer to deal with the demon we know rather than risk raising a demon we don't.

Understanding this process, sometimes referred to as a mechanism, is crucial for Shadow Work. As you raise your awareness of how your mind plots its course, you have the opportunity to recalibrate your internal tools, making them more aligned with your current reality rather than past traumas. These are the first steps in reclaiming your life from Shadow and then setting a new course toward healing and wholeness.

Do you recognize how you plot your demise? Can you see how your assessment is a projection? Do you "see" how you validate, compare, measure, and then blame?

Along my life's journey, I began to develop certain instincts. I got good at spotting someone who felt trapped. I got even better at noticing the patterns when people were about to snap. I developed a radar that constantly scanned a room, looking for traps and trapped people. I always size people up. "This person looks safe. That person looks like they are going to go off." I developed the ability to walk people off the ledge of emotional extremes. It was as though *my* life depended on it.

In contrast, I found myself more at home in a world of chaos. When the outside world was crazy, time slowed and my thoughts grew more pronounced. I felt more comfortable when things were chaotic than when things were "normal." Beneath that pooled feeling of suffering and dread. I describe the feelings using a term from the Matrix movie, "desert of the real," feeling so painful my mind works overtime to avoid, push, and bury it.

I continued to probe and finally recognized my problem. Seeing is not believing; believing is seeing. And because I constantly focused on looking for pain, pain's what I manifested.

I suffered years of addiction, divorce, homelessness.

I was the guy you crossed the street to avoid.

I never allowed myself to be close to anyone.

Eventually, I abandoned everyone and everything I held dear. I never finished anything, always blaming it on someone else. It's hard to take ownership when the cost is your freedom.

As I wrote this book, I had to address the part of me that I must lay bare before you. Turning Within is a subjective experience.

My Introduction to Shadow

My chaotic world continued to turn. Fast forward to April 15, 2000. I was twenty-four hours into a powerful and ancient process of initiation facilitated by a group within an organization called The Mankind Project (MKP). I found myself standing on a "magic" carpet, feeling energized, excited, confused, anxious, overwhelmed. Standing in the center of a sacred container with that group of men, I was given the opportunity to step out on the carpet. There I came face to face with the meaning I'd made, which had kept me stuck in a life I didn't want to live.

Hello, Shadow.

I was four months out of jail, living in a house full of active users, holding on by a fragile thread. At a 12-Step meeting, I was introduced to a sponsor working on his Shadow. Tom spoke with raw authenticity. It scared me. But something told me to lean in. Although I had zero understanding of the concept of Shadow, I understood I needed someone to show me the way out of my suffering.

I had no idea how to live on life's terms and didn't know how to survive. I was barely treading water in the ocean of shame from mistakes that destroyed all my relationships. Through one shitty decision after another, I found myself simultaneously exiled and trapped. I was willing to try anything. I was desperate to stop the painful cycle of my life.

Tom introduced me to a group. They swore me to secrecy. They explained, people wouldn't understand what they did was an ancient ceremony and a process for reclaiming my center, my power, my life. This tribe of men moved through the world with a deep sense of purpose—I *wanted* what they had.

In a crowded room, I could pick out which man was part of the MKP tribe and which wasn't. Without understanding what I was getting into, I signed up for a weekend retreat to meet what they called "my Shadow."

Life has shown me there are moments in our lives that define us. For me, being born wasn't living. Carpet work at the weekend retreat is where I finally began the journey to the land of the living.

However, before I could face the basement where I unconsciously lived, I had to find the power to stand. I needed to smash through self-limiting narratives I had etched in the looking glass I used to define myself. I broke through a gauntlet of "You'll never be enough" and "You are just a piece of shit" and "None of this matters so why don't you just quit?"

These narratives had plagued my life—all threads of work tied to the string of stories connected to the rope of belief attached to the chain of psychological imprints (or *samskara*) hooked to an iron anchor.

The anchor represented the feeling of being stuck, trapped in the basement. That feeling of overwhelming terror, left unprocessed, was an open circuit waiting for a signal the way a nerve is left raw and uncovered. This disconnection was the shame I recreated in every relationship I'd had.

Even though I gave it everything on the "magic carpet," it was only a flicker of light in the dark expanse of my Shadow. As if my mind knew I wasn't ready to tackle the more profound suffering I had been through, my thoughts swam and danced in and out of coherency, finally latching onto a bucket of work it felt safe enough to tackle.

Shadow Work starts where you are. The work is accomplished in layers, like peeling back layers of an onion. It's the start of the journey inward.

I managed just a sliver of work that day. However, when someone's starving, even a crumb becomes a banquet. I found something that finally cleared the path inside my experience. Something that allowed me to hit the reset button on my experience. Something healing in a way years of therapy hadn't accomplished.

I felt lighter.

I felt poised for liberation.

I found the thing I had been chasing *and* running from.

I found my purpose.

The experience on the carpet told me I'd finally discovered what would lead to real and lasting change. It would require me to be willing to go to the one place I had been programmed not to—my suffering.

I finally understood what Joseph Campbell, author of *The Hero's Journey*, meant, "It is the cave you most fear to enter that holds the treasure you seek."

Loaded with a glimpse of a treasure, I didn't care how long it took. I didn't care where I had to go. Didn't care what I had to step through. I was going to spend my life studying the art of Shadow Work. It was as if a more significant, purposeful part of me reached in and shook me to my core. Although I had only been shown a sliver of positive possibility, that sliver allowed me to make sense of the world in ways I'd never imagined.

I developed a personal mission of service. More importantly, I created a daily ritual to integrate this new identity. I found my mission *and* my purpose. I began chasing slivers of insights anywhere I could find them, launching my practice of Turning Within.

I realized my suffering existed because I was programmed to do so. Programming came from years and years of half-truths based on a lie. Years and years of mixed-up coding, all designed to keep me safe. Yet, safety eluded me.

I started to wonder if I was the only crazy one. Indeed, I thought it was because I had such a dark past, which prompted me to wonder how much Shadow was at play, and even more so, whether Shadow Work worked elsewhere in my life.

And nothing prepared me for the lessons I uncovered.

Asked a Simple Question

Turning Within is the process or practice of studying the unseen relationship between self, people, places, things, and events. By diving into deep conscious, you unlock insights, break through resistance, and heal wounds that have you stuck in cycles of suffering. When you want to improve in any area, Turning Within has the power to unlock a path forward where none existed prior.

- To begin the process, ask yourself the most basic questions:
- Where do you suffer?
- Where do you find yourself seeking validation?
- Where do you find yourself stuck in blame?
- Where do you find yourself trying to measure up?
- Is there a comparison you find yourself trapped under?

I believe the nature of all suffering is Shadow. However, Shadow is faulty programming. It's the distorted filter by which you and I view the world and then project back to it. It's an assumption based on a story, based upon a half-truth, taken for gospel.

Most of us are programmed through a lifetime of half-truths. We are clearing Shadow through generations of lies handed down like family heir-looms. Generation after generation, the imprint of half-truths deepens. It's not the external Illuminati holding you back. It's not your family. It's not Big Brother causing the problem. The problem is you. You hold yourself back more than any Illuminati could.

After I discovered Shadow Work, for the first time in my life, I felt a clear purpose. I refused to allow the how, where I had to go, or what I had to step through to keep me from my mission. I committed to spending my life chasing the light.

However, I still lived in the Shadow of the construct of being trapped. Being trapped became the fractal projection that I saw everywhere I looked. It became a self-fullfilling prophecy causing an internal pretzel I couldn't escape.

That feeling was realized in my relationships by pushing away those I held dear. In my suffering, I thought if I knew more, I had more knowledge, I could break out of the imaginary prison I had unconsciously put myself. Then I would finally be "good enough."

Turning Within is a practice. Working through lifetimes of faulty con-ditioning isn't an overnight gig. Anyone who tells you differently is trying to sell you something. I felt like I was on the right path with Shadow Work. I became a sponge. I started reading everything from the most practical books on change to the most esoteric texts I could acquire, though most I didn't understand. I traveled worldwide, taking workshops on Shadow, Neuro Linguistic Programming (NLP), hypnotherapy, Jungian archetypes, somatic change, anything and everything I could find on related topics to produce change within me at a deeper, core level.

I continued my practice, which has developed naturally into a skill to help guide others through their work. I spent a decade on a development track to hone my skills and ability. I sought anything I could find that offered even elusive slivers of insight, sliver after sliver would lead to another growth edge.

I deepened my practice, claimed my mission. That mission led me to work in the addiction field and then years as a youth counselor. I developed a chapter of the *Boys to Men* program, which leverages the same tools to help young boys successfully begin their work.

This made me wonder about the evolution beyond just wounding. Is our world built on pain? Is the only way to grow as an individual through suffering?

I began asking questions, delving beyond just healing wounds. Do these Turning Within tools still hold their value, helping in areas of fulfillment and peak performance? How about human development and business? What about evolution, both personally and collectively?

I discovered when my programing shifted, everything changed. My work began to move past patching up holes. I examined the nature of the holes themselves. I wanted to study the nature of insight.

At that time, I didn't understand, I had started the journey to chase the innate genius trapped inside of me, the one inside each of us. These sparks of light lit up whenever I witnessed someone's authentic piece of work. It was like watching a deeper version of them come online *instantly*. At that moment, for that person, a miracle happened. At that moment, they were changing the impossible to possible.

I was hooked. I mean, hooked bad.

Shadow Work can be highly magnetic. Whenever I watch the lights come on in someone's eyes, I'm gifted with an unexplainable reward. I began wondering how to collaborate, creating a community, a Shadow Tribe, to make an even more significant impact within the world.

The experiment grew. Could I gather enough people together, people practicing Shadow Work, to hit a tipping point in our world? The challenge is: Are we able to change the collective whole of society by changing an individual?

Read on, dear seeker, let us see.

I changed my approach. I used Shadow Work questions on sales calls. I found the inquiries helped my clients get clear on the fundamental blocks holding them back. I learned people don't buy products, they buy identities. Most times, customers were on a metaphorical hero's journey. And although they were seeking a fiery sword, they were looking for the deeper version of who they actually were. I learned that success is never a matter of resources; it's always a matter of resourcefulness. 99% of the block to that resourcefulness is Shadow.

It was about 2002 when I saw my first clip of Tony Robbins. He worked with someone, and within 20 minutes, I could tell he'd helped the person get underneath their negative programming that had them stuck. I saw he had developed the same weird skills that I sought to master. I had the realization that if I wanted to master the practice of Shadow Work, I had to be able to practice it all day long. I needed focused immersion. It wasn't about making it financially feasible; it wasn't even about making a living. It was about committing to developing a solid practice.

Immediately, I committed right then and there, much like when I saw my first piece of carpet work, to spend ten years and 10,000 hours of study underneath a master guide. So, I kept bugging the Robbins organization until they hired me. Then that small-time boy from Iowa headed to San Diego.

Working globally for someone as demanding as Tony helps cultivate a different skill level.

I wanted to see if this worked in business. I wondered if I could use this powerful insight tool in organizations. Tony commissioned me to run what we called "strategic interventions" on over 10, 000 business owners. I took this as a rich opportunity to practice Shadow Work to understand the reasons these businesses were succeeding, or in most cases, failing.

My "street smarts" gave me a unique ability to see what others were blind to. I leveraged it to help my clients look around corners.

Every day, I worked with eight to ten business leaders worldwide from every stage of growth. I experienced how Shadow shows up in business. With that knowledge, I developed tools to tend to the structure of my clients' lives and businesses.

I traveled around the world, sharing my insights with every type of business: executive training, business owners, corporation employees to contract employees to small independent business owners. I spent two years working with the homeless population in Colorado. I saw how the same root cause played out within every walk of life—all the while paying my bills and honing my abilities with my business clients.

I cross-pollinated Tony's strategic insights with what I had learned and been practicing, regarding Shadow and Shadow Work. This created massive breakthroughs in integration and implementation for myself and my clients.

Layers of insight lit up my understanding. I was a committed student, but still not free of my negative programing.

After well over 10,000 hours of study, facilitation, and mentoring, I still suffered from being chased by my Shadow, that deeply rooted fear of being trapped, even after sitting in front of some of the brightest names in the personal growth field.

The more success I found, the greater the feeling of impending doom blossomed. Traveling around the world, making more money than a small-town Midwest boy could dream of earning, the feeling of being chased by a monster trying to eat me still plagued me.

My suffering increased. Then in 2020, I reached the next stage of my journey, which presented as a breaking point. I was no different than any other hero on a journey, seeking, seeking, seeking. The portal to change often comes in the center of a dark night of the soul, and two weeks before the COVID-19 shutdown, I found another teacher in the most unlikely place—a plant.

Mother Gives Me a Vision

I sat cross-legged at the beginning of an Ayahuasca ceremony, surrounded by a group of people, all weary from seeking, searching, and learning. People don't come to one of the most powerful plant medicines on the planet by being dabblers. Typically, it's their stop at the last house on a very long street of seeking.

In the culture where I swam, most people turned their Shadow into the belief, "EAT OR BE EATEN!"

I was done running. I turned to the most unlikely of teachers.

While seated on a mat, I drank the most foul-tasting tea. I sobbed, begged, pleaded, "Mother help me! Mother, help me!" Then, in my mind, a loving, feminine, wise voice pops a question, one I'll never forget.

"When's the first time you remember pleading for your mother's help?"

BAM!

The trigger. The time-travel. Trapped. In an instant, I was imprisoned in the basement. I'm three years old. Filled with sheer terror.

"Fuck me!" I shouted. "I remember this! Let me out! I don't want to be here! This is too much. I don't want to do this anymore!"

In my mind, I started to struggle. I tried to break free of a hellish place. That place I had been imprisoned in as a child. The more I struggled to escape, the more immense the fear increased. My body shook. My mind started to blot out. My emotions exploded with terror. I thought, that's it... I'm shutting down.

I began to black out.

A whisper came. "Keep..." and then in the most loving and gentle way imaginable, that gentle voice guided me. "Keep moving forward, keep moving forward. The only way out is through."

I pushed. And then I purged. And I purged again.

I cried, screamed, shuddered. In the experience of a life-threatening terror, that gentle voice guided me to my strength, which permitted me to feel the terror trapped in my life. An awareness dawned, I realized THIS part of me felt this pain my whole life.

Covered in sweat, snot, and tears... and... well... I found myself at the door of something dark I had tightly held onto my whole life.

"What kind of person did this make me?" Something inside seemed to nod in approval as if I was asking the right question.

The medicine gave me another vision, showing me the impact of holding onto the fear of being trapped in the basement.

An image flashed. I watched as my wife and I discussed bills. I saw how I had made meaning and imprinted it. It was a filter, a blueprint, and it had tainted my view, twisting my wife's efforts to show me love into a dark and sadistic plan to suck the life out of me. I saw how my fear would create a wake, the ripples caused her to slip into her Shadow. The root of so much shadowboxing.

I saw how the terror of my imprisonment drove me to success. It made me push past what others felt was acceptable output because a deeply rooted fear caused me to believe any lack of performance would result in punishment and being locked in the basement.

This fear of being trapped became the root of my navigation around everything. I'd spent my entire life trying to escape the basement. It showed up in my beliefs about money, relationships, and success. And I realized escaping was futile—I had to dig deep to cleanse the structure of my belief—in order to get a breakthrough.

Understanding took root. I had been hobbled before I ever knew how to walk. And for the first time in my entire life, I began to understand the depth of Shadow. It left no area of life left untouched. There was no success, failure, or moment this construct had left untainted.

My life had been sucked into the gravity of a black hole. My little boy identity trapped in the basement needed tending. My life's survival, intimately and entirely, had been informed by the fear of ending up like my poor, abused, young boy who always looked at the world through the construct of "TRAPPED."

So once again, as I had done ten years ago with Tony Robbins, I quit my job, left a place I called home, started working with a plant. I devoted myself to supporting others navigating their path to healing through their profound experiences with the medicine. This has allowed me to take Shadow Work and practice it in a new setting with a new teacher. I could go forever about what I have learned and continue to learn while working with Ayahuasca.

Mother Aya, as I have come to call Ayahuasca, has helped me grasp things I couldn't have otherwise understood. I have learned to let go of things I wasn't aware I held tightly in my grasp. In the end, for most, Shadow Work is about releasing what no longer serves you, making space for you to grasp something that does. For those few, Shadow Work becomes Soul Work.

I hope the spirit of what Mother Aya has taught me will resonate within you as you continue reading this book.

Welcome to the ceremony that is your life.

Through learning to let go of what doesn't serve you, in that release, you experience and learn the best-kept secret of humankind. However, you must embrace the journey. Some things can't be taught; they must be earned.

Chapter 5

What is Shadow?

Your conscious thought sits at the edge of a unique and advanced system that creates meaning and then pushes all meaning to your mechanical mind. You "make up your mind" about something, and that belief becomes the looking-glass view that informs your reality.

Have you ever known someone who is always angry? Maybe intimately known them? Ever notice how they always find a way to be angry? They aren't conscious of this.

The first rule of Shadow Work: We lie to ourselves first.

That angry person, their looking glass only presents them with a plot based on anger: sadness, joy, fear... they are all the same.

The truth is, seeing isn't believing. You are about to learn how believing is seeing. The question isn't whether or not you have faith, but what do you have faith in? Most people have more faith in their demise than they do in their success.

What happens when we are "in Shadow"? The angry person is always tied to a feeling of being angry. The life data they receive is all true, but the story built around it supports personalized impacts that are always similar or the same.

How do you get caught just like the angry person does? If the only constant in life is change, how is your suffering the same story, yet a different verse, no matter where you go? Your mind craves patterns. Your suffering is no different. Your suffering is a pattern. Follow this truth, like a rescue dog tracking a lost child down to the Shadow and your liberation.

Consider a Broadway play. There is a director, stage manager, props manager, and other actors. Think of conscious thought as the stage, whereas Shadow is the influence of the performance. Work is taking place backstage during the entire performance. Like the play, your Shadow is all hidden underneath your conscious surface.

The parts of you that you notice "in Shadow" are only noticeable because of the pain they bring. Otherwise, you wouldn't even notice the imprint on your experience.

Then, there is the stuff that sits beyond your knowing. You're unaware and unconscious to that part of your mind, that part of your mind that keeps you from stepping out into dangerous traffic. Yet, somewhere deep in the recesses of your mind, calculation run, estimating whether you should stop or go.

You and I are so much more than "backstage at the playhouse" or even the play. Shadow Work isn't just for people dealing with trauma or those buried under debilitating levels of Shadow. It's not reserved for those suffering from an incurable bout of asshole-itis.

Our struggle with our personal trauma makes our invisible insides visible outside. It points to critical mental structures in need of our attention in a culture swimming in negative programming. This is not an insult to our world or culture. Instead, it's a recognition of the situation and each of us is offered an opportunity to grow. By learning to tend to our internal landscape, we find treasures—treasures that can't be explained or taught. They must be experienced and realized.

We only really experience two types of thought. New thoughts and thoughts already thought. However, exactly what is a thought?

After you make a judgment about a person, place, thing, or event, what does your mind do next? Your conscious thought stands on top of your judgement to reach its next meaning. This happens over and over and over.

48

The mind is obsessed with meaning. Each thought has the ability to have a life of its own. A thought doesn't disappear; each is leveraged, evolves, and then collaborates with other ideas in a mind. Once you make up your mind about something, you may find it difficult to let go. Even if you know it's wrong.

This is because making new thoughts takes much more energy than thinking old ones. New thoughts require a reassociation with all the other running ideas and constructs in your mind. If your mind can keep you alive with an old thought, it will do so to conserve energy. This isn't laziness, it's elegance. A mind evolved past what we can comprehend would operate from a place of maximized elegance and efficiency.

We have been lulled into the notion of laziness through a misalignment of orientation, which means, we are externally focused but internally generating our life experience.

The mind has three primary objectives: make meaning, elegantly evolve, survive. You know what meaning is: Meaning is the subjective interpretation that emerges from the interaction between our external world and internal mental states of emotion, cognition, and context.

Survival's focus is keeping you alive. Then the directive for efficiency is the purpose of the patterns and how such complexity is possible.

Just like in business, the mind's systems can be streamlined to make it more efficient by removing the unnecessary patterns. The National Science Foundation suggests 95% of an individual's ideas are repetitive.

Here are some additional questions to ponder:

- Over the past few months, what has been your default mindset?
- What is the narrative from which you live your life from? What is your emotional home—your predominate emotion?
- Now, be as honest as you're able and answer, "How much of that emotion do you think colored your day-to-day experience?"

In other words, how much of your predominate feeling—angry, sad, fearful, joyful, or whatever feeling—caused you to act such that your behavior made an impact on the world?

Consider, maybe you were short with someone who didn't deserve it. Perhaps you were scared to leap, so you made up a story of how dangerous it was. How much do you think your emotional home impacted your perception of reality? Be honest with yourself.

Since we know we lie to ourselves first, please give yourself the honor of being truthful here. How does your emotional home reflect your default mindset? How are these two facets of your inner landscape connected?

What happens when your mind is made up about something that causes pain?

For example, "I'm worthless," or "I'm the problem," or "I'm a victim." The mind looks for associations to protect "self" from these thoughts of judgment.

The victim is one of the core archetypes our society struggles with. So then, how does your victim show up in you? Maybe you create situations which require you to prove to yourself that you aren't a victim. Unconsciously, are you creating a hero's journey, trying to let go of the identity of worthlessness or victimhood?

Feelings of worthlessness, low self-esteem, victimhood have built entire countries' economies from people buying things to fill their emptiness, their sense of worthlessness. Too often, people's paychecks are spent maintaining an unconscious feeling of being a victim instead of pulling the problem up at the root.

Introducing Shadow into Modern Society

The Shadow concept was first articulated in modern society in the early 1900s in Europe. Carl Jung suggested anything outside the known parts of our personality was the Shadow.

Bringing the concept to modern psychology, Jung, a noted Swiss psychiatrist and researcher, considered to be the founder of analytical psychology, began developing his archetypes of personality in a series of books on the mind and human potential. Those writings are now the foundation of modern Jungian psychology and have dramatically impacted the global understanding of the psyche.

The start of the twentieth century was a prosperous period for psychology and human development as a field of science. Sigmund Freud was alive and practicing. In the pre-World War II period, intellectual debates spurred a particularly intense fire throughout the European continent. Jung corresponded with Freud, and for several years Jung traveled broadly as a speaker and researcher in Europe, the United States, Africa, and India. Students of Jung's work who examine the concept of Shadow will notice how Jung built on Freud's concepts of Ego, Id, and Superego, as well as other dominant personality theories of that time.

However, Jung's focus wasn't limited to pure theory and research. He practiced psychiatry for most of his life, treating private patients and working with institutions that housed individuals with severe psychiatric conditions. His family history of mental health issues provided him first-hand knowledge of schizophrenic episodes, depression, hallucinations, neurosis, and delusion.

As a result, when Jung shared his concept of the Shadow with the world, he offered practical and understandable elements for a person's growth and individual development.

Jung suggested the Shadow is a part of the unconscious mind that represents:

- Repressed ideas
- Unacknowledged beliefs
- Denied elements of ourselves
- Weaknesses/Shortcomings
- Desires
- Instincts

Let's put these concepts into meaningful thought. Imagine your consciousness as an ocean, teeming with unknown and ancient entities. The deeper you descend, the more mysterious and primordial the world becomes. Now, as you float on the surface, imagine a radiant light emanating from the ocean floor. You witness colossal creatures from the ocean's depths as they swim through this light, casting Shadows on the surface. These Shadows are then projected on the outside world. Turning within, examining your

Shadow, is a deliberate practice of diving into your deep consciousness to unearth insights, overcome barriers, and heal wounds causing loops of suffering. This is the structure of the way your mind experiences reality.

Your Shadow isn't merely the parts you hide or deny; it transcends the self you identify with. This is why people grappling with addictions often feel their urges, cravings, compulsions are larger than themselves. The Shadow, instead, is your guide to a more expansive version of you, encompassing your limitations and untapped potential. It's not a repository of beliefs you reject. It's a rejection of beliefs you hold.

Confronting *your* Shadow offers you a binary choice: reject this complex part of yourself *or* embrace it as a catalyst for growth.

The insights to be gained from this exploration defy verbal explanation because they tap into a realm beyond conscious understanding. If you reject this complex part of yourself, ignoring your Shadow will trap you in a loop of suffering. Rejecting this part of you causes a calcification of the Shadow in the outside world. Just like a windshield that doesn't get cleaned, it makes it harder and harder to see where to steer.

However, acknowledging your Shadow opens the door to profound self-discovery.

"The shadow is a moral problem that challenges the whole ego-personality, for no one can become conscious of the shadow without considerable moral effort. Become conscious of it involves recognizing the dark aspects of the personality as present and real. This act is the essential condition for any kind of self-knowledge." — Carl Jung, Aion (1951)

Evolution Of *Your* Shadow

Before addressing the need to choose how to tend to your personal Shadow, it is worthwhile to dig into the evolutionary roots of the Shadow. Where does this Shadow within us originate?

You were born with programing, though not every element of your programing has been with you since birth. You add pieces of yourself to it during your journey through a series of indoctrinations. These indoctrinations come from family, friends, culture, and other environmental stimulation.

We all have a side of ourselves we present to the world. This side is called the Persona. The word persona is taken from the Latin word for "mask." Your Persona behaviors and thought patterns reflect what you have been taught by the world, especially regarding cultural beliefs and the manners and behavioral scripts for life situations. This becomes your conscious "mask" to cover your internal turmoil. Yet, often it feels so real that you consider it your "self" throughout your life. However, it is merely the outer crust of your thoughts.

Let's consider your Shadow as giant filing cabinets of meaning you have been standing on top of since birth. The denser, less reachable, or less recallable meaning is pre-stocked with knowledge and impulses passed down through your genes—a part of the collective unconscious shared by all humanity—the very structure of thought, like archetypes and the monomyth. Mother and father passing on "information" to mother and father passing onto mother and father, etc., generationally. And while that foundation is laid, other contents of the cabinets develop throughout your lifetime. These layers of meaning make up the collaboration which is the experience of reality you call life.

Now, let's consider repressed ideas. At one moment in time, each was merely an idea. However, something or someone informed your upper-level consciousness, communicating how these ideas were unacceptable. In turn, these unacceptable ideas had no spot in your Persona, since it is the mask you show the world. In turn, you repress those ideas, shuffle them to the hidden file folder of the Shadow.

Yet, soon, you have a signal, coming from the inside the "self" you think you are, one you don't want to hear. The result: your mind starts looking for the cause of the signal in the *external* world.

The same pathway applies to unacknowledged beliefs. By way of an example, maybe deep down, you hate purple people. You utterly despise them. At some point, you may have been treated in a way or taught they were dangerous. Yet you may not acknowledge that belief on a personal level, even though you are inexplicably rude to anyone you encounter with purple skin.

If you were to give voice to your hate of purple people, owning this irrational resistance at its source, it might change your behavior. But since you hold that belief inside you, completely unacknowledged, it remains in Shadow. It becomes an influencer of your behavior without your conscious knowledge.

And we all have them.

To be clear, I do not suggest there is anything wrong with purple people. Your irrational belief that there is something wrong with purple people, based on the color of their skin, is an example of Shadow-based views. Many people store these sorts of beliefs. Most don't do the work necessary to investigate where they picked up that belief system. It's time to stop that monster before it eats anyone else.

Denied elements end up in shadow, too. Perhaps you once acknowledged them, but now you choose not to believe these things are true about yourself. You may weigh 400 pounds. And deny having emotional eating issues. You may be excessively generous or reckless with finances, but insist you are simply unlucky with money. Digging deeper beneath the surface, you may discover a belief—you're cursed and don't deserve to succeed.

What happens is the mind locks into a state of survival, and conscious thought blocks your unwanted beliefs, which is then left to find expression in Shadow. Denial keeps your conscious mind unaware, so you cycle around a black hole of suffering and shame, unable to release something you have no knowledge you're holding onto. Your mind keeps the suffering judgment from your awareness to keep you from harming yourself.

Weaknesses and perceived shortcomings are also trapped in Shadow. Perhaps you struggled with math. Unconsciously, you avoid numbers and arithmetic. When you were born, you had no concept of basic math, much less algebra, geometry, or calculus. Yet that element of perceived inability with math built up over time in your Shadow. Now, when you witness someone doing math very well, you feel inferior without pinpointing the underlying reason why. However, the construct of a time when you were bullied for having difficulty in school is running your behavior like a hot wire.

How about your desires and instincts? Our society teaches us some things are right to want and some are wrong to desire. Our instincts to eat, interact socially, to help others are honored as good. However, our instincts to conquer, dominate, or destroy are not welcomed in our modern-world culture. Other examples show modern art is an outlet for some, yet misunderstood by others. Our society sells sex, all the while shouting the way to God is through resisting desires. Entire generations are disconnected from their inner signals after being condemned for instincts and desires.

The judgements around your instincts and desires weren't with you when you were born or even when you were young. Some of those instincts were yours from the collective unconscious, and they may have tried to express themselves openly. Through indoctrination, we learn those parts of us are bad, resulting in our rejection of the fullness of who we are.

The net result is Shadow plays a big part in your life due to all the information and impulses it processes. However, since it is not openly acknowledged, explored, and tended to—the Shadow grows wild, causing you suffering, and becomes a hidden barrier in your life.

We find religion has been working with Shadow since the first written word. The Russian mystic P.D. Ouspensky wrote, *"Man is a machine, but a very peculiar machine. He is a machine which, in the right circumstances and with the right treatment, can know that he is a machine, and having fully realized this, he may find ways to cease to be a machine."*

What Ouspensky directs us to understand is that humanity is in Shadow. Being born isn't living. It's only an invitation to a life.

Any untended construct deemed painful will seek expression in Shadow. Your mind uploads suffering into the looking glass you use to make sense of the world, because that's what it's designed to do. The mind tries to fix the programming by projecting it for reidentification.

The issue is you have not been taught that this process happens. As a result, you experience the same suffering over and over and over again. This then feeds the very storyline you're living. You're like a dog chasing its tail, around and around and around you go. However, the suffering can come out from the Shadow. By pulling on the threads of your experience, you will find the whole tapestry of your life experience unravels. At the core of you, it's all just a story. Suffering doesn't sit in the data of your life experience; suffering sits in the story you've created.

Shadow is the gift of your discomfort. Through bringing awareness to your suffering, you gain insight into the programming of human beings.

Where do you suffer? Introduction To The Question

We are hardwired to shutdown pain and make it go away. This is rooted in the densest programming we have—our DNA. Turning Within starts with diving into the veins of suffering and following the pathway to its source. Sources include repressed ideas, unacknowledged beliefs, perceived weaknesses and shortcomings, instincts, and desires.

Once you know *how* you lie to yourself, you can gain power over the lie. When you willingly uncover the lies you tell yourself, you open yourself up to deeper meaning. In turn, you have the opportunity to improve the quality of your life, since deeper meaning directly reflects the amount of consciousness you bring to it. How you do anything in life is how you do everything.

The areas you work to avoid because they are so painful play a far more extensive significance in your life than you have any awareness of. They are buried in Shadow.

Therefore, Shadow must be experienced. Let Shadow Guide you as you dive into the depths to free your genius.

The ability to have an inner life is one of our superpowers, which sets us apart from other animals. Our minds run scenarios to make meaning out of the world and then projects that meaning on the outside world. Sacred XR goggles house your ability to recognize patterns in your environment and react to those patterns, which gets pushed down to the automated, another file of meaning to stand on. The mind automates ALL meaning

Each time meaning is leveraged, it goes more and more unconscious. This means the more our beliefs are confirmed, the more they become suppressed.

56

The trail becomes worn the more it is used. Thoughts seek to survive and grow inside the mind. If we give those thoughts attention, it's giving them energy to grow.

The other way meaning becomes automatic and unconscious faster is through experiencing high-level emotional or physical distress. Those situations charge the construct that holds the imprint and keeps the meaning closest to the surface of consciousness. However, because the distressed mind has been hijacked for survival, it defaults to simulations that stem from avoiding distress.

The challenge is how you start looking for what the mind is projecting.

It's critical that you don't mistake pain for suffering.

The mind is obsessed with avoiding what it labels as painful. It creates constructs to identify all meaning. Painful meaning receives priority. Then the mind evolves advanced strategies to avoid *that* pain ever again.

Our association to suffering is the very pain that doesn't go away. Untended to, this system traps us inside a looking glass that we forget we own and are left victim to its simulations. It's like a pair of XR glasses we forget we are wearing. But the simulations aren't just visual overlay. They are lifetimes of programming. Most of the constructs running are unconscious, and much of them are based on suffering.

Your mind leaves you in the waiting room of an experience you never want to happen again—all to keep you from ever having to enter that room again. We intend to change that from here on out. The mind makes a powerful collaborator but a terrible boss.

It seems more and more people suffer from a terrible emptiness gnawing in their guts. Internet, TV, sports, and political excitements may distract us, but we repeatedly return to the wasteland of life, exhausted and disillusioned. The realization that modern distractions will not fill this hole has become sobering. Many feel they're waiting for something that will never arrive, like a lover waiting at the docks, longing for a sailor who never returns.

This is the calling that a deeper part of you yearns for expression.

The inner adventure of the soul is the only place where these feelings can be quenched. The Western mind must unravel the Shadows that have kept us sick and twisted. That is utterly different from following a well-worn path.

It is the path that Jung spoke about when he said, "One does not become enlightened by imagining figures of light, but by making the darkness conscious." Most people will find this path too unagreeable because it leads to the nexus of the very agreement itself.

This book is designed to walk you through your limitations, to give you the insights necessary to create disruptive change in your life, to innovate your understanding of why you are stuck and start you moving towards a real solution.

Chapter 6

What is Turning Within?

Jolande Jacobi once said, "All too many people do not live their own lives, and generally, they know nothing about their real nature. They make convulsive efforts to "adapt," not to stand out in any way, to do exactly what the opinions, rules, regulations, and habits of the environment demand as being "right." They are slaves of "what people think, what people do."

The Three Eyes (I's)

In Ken Wilbur's book *The Religion of Tomorrow*, he speaks of the three modes of knowing, which all great religious traditions embrace. These three modes or eyes are:

    the eye of flesh,

    the eye of mind,

    and the eye of contemplation.

The first I can be seen as the eye of flesh. This is the knowledge we gain through observation. This way of "knowing" your world leverages your senses. All conventional science is based on the eye of flesh or observation. This is why materialists can't see past the surface of life—what they see, smell, touch, taste, and hear. We have developed telescopes and microscopes; both leverage the eye of flesh to accumulate knowledge. As technology advances, we blur the line between observation and interpretation.

The second I or eye of mind is where we obtain our rationality, logic, and reason. Mathematics, for example, comes from the eye of the mind. Because it is a higher form of knowing, it can only be experienced *in* the mind. You've never seen actual logic in the material world. You've only seen the impact of leveraging it.

This is an important note: *Each level above influences but can't be proven by the level below.* For instance, you've never seen examples of the square root of one in the tangible world. Therefore, math, like logic, is based on rules, but those rules are only experienced in our mind.

The third I is called the eye of contemplation. This is the eye humans use to have authentic spiritual awakenings. The contemplative eye is the foundation for waking up. Knowing at the contemplation level can't be proven by any level below it, neither through the mind nor the senses. Yet it defines and impacts the level of knowing on both levels.

Sensory experiences are the basis for natural science; the mental eye is the foundation for reason, logic, and mathematics. The contemplative eye is the eye we regularly used as kids; it's the eye trained in meditation and the reason the impact can be profound for those who commit to a regular practice of Turning Within. It will help you reorient yourself to the flow of your meaning and then you utilize that information to navigate through your resistance.

The Three I's: An Awareness Process

You've been introduced and now are familiar with the theoretical aspects of the Three I's. Let's ground your new-found knowledge with a practical exercise. For this, you'll need a simple object: a cup, or a pen, or a leaf, or even a piece of fruit. Place this object in front of you and prepare to engage with it through the lenses of the Three I's.

The Eye of Observation (Physical Eye)

Begin by looking at your chosen object with the Eye of Observation. This is your physical eye, the eye that sees form and color but doesn't attach meaning to them. As you look at the object, try to strip away any labels or names that come to mind. For example, if you're looking at a cup, try to see it not as a "cup" but as a shape, a color, a texture. Remove any labels you have for the object. The intention is to determine if you are able to perceive the cup with the eyes of a child.

Lesson: This eye teaches you to see things as they are, without the filter of language or categorization.

Limitation: Notice it doesn't offer any deeper understanding or context. It's a snapshot, not a story.

The Eye of Interpretation

Now, bring in your Eye of Interpretation. Observe the object again. However, allow yourself to see it as more than shape and color. What is its function? What is it used for? How does it fit into your life or the world around you? By doing this, you add a layer of meaning to your initial observation.

Lesson: This eye provides context and makes the object relevant to you. It adds depth to your understanding.

Limitation: While it adds depth, it can also add bias or assumptions based on past experiences or societal norms.

The Eye of Contemplation

In the third step, you engage your Eye of Contemplation by asking yourself, "What deeper insights or lessons can this object offer?" Perhaps the cup reminds you of the importance of emptiness and fullness and how both states serve a purpose. Maybe you contemplate the idea of utility and beauty and how they co-exist.

Notice how this object relates to other objects in the room. What deeper symbol might it reflect from your life? Is there a deeper meaning you have assigned to this object? Maybe it was a gift from a loved one, therefore it symbolizes love or worth. What's your story about this object? What feelings does it evoke from you? What is the meaning or value you've infused on this object? What is the origin of the meaning this object holds?

Lesson: This eye takes the object beyond its physical or functional realm and elevates it to a symbol or metaphor. It can offer wisdom and provoke thought.

Limitation: The insights gained are profoundly personal and may not be universally applicable. Your current level of awareness also influences the symbol it holds and can evolve over time.

By the end of this process, you'll find each "I" offers a unique perspective and a different kind of wisdom. Yet, each is limited by its own scope. This is a microcosm of your larger journey through this book and life—each layer of understanding builds upon the last but also sets the stage for deeper exploration and growth of the next.

Recoding the Western Mind

The Western mind has long navigated life without a comprehensive roadmap for understanding the intricate ways our consciousness projects itself onto the world. We're often left to make sense of our experiences without the tools to understand the underlying mechanisms at play. This lack of guidance can be likened to driving a car solely by looking through the rearview mirror—jarring, disorienting, and fraught with bumps. The only solution is to clean the windshield before you drive so the road ahead presents itself to you with a clear, direct view.

At the core, Turning Within connects you to the more profound truth that exists in you, in everyone. By utilizing your contemplative eye to its maximum advantage, you gain a path to liberation by rising above the part of you caught in the suffering. You feel a sense of enlightenment.

Turning Within activates what Jung termed "active imagination." It's a meditation technique that allows you to step out of the story you believe to be self-evident and into a more profound realization of who you are. Turning Within is the practice of bringing consciousness to the unconscious. It's the practice of stripping away lies to get to the truth. There are reasons, though, why you lie. You lie because the truth is uncomfortable.

Exploring more profound realizations offers more significant insights and it requires you to see through a more elegant lens than your rational thought can access. Einstein was right when he said you can't get out of a problem with the same level of thinking that got you into it. Think of your practice as active meditation. We face and investigate areas where we are resistant.

I have learned and experienced over and over again: *change is messy*. We have created whole systems set up to support our suffering. Because nature always pushes our minds and behaviors to the mechanical, the longer we've endured the suffering, then typically, the more unconscious we are to the system created to manage the pain.

These unconscious systems can respond to change as though it's a danger. Therefore, you will lie to yourself to keep from experiencing the risk you have worked so hard not to feel or face.

To free yourself from the bondage of pain, you must build something better. Something better only comes from tearing down the programming shackling you in pain, freeing you from where you are stuck. Only then can you produce something better to support the life you want to live.

There is a straightforward primer: *Strategic innovation first requires insight*.

Without insight, innovation is a waste of resources. The best place to start is looking where you would never think to and in a way you never thought to. It will continually and unconsciously control you without understanding what Shadow influences you. In the beginning, the work can be excruciating. You are facing parts of yourself you've worked hard to manage. Most people don't build the ideal self. Instead, they manage circumstances.

Turning Within is the practice of seeing through the surface of your circumstances to peer into the core. We learn to stop taking things for face value and develop a method of inquiry that transforms the fabric of our reality.

But, for all this seriousness, the practice of Turning Within offers an invaluable impact on your personal-growth journey. It is a value hard-won but worth even more than the effort you invested in obtaining it. The insights are profound for those who make it a lifelong journey.

Unleashing Disruption and Geometric Growth

Until recently, society attached negative values to Shadow in art and writing. Just look at Robert Louis Stevenson's book *The Strange Case of Dr. Jekyll and Mr. Hyde*. It's a masterpiece that still captivates readers' interest with its exploration of how Shadow can destroy. Hyde represents the repressed "you" and all those wild and unruly pieces of your psyche. Yet, while Turning Within first involves pulling out the dirty laundry of your inner mind—your wild and unruly psyche—there are also positive parts of your Shadow to consider.

Shadow isn't merely a repository of repressed emotions and thoughts; it's your wellspring of untapped creative and disruptive potential. By peeling away the layers of your perceptual filters, you unlock a realm of insights and ingenuity previously hidden from your conscious mind. Thus, Turning Within transcends mere psychological housekeeping—it becomes a quest for transformative growth and discovering the wellspring of your inherited genius.

William James once said, "Genius means little more than the faculty of perceiving in an un-habitual way." The deepest parts of your mind, the Shadow, is where your raw power sits. Unraveling and integrating these parts of yourself gives you deep insight and empowerment. You go from reaction to response. From take to provide. From consumer to creator. You become open to receiving the previously unknown parts of you. It is the opposite of those patterns, constructs, frames, built up over years of indoctrination.

Think of your life like a business. In business, there are two types of innovation—incremental and disruptive. Incremental innovation is essential to cultivating cash flow, which is required for a company's growth. Likewise, improving how you show up through constant incremental improvements has the same impact. More importantly, incremental improvements require you to be engaged in cultivating *where* you are and not where you wish you were, it supports the second directive of your mind, which is to evolve efficiently.

More importantly, incremental improvements require you to be engaged in cultivating where you are and not where you wish you were. This supports the second directive of your mind, which is to evolve elegantly.

In the book *Atomic Habits*, James Clear teaches, *"True long-term thinking is goal-less thinking. It's not about any single accomplishment. It is about the cycle of endless refinement and continuous improvement. Ultimately, your commitment to the process will determine your progress."*

On the other hand, disruptive innovation changes the rules of engagement and the entire playing field. Whole industries have been wiped out by disruptive innovation. But where does this powerful innovation come from? It comes from geniuses who are willing to perceive the world in different ways.

Remember Steve Jobs' "Think Differently" campaign? There is a reason it resonated greatly in the minds of consumers. Steve's innovation exceeded what we thought we wanted and passed the collective understanding of technology. We all gave a collective "Yes!" when we saw the first iPhone. We felt intimately connected to technology because Jobs leveraged our collective, calling us to breakout of our programmed flat existence and break through to a life of color. Then, he delivered a product that gave an intuitive experience. We collectively upgraded our experience of reality. He shifted the game for an entire planet.

Modern society talks much more about the power of "disruptive innovation" than was discussed during Jung's day. He didn't have the reference of digital music upending the recording industry, email upending written communication norms, social media and all its disruptions and impact. Yet he referenced that kind of intensive disruption of old systems and the creation of new operational pathways when he discussed how the Shadow allowed you to reshape your self-perception and self-concept.

By Turning Within, you send awareness deep into your roots. Like an archeologist delving downward, you search for cornerstones and, once tended to, regain compacity, or what is referred to as "agency," to rebuild on them or rewrite as you choose. You will wake up the inner parts of you that have fallen asleep or numb. The experience might cause you to feel some internal pins and needles, like legs stretching for the first time. This is natural.

Your repressed ideas and desires may shock your conscious mind and your old way of thinking. Facing laziness, spitefulness, gluttony, or hatred within yourself may feel uncomfortable, especially when realization of how you projected a victimhood identity is causing you to suffer. Facing an imprint you've spent a lifetime avoiding can hold the internal weight of fighting a fire-breathing dragon. Yet, recognizing and tending to these aspects of yourself and how you project on the outside world gives you the wings and power of the dragon inside you. That which had unconsciously held you back transforms the power by which you design your world.

By doing your work, you uncover parts of yourself and seek an understanding that offers peace in place of conflict. However, left unchecked, Shadow desires and instincts will find expression through the chinks in your conscious mind and Persona-created armor. You can resist or choose to do your work, tending and leveraging parts of your whole self. Either way, the Shadow part of you exists and isn't going away.

However, by choosing to expose your inner self, through Turning Within, you discover a more actualized self-awareness and complete self-acceptance. In other words, found gold.

You may also find raw energy you previously didn't know existed. This can be a positive force coming from a place you hadn't considered to be a good part of yourself. You have the ability to harness this energy as your spark for a disruptive innovation. This disruptive innovation will help you break through to your development goals and your understanding of yourself as an individual. In other words, found gold.

Choosing to integrate a part of yourself previously you warred with, your life becomes more effortless, targeted, and energized. In other words, again found gold.

What's it like to find gold? I ran a first-time integration session with a seeker coming from a powerful Shadow Ceremony. This session is important because without integration, insight can become insanity. In this seeker's session, she expressed that she experienced a waking up, realizing she had been living a nightmare for so long (twenty years, in fact) that she had forgotten. All those years were consumed with her navigating from suffering. Unconsciously, she learned to carry it, use it to drive her to external success, but the angry, anxious, unsettling feelings only grew.

Through her Shadow Work, she reclaimed a part of her soul locked in unconscious suffering. Her gold was a level of clarity of direction she could not previously perceive. The ability to move through the world effortlessly seemed miraculous to her. Gravity of an impending doom no longer clouded her everything.

Carl Jung once said... "To confront a person with his shadow is to show him his own light. Once one has experienced a few times what it is like to stand judgingly between the opposites, one begins to understand what is meant by the self. Anyone who perceives his shadow and his light simultaneously sees himself from two sides and thus gets in the middle."

A second piece of self-knowledge created from exploring the deep consciousness is the ability to allow your genius to shine through as a unified light in your soul. There comes a point on this journey when you will tap your genius and understand why you have suffered through what you have. The answer will raise a whole new level of questions.

Seeking to know and be yourself is a fundamental drive we have in life. This is the core motivation for the first directive of the mind. Think how many different workshops, seminars, and books exist to help you "find yourself." Young people set out on year-long travel experiences, older people churn through a mid-life crisis, and people of all ages try on different religions, diets, hobbies, and lifestyles to uncover the answer to the question "Who am I?" This "I am" sits in the core of every construct you live out of.

Jung referred to these activities as the "individuation process or becoming unique in the collective." The community dictates sameness among its members, and you must rise above what the world has programmed you to be. This requires a willingness from you to love who you are in order for you to unlock the parts you have resisted integrating.

Now, a caution. You do not want to devolve into a base creature of your Shadow—Mr. Hyde, but neither do you want to live 100% behind the false mask of your Persona—Dr. Jekyll. This is your opportunity to be you, which is only possible with light and dark mixed and mastered. This is only possible by investigating what you have been taught life means. In that investigation, you learn to develop the insight to choose meaning instead of reacting to it.

This is what the gurus and masters mean by balance. Reorientating yourself from within creates this feeling, sense, and knowledge of balance. However, the whole is greater than that. Balance is the byproduct of your realigning based on the natural genius trapped within you.

Jung described this process as taking the problematic "it" and turning it into an integrated "I" understanding. Instead of thinking of your Shadow as a separate thing, a problem to be controlled, you pull your conscious-self on top of or in the center of layers and layers of meaning.

In this way, you engage to your best advantage the power of the Shadow for the greater good of your holistic personality. You make its power your ability. This pivotal change prevents Shadow from continuing as a part of you which challenges your internal stability and self-concept. Your *Axis Mundi* becomes balanced and centered in your core. It opens you to the feel of the flow of love and life coming through you.

The net result is a "you," which is mindful and understanding. You may experience a sensation of deep healing and resonance as the different parts of your psyche are melded together. What then shines out to the world is a unified Being, strong and more powerful than your previous fragmented self. It is a personal difference, providing you with the self-assurance to thrive as your own person in a conformist-oriented universe.

The mindfulness and strength cultivated are your tools to build on your development. Your work will ignite your creative spark of self-discovery and self-knowledge, transforming your personal journey to a higher state of self-expression. By connecting within the community, all who witness your enlightenment receive a release and awareness by integrating the same insights into their lives. "Isn't that interesting," we say.

It is worth mentioning that Shadow Work necessitates a particular breaking down of the Persona elements. Your Persona stems from outside of yourself, in the lessons of the society around you. Your commitment to the collective ideal smooths your road through society, in the same way that conformity to accepted norms is needed for any culture to function effectively. However, living through this Persona and continually conforming to outside standards masks your individuality. It's like pinching off a massive reservoir of data, insights, meaning, and energy. Instead of coming from within, you are forced to manage a life without. Over time, this develops into a feeling of numbness.

So, it's important to be cautious. At times, the mask you wear will slip or even break down. This can be very disorienting if you are unaware of what is happening. Spiritual emergence can look similar to a spiritual emergency. For example, what happens when you discover you don't share your parents' religious beliefs? Some might call it a crisis of faith, a moment of intense distress or chaos. Others will say the identity of a believer given to you by your parents has transformed, and a more authentic version of you has found its way to realization.

The same goes for your life goals. What if you wake up to the realization that your 9-to-5 job is something you hate deeply? For some individuals, this is a profoundly emotional time. Often, they will seek to find a way to re-conform to societal taught norms about working. James Clear wrote, "Goals are good for setting a direction, but systems are best for making progress." What happens when your spiritual progress meets your lower identity trapped in survival-rooted programming? The result is often profoundly distressing.

These examples can trigger a fear-based reaction. One that could cause you to run even farther the wrong way. Awareness of what you are doing and a guide to help you with the Turning Within process may keep you from running in fear of your power. Then you'll no longer need to conform to societal norms simply because you will have other choices. The key is, as your mask breaks down or is deliberately punctured by you, there is an opportunity for you to grow your individuality.

Instead of mindless living, you can choose between societal teachings and your internal dreams and desires. Your decisions in response to these moments represents the engine driving your growth as an individual. Your decisions inform and are reflected in the structure of your life. You are empowered by leaning into where you find your suffering. As Mother Aya teaches, the only way out of suffering is through.

What to Expect

For those who engaged in this work, we can point to certain feelings as bookmarks. Many seekers report feelings of enlightenment, they grew wings and were no longer trapped by the gravity of their problem. My greatest joy is witnessing awe—awe from a seeker who finally understands their power. I commonly hear, "Wow." It brings me to tears when witnessing as their mind restructures their decision-making process, and I know they see a change.

Something that boggled a seeker now makes perfect sense to them. A cloudy path has cleared in front of them. They receive an "Aha!" moment. I look forward to hearing what "aha" moment this journey brings you, and I hope you'll write it down and share it with me.

The insights gained during Shadow Ceremony serve as the foundation for this book, unearthing wisdom tools long concealed until we're prepared to wield them. Your mind already holds the keys to cleanse your ingrained beliefs and reconnect with a more authentic version of yourself. Your mind is capable of enabling transformative shifts akin to psychedelic experiences without the need for plant medicine. Affectionately dubbed the "Weekend of WOW," Shadow Ceremony is punctuated by moments of revelation, where seekers suddenly unlock answers to long-standing puzzles in their lives.

Shadow Work is like peeling back layers of an ever-expanding onion, which makes sense when you reorient life from within. Whether it's a personal or business problem, Shadow Work lights up the area of any issue usually overlooked.

As a practice, Turning Within is a life-time journey to mastery. Turning Within brings a feeling of blinding clarity. It is finding answers that were overlooked and right before you the whole time. As a result, feelings of "aha, eureka, wow" are all born out of finally solving some long-worked formula. The formula is then jettisoned for a more profound, authentic part of you.

This is the reason I remain excited about the journey of discovery.

The Woo Vs. The Material

You will find Shadow Work exists in practically every religion. The Christian Gnostic faith gave Jung much of his framework for understanding the unconscious. These faithful believed it was possible to know God personally. The word Gnostic means "to know." What if few people found the path to self-love because it was on a path they were programmed to avoid? What if we can find liberation not by imagining light but by taking the dark path into the depths of the soul?

Jung wrote in the now infamous *Black Books*, "We have to grapple with the knowledge content of Gnosticism and new-Platonism. These systems contain the materials destined to become the foundation of a theory of the unconscious." He referred to the confrontation with the Shadow as a "gnostic process."

The Hindu tradition is steeped in Shadow Work. Later in this book, you will learn more about *samskara* and how Shadow manifests as a physical charge in the body which can be tracked and must be released. In the book, *Feeding Your Demons*, Tsultrim Allione brings an 11th-century Buddhist Shadow-Work process to the West. She teaches a simple method to release you from your demons trapped within. This profound, yet counter-intuitive, process brings you up against your Shadow. Rumi was a famous Muslim poet who wrote extensively about Shadow and what it felt like to do Shadow Work. "I have a thirsty fish in me that can never find enough of what it's thirsty for!" Rumi wrote, "*The wound is the place where the Light enters you.*"

This Sufi quote by Rumi encapsulates the essence of the work. The "wound," or the construct, imprinting reality and causes suffering, is not just a point of pain—it's a gateway. It's where the light of awareness, understanding, and transformative potential enters, allowing us to see and engage with the deeper aspects of our consciousness.

Turning Within is a path that exists in every religion because it's part of every human's path. Shadow: Our purpose is meaning itself. As the ever-awakening, dancing glitter of the universe, our path is forever lit up by the meaning we make.

There are four levels of gnosis with your Shadow. Each stage is rated on your level of consciousness and ability to respond rather than reacting out of your suffering. Think of an area of your life in which you are currently experiencing resistance. Someplace where you aren't your ideal self.

4 Stages of Gnosis

Stage One: Asleep and Trapped in Feeling

This stage was referred to in the movie, *The Matrix*, when they talked about people being a slave to the Matrix. Morpheus said, "That you are a slave, Neo. Like everyone else, you were born into bondage. Into a prison that you cannot taste or see or touch. A prison for your mind."

By Turning Within, you become conscious of these sub-routines running in the background, directing your very experience of life. It's your life and you live from where lies reside.

At this convergence is where most of us will wake up to find the Shadow Work waiting for us. Treasures waiting to be found trapped within Shadow, in the deep-frozen tundra of our mind. These Shadows provided us with an algorithm effective for navigating reality.

This is the first layer of *you*, completely unconscious and reactionary. Your Shadow is activated by stimulus-response. At this level, you entirely deny the suffering you created. You may have the subjective experience of never breaking free of suffering. You might feel caught in a loop, like a mouse running around wondering who moved their cheese.

More than likely, these Shadows never cross your conscious thought. The deeper the Shadow goes, the less you will know its control over you. This allows your mind to retrieve and deliver meaning—the value you borrow or give to life, creating the very building blocks of your experience—already efficiently made. As such, you spend your energy focused on higher thoughts, like metaphors and symbols used by the mind to navigate life. You unconsciously take this Shadow for granted. If it causes suffering. The strategy to alleviate your suffering runs unconsciously within you, avoiding it. Just like avoiding the oncoming bus is removed from your decision-engaging process.

What If Will Smith goes to the Academy Awards with fear and powerlessness around his wife's illness? He sits down, hoping he will have a night free from his crushing feelings. He ends the night by creating what he is trying to avoid.

Stage 2: Awake to the Feeling but Still Controlled

This is the danger zone.

One of the challenges with tending to Shadow is the pain it produces. Your programming to avoid pain runs deep and includes emotional pain. The first step to change is awareness. Awareness of your suffering. However, you can't find peace until you let go of suffering. You can't let go of grief unless you know where it resides within you, where you hold it. You must stop resisting what you have programed to unconsciously avoid. This will feel uncomfortable and could cause you to feel as though things are getting worse, not better.

You now feel the feeling you have been avoiding, but you're still under its spell. Your awareness of your suffering is awakened. However, since you just became aware of the emotion and the control, you may likely feel as though you're in a worse place. Before, you may have felt like you were on solid ground. With awareness, you have no place to hide. This is the sign of movement in the right direction, going through the normal assimilation process. Before this, you couldn't fix what you didn't know was broken.

Stage 3: Awake to the Feeling and In Control

By remaining vigilant in your work, you maintain an awareness of the space between yourself and your programming. You are now in control of how you show up; you are awake to the feeling. You feel emotions and step through the distress anyway. This is a red-letter date because you are reclaiming your agency. Miracles and magic lift these moments for us. We witness mountains in our lives being moved.

In one example, you may find yourself angry, your mindset may be jarred. However, you maintain composure and don't react. Maybe you mutter under your breath or even call someone to vent right after a distressing engagement—but you don't add to the situation and worsen it. You are learning, thinking, and acting outside of your prior reality.

The system that is you is now open to response instead of reacting. You're still triggered by the situation, but the trigger doesn't control you. You may still be challenged in how to respond and not react. The challenge may drain you, since you're fighting a war on two fronts. However, remember, keep moving forward. This is a process. When you do not allow the trigger to dominate you, then you start to rewrite the path the mind uses to describe and make meaning of your world. You either control the mind, or it controls you. You are now in control.

In the What If story, Chris Rock comments on Jada Smith's hair. The camera may reveal the visceral feeling of anger that came over Will. However, he doesn't react. He responds. Maybe he will meet Chris backstage and be clear with him. But by not reacting negatively, he doesn't create more karma or momentum for the Shadow to grow. Will transmutes it. After which, Chris may face the wrath of the cancel culture, rather than receiving the blow from Will.

The learning is: We have work to do.

Stage 4: Freedom

Freedom only comes when you let go of the feelings that keep you stuck in suffering. Someone else's behavior belongs to them. You are not responsible for their suffering—don't seek to be their savior—when you're triggered by their desire or cry for help. From this vantage point, your Axis Mundi is centered. You're no longer triggered by the situation. You are no longer in a relationship with others *through* Shadow. You can better see that person for who they are. This frees up all the energy it took *not to react* as

74

your previous programming demanded. It also frees you to respond how you choose.

Remember, every action is a loving response or a cry for help. Now that you aren't suffering, you may be able to help this person by showing them behaviors outside the system in which they are trapped.

In the *What If* story, Chris' ill-informed joke falls flat. He and Will use the situation to raise awareness for alopecia and the importance of humor in our society. No one is impacted, and the world is better for the misunderstanding.

Stage 4 is rarely permanently etched within. Your mind is powerful and has created various relationships and associations through which you operate in our society. Shadow presents itself in "the now" as an echo of the past. It's the result of faulty programming the mind is trying to reconcile. Therefore, Turning Within is a practice, not an event. You never know when you may be triggered by something in the present. However, I believe this is another finger pointing to yet another insight.

The journey of Turning Within through Shadow Work is not a linear path but a spiral journey. This process is not about finding quick fixes but about engaging in a lifelong dialogue with ourselves. It's about uncovering, understanding, and ultimately transforming the deepest aspects of our being.

Chapter 7

Fruit of Your Work

The Three Great Directives of the Mind

We can break down the coding of the mind to find core directives, the baseline of thought. These directives are the undercurrent driving your everyday experience. By uncovering and integrating the awareness of these directives, much of the underpinning of suffering and success you experience begins to come into focus. The key to Shadow Work is awareness. The more aware you become of the way you design your world, the more agency you gain to live the life you desire.

Core Directives: Meaning, Elegantly Evolve, Survival

The Three Primary Directives of the Mind

1. Meaning
The primary directive of the mind is making meaning. Meaning is the value you borrow or give to your life. It's the building block of your

experience. You navigate your life from this dictum as it supersedes, drives, and informs you. Know that the question at the bottom of each question the mind strives to answer is: "What does this mean?"

Making meaning is the starting point of all thoughts. But you don't take my word for it— check your tape. Look at what you have done today. Examine how much of the makeup of your mind has been about meaning. Step back and look at your narrative and evaluate what you told yourself. What was your mind doing all day? It was making and navigating meaning.

Whether good or bad, right or wrong, your mind is designed to make meaning to enable you to navigate your experience. What were you navigating to? The answer is more meaning. Every meaning made is branched out of meaning already made (layer upon layer upon layer) and often unconsciously leveraged. This new meaning supports the budding of the meaning you will grow next. For example, you can't experience being mad without knowing there's something to be mad about. At some point in your life, you gave meaning to "mad" and applied it to any situation triggered by that feeling.

You are so good at making meaning you do it in your sleep. Unconsciously, you're doing it right now as you read these words.

Please take a pause in your reading right here. Try to clear your mind. Try to stop making meaning just for a second. You can't do it. Even the act of trying to pause is making meaning of what the pause means and feels like.

Finding Purpose in Design

When watching a young cat, you see it practice what it is designed to do. It chases the other cats, hunts, and stalks everything in its environment. As humans, we witness the fundamental attribute and programming of the archetypical cat coming online inside our four-legged feline friends. They are bred to be predators. It's in their programming.

Examine trees. You define a tree by the fruit it bears. An apple tree only makes apples. But what about humans? Do we have a fundamental attribute?

What did adults tell us to do when we were kids? "Go play." Remember what it was like to play as a kid? What did you spend your time doing? What games did you play? What did you pretend was real? You would design meaning and then live out of that meaning as if it were real. Cops and robbers. Pirates finding treasure. Ballerinas dancing on stage. Flying jets across the sky. Many of us survived lava flowing through our living room, jumping from a couch to a chair. Some of us pretended to be superheroes, activating the hero's journey architecture embedded in our minds.

We practiced holding meaning in our minds and simply doing what humans are programed to do. At a young age, we practiced what big people do at an extraordinary level— we forgot we were doing it.

We hold onto meaning. Meaning of what it means to be you. Constructs of reality so deeply engrained that you forgot how you are lying to yourself. You do it on multiple levels. You've woven meaning so tightly that questioning it is impossible, because you don't even recognize it's there.

Those pretend monsters are forever poised to eat you, materializing as a financial ruin or relationship Armageddon. Your universe isn't made up of atoms. It's made up of constructs.

This dynamic is one of the core reasons Turning Within has such a profound impact. Through Jung's concept of active imagination, you step out of the story you believe to be self-evident and step into a more profound realization that empowers you to make the changes you seek.

One of the ubiquitous fears in the human dynamic is the fear of not being good enough. Activated, this fear will be validated externally by experiencing anything that resembles or is interpreted as failure. This is especially important to understand because no one is perfect at anything the first time: Learning to walk. Learning to talk. Learning to dance. Learning to play a sport. Learning to…to…to….

You navigate life through representations of meaning. These constructs are like holograms from which you then live your life. However, by leveraging your Turning Within superpower, you can move mountains.

If you allow your fear of not being good enough to consume you, you will block access to your genius. This is where the second directive comes in.

2. Elegantly Evolve

You experience evolution, a gradual development, in every moment and in every facet of your life. It is one of the primary directives of the mind.

Everything evolves, and if everything is mind, then, by design, your mind must be more evolved and elegant than you could possibly know it to be.

Greek philosopher Heraclitus is credited with the idea that change is the only constant in life. Consider the idea that everything is in a constant state of development or evolution. As author Scott Olsen suggests, we can see how we are wired for evolution through the Fibonacci sequence and other patterns that exist in our physical bodies. How could our minds be any different? The mind must follow the same fundamental attributes of everything else in creation.

Most people believe that because we can only recall the experience between the bookends of life and death, our individual experience is the only meaning that makes up the "River of The Story Called You." Turning Within is an endeavor to dig beyond the surface of your experience. What if there was more to it all? What if you are much more evolved than you could ever know? Don't fall into the trap of thinking, your mind just got here. What if the meanings you have developed are created in a much greater well of meaning that has evolved over billions of years? AND is still in process.

Embodiment, Efficiency, and Evolution

One of the obstacles the mind has evolved through is embodiment. The brain is the most significant resource consumer of all organs in the body. It takes enormous amounts of energy to process thoughts, over 20% of your caloric intake, in fact. New ideas are much more energy expensive than old thoughts. New imprints and grooves need to be created. New thoughts are the VIP of thought, taking more energy.

Our prefrontal cortex is another considerable bottleneck. Your brain can process an estimated 11m bits of sensory information every second. But you are conscious of only around 40-50 bits of data per second. What if creation solved our bottleneck by creating an elegant way to present itself?

Consider that once a meaning is made, it's held against other meanings to see if it lines up. This process is called **confirmation bias**. When meanings line up, they begin the journey to a calcified belief. Beliefs are then "stored" in the Default Mode Network of the Mind or DMN.

You experience the present moment in a construct formed by a collaboration of previously made constructs. Your conscious thought is your creation (we believe what we are programmed to believe) and you are the creator.

Like zip files of meaning waiting to be leveraged, these files hold meaning and are how you interact with the outside world. This elegant solution to the creation process and powerful tool to navigate life is how you drive and think at the same time. You both evolve and experience evolution. This ability to leverage evolution is one of our superpowers. Evolution is the great "and therefore," which I call the "And so..." affect.

Your life challenge is initiated when meaning blocks your evolution, causes too much suffering, or the previous meaning inhibits you from living life. To check its work, the mind projects a Shadow of the suffering-rooted construct onto your present experience. Then your goal is to unlearn and relearn new ways to experience the present moment.

Unacknowledged, it manifests as cycles of suffering experienced over and over. We are like toddlers driving the most advanced navigation equipment in creation. When you're stuck in a cycle, it's because you are somehow wrestling with the Shadow of a construct your mind is trapped in.

When we finally grasp this and acknowledge it, we can finally begin to mature our understanding of the vehicle called the human mind. We can clean up the mess and recreate our creation.

3. Survival or Self-Preservation

The bookends of life and death create another directive: survival and self-preservation. It's not that the mind is built to survive; the mind makes meaning based on its limited perspective. The primary perceived limitation presented while living is the end of life.

This challenge has been compounded over the collective existence of mankind for eons. Most of mankind's existence was hand-to-mouth. If someone had a good day, maybe they shared some extra berries with those they cared for and loved. On a bad day, their day could result in "game over; thanks for playing!"

Lifetime after lifetime, generation after generation, the mind became hijacked to anticipate and focus on the danger life poses.

The Toddler Society

Add the reality that human beings have only lived in our current society for around 7,000 years, and then you understand what survival-rooted programming in your mind is made of. Although a T-Rex isn't chasing you, your mind is still conditioned to anticipate the chase through the calcified meaning made over countless lives. Because believing is seeing, your advanced mind upgrades the deeply rooted algorithms to the modern world. The chase arises from a risk of losing a relationship, or being financially devastated, or being physically attacked.

That ancient dinosaur is now transformed into the intangible weight of impending doom. The mind reasons that too much pain equates to death, so pain should be avoided. When you experience pain, your mind creates strategies to avoid whatever you decide caused it.

Shadow Work cleans your looking glass and rewrites lifetimes of misinformed, survival-rooted, or trauma-informed meaning. We can move past our survival-rooted mode only when we work to get under our established programming. By learning to face your suffering, you get a glimpse of something past the surface of thought and recode the meaning you live out of. Again, if this is true individually, the same should hold true collectively.

The experiment is to see if we can shift the collective. Can individual work rewrite our survival-rooted programming at the collective level in a way that changes how society values and experiences life? If your individual projections are a manifestation of the collective Shadow being presented to you intimately, then I believe the work you do individually has a marked impact overall.

Rules To Practice By

Sitting with my Turning Within practice for over 20 years, I've learned to use specific rules to help unravel the messes I could find myself in. What-ifs create a buffer just big enough for me to get a second chance before getting sucked into a story. I needed to make rules because I kept forgetting. Interestingly, the root word for *human being* in Arabic is to **forget**.

These rules help develop a deeper faith in your mind than the surface-level faith you use to cover up your fear of inadequacy. They act as symbols on

82

the map, yet they're not the map or the terrain. They are not dogma, that's what they are meant to avoid.

Every practice has a set of rules or guidelines. These are principles you can leverage to deepen your practice, deepen your understanding, to make your practice more impactful and improve the integration of your practice in the "real world."

The 4 Rules of Shadow Work

In the journey of self-discovery, one of the most transformative processes we can engage in is Shadow Work—the practice of delving into the deep conscious to unlock the structure of our being. In Turning Within, we embrace this journey with a unique approach, guided by four fundamental rules that serve as reference points to help us do the work. These rules are not just principles to understand; they are lenses through which we can deeply engage with our inner world. Let's explore these pillars, each a beacon illuminating the path to true self-awareness and transformation.

1. We Lie to Ourselves First

The first pillar confronts us with a stark but liberating truth: We lie to ourselves first. This isn't about deliberate deception or malice but a fundamental aspect of our human experience. From our earliest moments, our minds, in their quest to make sense of the world, construct narratives. These narratives, while essential for our survival and functioning, often lead us away from our authentic selves.

In the theater of our minds, we are both the playwright and the lead actor, often enacting scripts based on past experiences, societal conditioning, and inherited beliefs. These scripts dictate our reactions, relationships, and even our sense of self-worth. By acknowledging that we lie to ourselves, we start peeling back the layers of these narratives, revealing the core of our true being.

This realization is the starting point of Shadow Work. It's an invitation to question our deepest convictions about who we are and to challenge the stories we've been telling ourselves. **As we turn within, we learn to differentiate the voice of our authentic self from the cacophony of internalized scripts and societal expectations.**

2. There Are No Accidents in Shadow Work

The second pillar reminds us of the purposeful nature of our experiences: There are no accidents in Shadow Work. Every encounter, every challenge, and every joy we experience is a thread in the intricate tapestry of our lives. These threads, when woven together, reveal a pattern, a purpose, and a direction.

Turning Within, we begin to see the threaded connections between seemingly random events in our lives. We understand that our most challenging experiences are often our greatest teachers. This perspective fosters resilience and empowers us to face life's challenges with a sense of purpose and openness.

In the theater of life, every character we meet, every scene we encounter, is there for a reason. They are mirrors reflecting aspects of ourselves, opportunities for growth, and invitations to deepen our understanding of who we are. By embracing this rule, we move from a place of victimhood to one of empowerment, recognizing our role in co-creating our life's story.

3. Every Charge Begins and Ends with Me

At the core of Shadow Work is the principle that every emotional charge—every reaction, feeling, and emotion—begins and ends with us. This rule invites us to take ownership of our emotional landscape. It encourages us to look inward whenever we are triggered, to explore the underlying reasons for our reactions.

This inward journey reveals much about our unhealed wounds, unmet needs, and unresolved conflicts. It shows us how our present emotions are often entangled with past experiences, influencing how we perceive and interact with the world.

In the theater of our emotions, we are not just passive spectators but active participants. We have the power to change the script, to respond rather than react. This shift requires mindfulness, a willingness to sit with our emotions, and the courage to delve into their origins. By mastering this rule, we transform our emotional responses from unconscious reactions to conscious choices.

4. Black Hole Sun

The final pillar, Black Hole Sun, addresses the self-reinforcing nature of our mental constructs. It speaks to the tendency of our minds to create and get trapped in cycles of thought and belief that reinforce themselves over time.

This rule invites us to examine the patterns and cycles in our lives. It asks us to question the beliefs and assumptions that drive these patterns. Are they truly reflective of who we are or remnants of old scripts and outdated narratives?

In the theater of our mind, we often find ourselves playing roles that no longer serve us. We repeat the same scenes, expecting different outcomes, unaware that we are following a script written by our past selves, society, or our families. **Recognizing these patterns is the first step in breaking free from them.** It allows us to rewrite our narratives, choose different roles, and create new, more fulfilling life stories.

The Cosmic Inside Joke: A Journey Beyond Belief

In the vast tapestry of our lives, interwoven with beliefs and narratives, some moments stand out—moments of profound clarity that reshape our understanding of reality. I recall a conversation with a client and friend, a fellow traveler on this journey of self-discovery, who shared a dream that became a threshold moment.

Every hero's journey has a pivotal moment where the hero stands at the precipice of change. This moment, often referred to as a "threshold moment," is a turning point, propelling the hero into a new phase of their journey. It's a moment of profound realization, a sudden clarity. Previously held beliefs or perceptions are challenged, leading to transformative growth.

Threshold moments can be both subtle and monumental. They might come as a chance encounter, a dream, a loss, or even a simple realization during a quiet moment of reflection. Regardless of their origin, these moments are characterized by a significant internal shift. They act as doorways, leading us from one state of being or understanding to another. They are often accompanied by a surge of emotions, ranging from exhilaration to fear.

The power of threshold moments lies in their ability to disrupt our status quo. They can redefine the very structure of how we make sense of reality. They can redefine aspects of ourselves. They can alter beliefs we might have previously ignored, or even been unaware of. In doing so, threshold moments offer an opportunity to grow, evolve, and step closer to our true selves.

The River of the Story Called You

Your body is floating down the river of *The Story Called You* in the boat called *Now*. From the perspective of Kronos time, you've been drifting down this river since birth. Notice where the boat called Now is in the river of The Story of You. Do you feel as though you've been on this river for a while? How far down the river are you? Are you just starting? In the flow of time, where is this boat called Now?

Pause to notice if you are in the deep of your life? Or are you about to run aground? Is the water calm, or does a storm rage? How clear is the water? Are you able to peer down into your depths? Or is the water toxic and murky? Is there enough fish to feed you? How fast does the flow of the river feel? Maybe there are rapids ahead. Or perhaps you're in the rapids now. Are there any wakes? Are they menacing? Do you feel as though you're constantly trying to paddle upstream against the current?

Where is the boat called Now if your life were a mighty river? Take a moment to allow this metaphor to build in your mind before you move on from here.

At this moment, think of a significant life's traumatic event or high-stress moment a storm in your life. When in the face of it, going through the experience, you may have experienced a sensation similar to your boat about to fall over a waterfall or run aground. Maybe for you, it's a fear of falling off the ship or breaking up in the rapids. Like a knot in a muscle, after too much stress, your mind knots up. Your risk manager comes online. This identity lives in you is always scanning for trouble. However, that fantastic voice has saved you from more than you could ever know. You tighten up, drop anchor, immediately seek a safe harbor.

"*Make this stop!*" you shout, scrambling to survive the storm.
Your risk manager took harbor and dropped anchor. At some quantum level, your boat is stuck or imprinted there. Right now, notice how some part of you stayed back, back where the storm never ends. That part of you took root at a quantum level. However, "time" continued to flow, in the physical world you continued your float down the River of The Story of You. Because the mind has a mind of its own, it's built to survive. It creates a flow to avoid pain. It wants to avert anything and everything that hints of pain. The mind concludes pain equals death. It seeks to protect your mortality. The construct, the boat called Now, rudders away from dangerous shores.

When the mind creates a construct, one built to avoid painful moments, then a split can happen. A part of you sits back there in the waiting room, waiting for your pain. It's a sacrifice to the time when a part of you became an orphan, abandoned by you, and left in its wound.

The mind is now both navigating from the wound and simultaneously denying the very thing which is causing the pain. A false self emerges. Now you experience life through avoidance. The Shadow comes online to protect you. Concurrently, your mind forgets how it is the root cause of the construct.

How This Impacts NOW

Part of you unconsciously took harbor upstream due to the storm. This may leave you feeling the existence of a life half-lived. Your life experience now becomes more difficult to navigate. You may be left with a sense that the river no longer flows as it should. Pause and notice how your anchors now impact your ability to navigate your ship. Notice how echoes of past moments are trapped inside you. Notice how do they affect you? How much work, energy, control does it take to resist succumbing to the urge to jump from ship? How do triggers limit your ability to clearly see what's right in front of you?

Consider how many harbored ships you manage at any given time. Notice the amount of your resources are allocated to address the impact of harboring due to your past. Notice how those echoes have programmed you to navigate your ship now.

Notice how your risk manager is running scenarios all the time.

The scenarios are based on those harbored ships, like artificial intelligence with access to only doom-related equations. All it sees is troubled water. That is your risk manager's job.

Let's pause and get curious. Without judgment, ask yourself. "How much of the makeup of your narrative is unconsciously identifying from scenarios that mirror back there?

Permit yourself to notice that a part of you is always here. There is a part of you that doesn't feel your age. Notice how that part of you never felt their age. Albert Einstein once wrote, "The distinction between past, present, and future is only a stubbornly persistent illusion. He said, "Time, in other words, is an illusion."

When you dig beneath your experience, you understand his words.

PHALTS

The mind makes meaning. That's the gig. When we feel uncomfortable, the body is trying to tell us something. The challenge (and opportunity) occurs when we mis-translate what we are experiencing based on Shadow. To gain clarity, we need to check the gauges to get an accurate reading. One of the tools some in the recovery world use is the acronym HALT. This handy acronym reminds us to take a moment (HALT) and ask ourselves if we feel Hungry, Angry, Lonely, Tired. It seems simple enough, yet we become susceptible to self-destructive behaviors when these basic needs are unmet. Fortunately, hunger, anger, loneliness, tiredness are easy to address and serve as a warning system before you reach a breaking point. In further contemplation, Turning Within adds book ends to the HALT process to add awareness to something we all seem to be managing.

P is for Pain in PHALTS.

The S in PHALTS is for Stress.

Pain is an unavoidable part of our human experience. The human body is magnificent AND fragile. The central stimulus we humans are all programed to avoid is pain. However, pain can color our narrative and re-write the best experience into a horror plot.

Sometimes, just acknowledging your pain and any associated condensing feelings may be enough to break you out of a trance and provide you with a space to respond to the pain-stimulating situation rather than you reacting out of the pain. If that isn't enough, then the pain needs to be managed in a way which allows you to maintain the authorship of your narrative.

It's your responsibility to yourself, an act of self-love to maintain author-ship of your narrative. It can begin with basic behaviors. For example, hunger can be a physical or emotional need. Understanding the need to eat is relatively straightforward. However, you should remind yourself not just to eat, but to eat well. Meeting nutritional needs allows your body to operate to the highest potential and helps you maintain good feelings.

When we assess our situation, we can describe a hunger for less tangible things such as affection, accomplishment, and understanding. Hunger can also be a longing of the soul. To ease hunger, do not turn to destructive habits or negative people. This will not fill the physical or emotional emp-tiness that you're feeling.

This is why having a support system is so important. Find something wholesome to eat with a good friend or loved one. Spending time with those who love you will give you food for your soul and may ease the emotional hunger you feel.

Let's examine anger. Anger is a normal, healthy emotion to experience. Yet, it's essential to take a pause to understand what is causing your anger and then know how to express it adequately and appropriately.

Perhaps you're angry with a situation, or a person, or yourself. It might be one little thing spinning out of control or an ongoing event. No matter which one is bothering you, assess whether or not you can confront what angers you. Calmly talk to the person with whom you have an issue or fix your problem. If what angers you is beyond your control or you aren't ready to confront the issue, try to express yourself in other ways. For example, exercising, punching a pillow, or even cleaning are active ways to eliminate the excess energy anger can produce.

Creative projects such as painting, singing, or writing might be more compelling activities for you to dispel your anger. Meditation or prayer are ways for you to calm yourself anywhere and at any time. Finally, talking to someone not involved in the situation may be beneficial. It may help you think through your anger. Regardless of how you expel your anger, start by acknowledging it, then reflect upon its cause, leaving you to release your anger in constructive, not destructive, way.

Another emotion to examine is loneliness. It can occur whether you are alone or surrounded by many people. Often, we isolate when we don't feel as though others understand us, withdrawing into self out of fear or doubt. Being alone is a self-imposed situation. If you're feeling lonely, pause, ask yourself if you have contacted anyone lately. Your support system is there when you feel depressed, overwhelmed, or anxious or need someone to talk to. Find ways to cultivate energy in ways that are comfortable for where you are beginning. We receive a lot of energy by being around others, even when it feels tough to do something. Call someone, run an errand, go for a walk, or go get coffee—begin to monitor how you feel before and after and reflect on the shifts in your energy.

Again, don't be afraid to bring in professional help when needed.

Another physical sensation linked to our emotions is tiredness. Tiredness takes a toll on our body, mind, and spirit. When our days are filled with go-go-go, such as errands, meetings, and activities, we ignore how tired we become. However, running on low energy compromises our ability to think and our capacity to cope.

Noticing your PHALTS is particularly important when you're tired. Satisfying the physical need to sleep, rest, and rejuvenate is critical to maintaining physical, emotional, and spiritual health. A good night's sleep or a power nap may be all you need to change your outlook for the day. If your day is particularly hectic, take a short break to listen to music, walk, or take a deep breath. Build into your schedule time for your rejuvenation. Take a trip to your favorite park, movie theater, or restaurant. Recharging your body, mind, and spirit will help you overcome challenging moments.

Stress is becoming a bigger and bigger and bigger part of our society.

According to The American Institute of Stress:

- About 33 percent of people report feeling extreme stress
- 77 percent of people experience stress that affects their physical health
- 73 percent of people have stress that impacts their mental health
- 48 percent of people have trouble sleeping because of stress

Unfortunately, for about half of all Americans, stress levels are getting worse instead of better.

The Global Organization for Stress reports that:

- 75 percent of Americans experienced moderate to high stress levels in the past month
- Stress is the number one health concern of high school students
- 80 percent of people feel stress at work

PHALTS will serve as a reminder of how signals can be misinterpreted from the inside. Take a moment to check-in with yourself. Ask, "Am I in pain, too hungry, angry, lonely, tired or stressed?" Assessing how you feel takes only a moment. Doing so will help put the signals you feel into perspective. It may help alleviate the gravity the Shadow has on you. Just a breath is all you need to dive down and see where you're stuck in Shadow. Realizing you feel uncertain, uncomfortable, or unsteady because you haven't slept or eaten well will help you regain your agency.

As a Shadow Practitioner, PHALTS are a great place to see where we fall into default patterns of suffering. These threshold moments become powerful opportunities to break free. Suffering is sacred. Yes, you're tired and hungry. Yes, that is the reason you were short with someone or even yourself. Yes, you pushed your mind, body, and spirit beyond your energy limit to overwhelm. However, you can use this threshold of Shadow to do work, pull the thread of the stories where you're stuck. Then, maybe next time, tired can just be tired. Hungry can be just that, hungry. You don't have to live out of the suffering in loop after loop where you've been caught.

Remember, your suffering moments are the direct result of a story you bought into that drive your suffering and keep you anchored there.

Chapter 8
Catching Monkey Mind

The Mastering Change website has a video showing the effectiveness of the age-old South India Monkey Trap. The trap is used to keep monkeys from stealing food from the villages in India. In the video, a soldier takes a hollowed-out gourd with a hole just small enough for the monkey's hand to fit and places some fruit inside. The soldier then walks up and ties the trap to a tree. He doesn't even hide; he walks away from the tree and waits.

The monkey is a curious animal. So, he climbs up the tree to the trap to investigate what's there. After noticing the sweet fruit inside, the monkey reaches in to retrieve the fruit, what he thinks will be a tasty meal. The thought of the sweet fruit creates the anticipation of joy and satisfaction in this monkey's mind. The monkey can't see his fist closed around the fruit is too large to fit through the hole. Because the monkey doesn't know the lynchpin to the trap is a closed fist, he doesn't realize all he has to do is let go.

In analyzation, it's suggested the monkey doesn't let go because he doesn't want to risk losing his bounty. As the soldier calmly walks up to capture the monkey, there is terror in the monkey's eyes. He yanks on the trap, pulling with all his strength. He bites deep into his arm to try and break free. At that moment, I wonder if there is anything the monkey wouldn't do to get free. The soldier unties the trap from the tree, then places the monkey in a cage with three other monkeys he just caught using the same trap.

Do you know what it is like to be caught in such a trap? Of course, you do. You're caught in one now. This trap doesn't exist in the physical world. It exists in your mind. You created it. It has been created by the very aspects which allow you advanced thought.

We are prisoners in our minds because we don't understand the dynamics of having a mind that evolves. The meaning your mind makes is like grabbing the fruit inside the trap. The mind automates all meaning. It runs that meaning against what it already holds to be true, (meaning it already contains), which are beliefs, and makes more meaning.

Each layer is given validity based on the previous deeper layers of thought, like a never-ending stairwell your mind climbs endlessly through time.

See, your mind isn't composed of mostly "unconscious" thoughts, but "deep conscious" thoughts. These are thoughts that have already been thought—for example, when it rains you might anticipate the need for an umbrella based on prior thought. Your ability to navigate life is paramount in your mind, constantly assuming and leveraging belief. This is vital. This is the reason you need to remind yourself to have gratitude and say, "Thank you mind for keeping me safe."

By automating thoughts, those thoughts become beliefs and hold up the construct you leverage to live out your life. Most people don't spend the time examining and redefining this deep conscious thought. As such, each meaning becomes the fruit your mind will hold onto without you ever realizing you have to let go.

Most people don't have thoughts. Most people's thoughts have them. You've seen this monkey-mind caught in a belief. Ever have friends and acquaintances so married to a story they'd argued the sky was red and not blue. Consider and review some of your past arguments to see where this is true. However, know that if it is valid for them, then it must be true for you. Why? As human beings, there's not much tragically hip or terminally unique in any of us. The truth, which is hard to swallow, is most of our thoughts have us, hold us, capture us. We don't have them. No one is immune.

Just as you float down the River of the Story Called You in the boat called Now, that river is your deep conscious meaning. Layer upon layer of coding, all designed to hold the boat of consciousness on top of it. It's not just assuming you aren't good enough or lovable. These are stories causing you enough discomfort to allow you to pierce the veil of thought to see what you are floating on in life. Your suffering is sacred because it gives you a glimpse of your divinity. By delving into the depths of your mind, you start to understand what the gurus have been telling us all along: YOU are the author of your reality.

Now that you are aware of the River of The Story Called You, this is the time to upgrade how you see the world. The velocity of change has sped up. This means the beliefs and stories you live out of will become less and less valuable. For example, the faster a vehicle goes, the more dangerous it is to drive with a dirty windshield from years of buildup.

How do you clean the windshield? By identifying the cycles deluding your perception of your life. Recognizing the cycles brings insight. Learning to unlearn or redefine your worldview returns your agency back to you. You're no longer owned by stories. Stories that have you rooted in suffering because now you know where to let go.

Yet, just like hunting for treasure at the bottom of an ocean, if you miss by an inch, you miss by a mile. You can't let go of something you don't know how/what/why/when, or where you are holding it. You remain trapped like the monkey in the trap, biting your arm and trying with all your strength to break free. However, by developing a practice of Shadow Work, you learn to dive into your suffering to unlock the insights and healing which is trapped in the murky depths below. You free the monkey-mind and uncover a treasure of immeasurable wealth. But it is only for *you* to find. And only *you* can own where you are in Shadow.

What can suffering teach you about why You Do What You Do

Certain painful experiences take root at a quantum level, below time and space. That is beyond time, language, and identity, below your conscious awareness. It takes root, and you develop *samskara* (psychological imprints). Suffering is often not past, present, or future but always sits below, within your conscious awareness. It sits below the ego, and it projects a Shadow onto the surface of your life. This causes you to continually and compulsively re-create the trauma and live the suffering through a "repetition compulsion" process.

In these instances, you are no longer experiencing the present. Instead, you're trapped in scenarios of "what could happen" if the trauma were in the present moment. Consciousness takes the form of whatever it is presented with, it wraps you in Shadow and looks for an exit. At some level, these scenarios become the yardstick with which you measured and navigated your reality. Your story is the only story you know. You're a sailor at sea, and your map is the only navigational map your mind knows, although a map is not the territory any more than your story is the truth. Therefore, the meaning you make is the only meaning you have.

In my personal experience, some part of me remained entombed in that basement my Boogie-Mom had locked me in long after she released me. In navigating my experiences, I would find myself feeling trapped in every area of my life. I created scenarios where I would be trapped, overwhelmed, smothered, and imprisoned at every level, in moments, loops, and all seasons. This Shadow tainted my career, family, health, finances—no part of my life remained unscathed. Then my mind worked to resist running or lashing out inappropriately. I was forced to carry these heavy, invisible chains. The loss of resources I could have used to navigate or manage my life caused a cascading effect, setting off an avalanche over everyone around me.

It wasn't until I became conscious of my Shadow that I could begin the journey out of the cellar. This is the same journey everyone must take at some point if they desire something new in their life. As stated before, being born isn't living. Being born is the invitation to live. It isn't until you learn to unravel the coding that predefines your experience that are you able can begin the journey to living. Otherwise, the cycle of suffering repeatedly loops in your life, providing your experience with the same suffering over and over and over.

Eons of programming

Think of your mind as a bundle of algorithms. An algorithm is a process or set of rules to be followed in calculations or other problem-solving operations, especially by a computer. Although the process is similar, the building blocks aren't. For one, your code is different from a machine's. Yours is based on story and not mechanical 0s and 1s. Your mind makes up a story of what something means and then begins its journey deeper into your consciousness, like a bite of chewed food traveling through your digestive tract.

But the greatest kept secret of our time: You Can Self-Correct Your Code.

But why must we relive the most painful moments to begin with? Are we trapped in some sick hell where we are forever recreating our most painful experiences? Does God hate us so much that we must repeatedly endure the same pain?

The surface-level reason is the most basic: survival.

Civilization has only been around for a little over 7000 years. Before that, we were food. On a good day, you might find a couple of extra berries to share with your family. On a bad day, "game over...thanks for playing!" Dead. That was it. Human beings have lived on the razor's edge for most of our existence.

Think on this for a second. The version of The Mind in your head has been updating every second of your life. Every second. It validates and tests best guess scenarios over and over. Your mind is doing it right now.

Stop. Here. Notice.

Notice how your mind is analyzing these words on this page, in this chapter, in this book.

PAUSE: HAVE the EXPERIENCE

You are noticing…some may. Some of you reading this now ARE noticing. Isn't that interesting?

This version of you (maybe version 347) didn't start with the you reflected in the mirror today. You evolved and are evolving. You're not at the beginning nor at the end of you. You possess a vast number of different versions of you.

Your genes and DNA were passed down from your parents. That DNA, we now scientifically understand, is the basic information needed to create your version. So (and I think this is mind-blowing), your version of "The Mind" has been running and updating since the beginning of creation. Most of your programming is survival-based, and it does not fit our current civilization. This means the predator in you will still eat and kill. It means you have a collective wisdom that is both profound and intelligent. It sits just under your conscious thought. In other words, you know way more than you are telling yourself.

The system that learns expeditiously will quickly learn it pays to anticipate risk. One of the ways we have become the planet's top animal is our risk manager's ability to come online and run scenarios. We problem solve. Yes, we have an enormous ability to think through scenarios. If you can predict something will happen, you can avoid repeating it.

Our minds are addicted to running scenarios. It runs worst case, best case, and any case it can imagine. Over and over and over. This process has been so effective it has taken residence in the deep conscious and become one of our primary ways to solve problems. Therefore, it is one of the core identities from which we live our lives.

Deeper than logic, more profound than the *You* that you are right now. You have a risk manager running scenarios, both consciously and unconsciously. Once a scenario is picked as the most likely, your consciousness forms into that container. It becomes what you experience.

The mind validates and then automates meaning. The validation process causes confirmation bias. This is the tendency to search for, interpret, favor, and recall information such that your mind confirms or supports your prior beliefs and/or values. All your meaning has been made by standing on a previous meaning to make the next. You're like a child standing on a stack of books, stretching to grab the next one.

Your brain is the most energy-draining organ in your body. The human brain makes up a mere two percent of total body mass but consumes twenty percent of your energy supply. That's a lot. To help manage thought efficiently, your mind automates systems, patterns, and habitual or systematic behavior. Your mind craves patterns at every level. It will create a pattern out of total chaos. It contains default identities, language patterns, stories, blueprints, insights, and behaviors. These imprints load into what neuroscientists call the *default mode network* or DMN. This part of the mind allows you to act without thinking. Ever return home from somewhere and not remember the ride? Thank you, DMN.

The unconscious playing out of the scenario, again and again, is your mind's attempt to re-experience something differently, trying to assimilate an experience in order to liberate the part of you trapped within the scenario. That is, you are unconsciously reliving a trauma to give yourself a chance to free some lost part of your soul—some part of you is frozen in time.

Imagine if the mind has its own immune system, which has the capability of separating a virus within your system. Then it circulates thought, virus-free, and projects back into your life, giving you another chance to rewrite. Even as another part of you refuses to look at the opportunity for change.

A computer trying to free itself from the pull of a virus will rerun the code repeatedly. In human beings, this repetition becomes the very symptom and pathology of trauma. Once you become aware of how your mind process works, invest in yourself by doing the work to get under your programming, you become free to release yourself from a lifetime of suffering. You open the door to real change. Old patterns that used to baffle you will burn away, leaving only traces of ash. You regain control of your system. You begin the journey to real healing and transformation, to living.

The Holographic Universe

In his classic book *The Holographic Universe*, Michael Talbot argues the universe is like a giant hologram. He explains the connection between the mind and body through understanding hologram theory. He says, "The universe no longer appears to be a machine composed of innumerable parts but an interconnected network of patterns that manifest themselves everywhere."

If everything in the universe is made up of patterns, then your mind would also be made of the same stuff. Inside your mind, you have a meaning-making machine that is layers-deep of meaning. Talbot explains how memories are stored through specific patterns in the brain, not in any particular spot. Like a holodeck or your own personal matrix machine, you collaborate with your story-informed and survival-hijacked-meaning-made machine operating inside a vast amount of pre-made meaning.

From Talbot's theories, I started to wonder what the implication of a holographic mind had on Shadow Work. If the universe is conscious, and there is a quantum field from which we draw upon, then it should be possible to open the channel of consciousness wider to change the scenarios where we are stuck. Shadow Work is a path to liberation. It opens you up by allowing you to take in the broader view of the holographic universe we are living out of. By practicing Turning Within, you learn to own your Shadow and stop projecting on the screen before you. And navigate from a more self-generating center.

Shifting the focus of your Shadow Work from trying to cure the pain to understanding the nature of your existence deepens your practice. Turning Within raises questions that a suffering resistant mind doesn't have the resources to ask or understand. What would your life be like if … suffering was sacred?

If you could get a glimpse of what sits beyond the programming where you're trapped? We know the adage of "thoughts become things." If you have thoughts rooted in survival and suffering, you can't not create that experience externally. Your survival and suffering thoughts manifest for you, whether you consciously acknowledge them or not.

What would your life be like if you no longer suffered through the projections of past horrors lived through? More importantly, what if you could reclaim the trapped part of you and finally connect to your genuine authenticity and genius?

Shadow Work changes nothing. And Shadow Work changes everything. Because, at some level, we are all living out simulations in our mind, best guess scenarios of this thing called life. Ram Dass said, "The shadow is the greatest teacher for how to come to the light." This is because we can track suffering through Shadow Work down to its source.

Subjective Practice Vs. Objective Lessons

Shadow Work is the tuning of the subjective experience of your world. When leveraged with integration, the results can profoundly affect your life and the lives of everyone around you. How do you leverage it? By learning to let go of the story you're trapped in, you become empowered to create a new story, redefining your journey. When you change how you show up for things, the things you show up for change.

Shadow Work is a subjective practice. This means the impact it can have on your life must be experienced in order to be understood. Reading about integrating Shadow will produce little change for you. Your objective lessons learned may be considered matter of fact. However, the subjective experience of integration—the twining of insights gained through Turning Within— will lead to profound results and produces a new reality.

You might read a book about what it's like to visit the temples of Jerusalem. But until you sit in this holiest of places, you don't know. You can be told how to care for a baby, but raising a child is another matter. Objective lessons mean nothing compared to subjective practice.

My uncle teaching me how to swim on the couch meant nothing until he took me out into the water and tossed me. Once my body hit the water, it crystallized the knowledge into the body. I was officially a swimmer. Identity is formed by activating meaning. Following a process creates an awareness of deeper meaning beyond your understanding. Just like a recipe for a dish doesn't make the meal itself, you must follow the recipe to fill up on the fruits of your lessons.

Axioms of Shadow Work

By being immersed in the practice of Shadow Work for over 20 years, I've learned that we are able to embrace and utilize specific rules or axioms to untangle ourselves from the delusions and cycles where we are caught. These accepted truths are only suggestions. They are symbols on a map, yet not the map or the terrain. They are used to offer you a doorway to get underneath the outer layer of your experience and then sink into the depths of the meaning where you swim.

Any effective practice benefits from a set of axioms. These forms are ways of moving through the practice to provide a solid foundation. These are principles a practitioner can leverage to deepen their practice. By developing your own set of axioms to follow, you deepen your understanding, make your Shadow more impactful, and improve the integration of the practice in the "real world."

A half-truth is more dangerous than a bald-faced lie.

We lie to ourselves first.

A student of mine is stuck in the lie that he is a phony. He finds many reasons to believe he is a fake at every turn. I deal with many successful people who suffer from imposter syndrome. The condition may have many faces, yet underneath is the same, this is a feeling of not being good enough. It's a sacred fear. Say, "Hello, Sacred Fear."

The mind tries to avoid being discovered, so it looks into the world to see where you are living a lie. "I'm *not* good enough" is often a deeper-held belief than any confirmation of "I *am* good enough." It sits farther down in the roots of the tree of meaning, beyond your awareness.

Validation is made over a lifetime of avoiding being found out, it's those moments of suffering attached to other examples of when we fall short. All these suffering moments create a dense and deep conscious subsoil of judgment. Conscious thought sits on top. The mind then searches for ways that we are living a lie. Well, again, it's all story. It's *all made up* at some level.

As a result, your mind will always find a way to pull apart the certainty that you are truly meant to be here. Know that if you were meant to be someplace else, you'd be there—not here.

Consequently, a half-truth is more dangerous than a bold-faced lie. The reason for this is because something you know to be untrue is easily dismissed. But if something you know is partly true or you believe it's true at a deeper level, then your mind operates out of *that* meaning and uses that meaning to justify the narrative. Thus, it feeds you a corrupt truth. That fallacy perpetuates your rotting experience of the plot from where you live out your life.

A great example is when a friend is angry. We assume they are mad at us. Or maybe when something goes wrong for them, we assume it's about us—our fault. Yes, the friend is mad, however, remember—if someone has a charge around something, that charge is about them, not you. However, you need to take accountability for your actions. Because there is always a hook.

The deeper and more meaningful question is: Why are you experiencing a charge because someone else is mad? What's underneath the story that makes their story about you?

There are two types of thoughts

Human beings generally experience two types of thoughts. There is the new thought. This is a new perspective, insight, or meaning—one that you created. These new perspectives come in the guise of insights, moments of clarity, data downloads, and intuitions. New thoughts may feel "like a bolt of lightning" strike. Yet, even new thoughts are based on meaning you've already created. However, these are fresh and never thought about.

The second type of thought is thoughts that have already been *thunk*. These are pre-existing avenues of thought, grooves already made in the mind, imprints and meaning made and confirmed. This is the root of the narrative from which you live daily. The National Science Foundation suggests over 95% of our thoughts are repetitive. Forget the number, instead examine your life over the past week, month, and year. Isn't it true that the makeup of your mind consists primarily of the same thoughts repeated in your mind? Your default mindset is a set of beliefs and expectations you live out of daily. These thoughts load in the DMN and make up most of the daily content of your experience.

By learning to mine your default mindset of pre-supposed beliefs, and thoughts, you unlock a wealth of agency and have the power to finally take control of the story you have been living out of. When you're suffering, learning to ask yourself, "Is this a thought that I have already *thunk*?" gives you the space between you and your automated meaning to begin to make new thoughts and perspectives.

Being a Human Being

Narrative Transportation is a concept rooted in psychology and storytelling. It describes the phenomenon of becoming deeply engrossed in a narrative, temporarily losing awareness of our surroundings and personal identity. How do you know if a book, story, movie, or tale is any good? You can tell by how much you are swept up in the story. You forget you're being told a story and live out of that narrative.

We see it in movie theaters when the crowd jumps at a scary scene. We experience it when we cry during a sad one. The exact mechanics happen during hypnosis, psychedelic journeys, Shadow Work sessions, meditation, and when children play. In this state, we become profoundly open to new programming. Our deep-conscious programming becomes available to change since we have forgotten or let go of the identifications of what we deem as reality. New constructs are formed. Effective artistry in these areas have guided society for eons.

It's interesting to note the Arabic word for human being is 'insane,' which is derived from the word 'nasiya,' which means 'to forget.' This is a decisive necessity for your everyday experience of reality.

In this state, you can be profoundly affected by story, experiencing emotions, and adopting perspectives as though you were part of the narrative. Narrative transportation can inspire, enlighten, and transform us by allowing us to empathize with characters and situations beyond our own lives. Uncle Tom's Cabin greatly furthered the abolitionist cause in the north, ratcheted up tensions with southern slaveholders, and, as President Lincoln himself suggested, helped tip the country into civil war. How? Because of narrative transportation.

Your mind is coded through stories, symbols, and patterns. The pattern the mind anticipates and is wired for is story. Joseph Campbell stunned the world when he revealed that every mythology and religion had embedded within it the same code, the monomyth. This makes perfect sense when we tie our current understanding of the holographic nature of reality and the first Hermetic Principle that all is mind. You are living out your own personal mythology. The challenge is that most of us have lost the plot. You are living out the extraordinary story of your life. Myth is just a reflection of life.

Michael Meade teaches that story is the telling of lies to uncover a more profound truth. We tell ourselves stories or scenarios over and over. This fits perfectly in a holographic universe that is looking back on itself. Look at your day and notice how many stories you tell yourself. Now, notice how much narrative transportation plays in the subjective experience of the story called you. Now, consider that is just how much you are aware of. How much do you need to "forget" to live out of the narrative that you do? What if narrative transportation ran deeper than you thought? Notice how, in your mind, your life is a story. What is the storyline you have been living out of? This is your personal mythology. The River of The Story Called You. What happens when the construct is so painful that our ego refuses to experience the pain from the story that we have made up?

In Timothy Wilson's book, *Strangers to Ourselves: Discovering the Adaptive Unconscious,* we learn, senses gather some eleven million bits per second from the environment. But our conscious minds can handle only forty to fifty bits of information per second. Your mind constantly decides what information you should be aware of, how it should be presented, which "facts" should be the most important, and which are viewed as too painful to keep the boat floating downstream. That stuff is offered up based on constructs you created through life.

Because you are living your own personal story, *you* are the hero of your subjective experience. Anything too painful or that upsets the applecart of your meaning is avoided, forgotten, or flat-out denied. However, while avoidance may provide temporary relief, it most frequently perpetuates a cycle of suffering in the long run. Avoiding challenging experiences denies us the opportunity to learn and grow.

Avoiding Experiences

Experiential avoidance is trying to avoid or escape unpleasant thoughts, emotions, and experiences. It is an automatic mental process meant to protect us from discomfort as too much pain equals death in a mind programmed for survival. Avoid any discomfort is one of your mind's basic subroutines. The greater the hurt, the harder your mind works to prevent it. If a construct is too painful to take in, too much to process, or seems too big to the fragile ego, the mind seeks to manage the weight of the meaning while keeping the boat afloat. Management of the "too much to handle" is accomplished as it hides, represses, or denies that you are trapped inside and yet living out of the construct of the trap.

Ironically, in the very attempt to avoid pain, we calcify, cultivate, and strengthen it. The survival-hijacked mind begins to navigate away from what it doesn't want to experience.

If you pick up the construct, tell yourself the I'm-worthless lie, you will find yourself endlessly trying to prove the construct wrong. The consequence of the lie is your inability to fix something that isn't perceived as broken. This becomes the black hole of suffering where you're trapped. You unconsciously project the message of worthlessness into the outer world.

Now, you're caught in a double bind. The construct of worthlessness is an imprint always running and informing your experience of reality, therefore, any success you may experience can only lead to greater feelings of worthlessness. Like a rabbit chasing a carrot on a stick, you chase success, hoping to satisfy a zombie-hunger, which in turn, becomes an ever-increasing drag on your reality experience. Equally important to understand is your mind's need to stay consistent. The mind fears and resists change. Any attempt you make to sail away from the island of worthlessness is unconsciously resisted.

Lost in Thought

Cognitive fusion, closely related to experiential avoidance, occurs when we become overly attached to our thoughts and emotions, believing them to be absolute—having no restriction, exception, or qualification—truths. Like inner narrative transportation, we fuse with our internal narratives, allowing them to dictate our actions and shape our perception of reality. These fusions limit our ability to step back and observe our thoughts objectively. There is no objectivity. Instead, we become entangled in a web of self-created stories, which can lead to distorted thinking patterns and emotional distress.

Learning to See What You Can't

When you find yourself stuck in the victim archetype, you will find the narrative always lines up with being victimized. If you are stuck in the Shadow of shame, you won't be able to see your power. If you judge that you can't be right, you will find it difficult to see any right way out. Remember, seeing isn't believing. Believing is seeing.

One of the most amazing things I find about the mind is how we can be blind to that which is right in front of us. One of my clients is a top-notch doctor. She needed to grow her business. The only way to accomplish her goal was for her to increase her staff and lead them. Yet, she felt she couldn't teach anyone. Thus, the strategy to scale her business was hidden. Her mind hid her suffering-rooted belief that she wasn't good enough. In the meaning she'd made, no one could do what she did.

I asked her, "Not one person in the 7 billion people on the planet can do what you do?"

She couldn't see it.

After some digging, she realized, she saw her fear of not being heard kept her from engaging the staff she needed. Once she stepped past the fear, she woke to her new reality and started seeing resources right before her. In reality, she had several strong candidates, and she reached out to them. She recognized because she held the belief that no one would come to her, it prevented her from seeing anyone that would. By learning to see where your perception is short, you can trail yourself down to the root of your Shadow and see how you are stuck. The trail is quite simple: look for what your mind is holding back from you as it distorts your reality to align with the belief, causing you to live in Shadow.

As I wrote this book, I had to step through multiple stories of my own, all rooted in survival-based thinking. I had to let go of any judgment of perfection, knowing it was never reachable. I had to step through any questions I had as to whether or not I was qualified, crazy, or good enough. When those moments arose, they left me motionless and unable to consider writing.

All my questions were based around and rooted in "not enough," always something lacking. It forced me to get to the core of what I know and trust: What I am offering is the best version of my understanding of Shadow. I resolved to offer something clear, an opportunity for someone to break through, wake up, come online, step forward. If I trusted what I knew, then all of the effort would be worth it.

What was this "enough" that I was being confronted with? I asked, what if "not enough" wasn't a deciding qualifier of our reality? What if I accepted the possibility of all assumptions as a story? What if I chose to have radical certainty and trust? I would have to let go of the whole sub-routine of weighing something because it constantly distorted my perspective. I asked the next logical question, "What are ways I limit my perspective by qualifying and coming from not enough?"

Suddenly, I saw how I had been limiting my perspective by assuming insufficient was in the equation. I saw the limited view of what could be stunting what was. There it was, like a virus draining valuable resources. Like an invisible prison. Like trying to break out of the problem by recreating the same problem again and again.

I saw the ever-familiar pattern of judging that the resources I would need would not present themselves. Like living paycheck to paycheck but confident every check was the last. I saw how this view was counter to the way that life worked. I found a level of certainty that came from within, not from without. I suddenly found myself able to reconnect with the words to begin again. I was able to step into that space I find myself in when doing Shadow Work, an area beyond any limitation. All because I saw what I wasn't allowing myself to see. Shadow Work done in real-time while trying to get this book into your hands. Thank you, readers, for being my teacher.

By learning to see when you are in Shadow, you gain the agency to transmute the Shadow into light. This is a sacred moment being masked as danger. Learn to see where you have been blind. Learn to hear where you have been deaf. By noticing the limitation, we bring awareness to the resistance.

Listen to me, for they who have the ear to hear… all of your sufferings can be tied to some part of yourself that is holding on and has yet to let go. You can't see where you are holding on because the mind is not tangible; it navigates, controls, and traps you like the poor monkey caught in the trap.

The key is learning *how* and *where* you are holding on.

You can't heal what you don't feel.

Awareness will do most of the work for you. Finding the sacred identities you have created to solve the problem and connecting them where they can heal you unlocks insights that will dissolve barriers in front of your eyes.

Shadow Work Never Ends

A statement I emphasize with everyone before we begin any Shadow Work is about how things, once learned, can't be unlearn. With Shadow Work, the statement, "Life will never be the same," is required understanding. One of the reasons for this is that once you become aware of the Shadow driving your behavior and experience, it then becomes your responsibility to keep that awareness, monitoring when it appears again. There is a lie in our current zeitgeist which suggests work gets done and doesn't come up again. Like you take a pill, and it all goes away. That is a lie; it sells books, it signs contracts, but nonetheless, it's a lie. The truth is more complicated and much more interesting. You learn to keep your Shadows out in front of you, therefore, when they appear, you are aware of them.

Shadow Work is never done. It is either doing or not doing, but it is never done. Each Shadow will lead you to the eventual next layer of the onion. You peeled back a layer to expose a new layer, a deeper understanding of yourself. Each layer offers up another gift waiting to be unwrapped. By developing a practice, you witness meaning deeper than solution-based, suffering-rooted programming. You see how you're part of a larger story being told through you.

As you step into your authenticity, your genius emerges through you. The boat called Now grows, changes, and becomes less important. The "aha" moments you earn through diving into deep conscious are nothing without integration, which can take a lifetime.

Augmented Armageddon In Your Life

Over the past couple of years, an interesting form of entertainment has appeared across America—Ax throwing. My wife and I enjoyed a date night at a bar serving alcohol while simultaneously giving us big axes to throw at a target on the wall. Ax throwing and alcohol. Ax throwing. And.

Alcohol. Yes, It's a thing. Mind you, I don't drink. (If I did, someone would have undoubtedly been harmed that night.)

My wife and I spent several hours enjoying this new-found sport. There was something about it that put me in an other-than-normal state, a Zen state of thinking but not thinking. This state unlocked an awareness within me and taught me much about how the mind constructs reality and anticipates pain.

The throwing area was sectioned off by chain link fences, creating throwing lanes. The thrower stands behind a line and tries to hit the bullseye on a target. I noticed right away the worn-thin spots on the floor from people readying and taking their aim. By standing in the sweet spot, I was at the proper distance for the ax to hit the target in the right place *and* stick the landing. There was a spot that was more worn for right-handed people and a less worn spot for left-handed. Both types of throwers considered the distance it took for the ax to spin so it could stick.

I began to wonder, if we operate out of survival-rooted programming, and the mind is patterns and stories, could I track Shadow by noticing the worn spots in my experience? This analogy initiated several layers of awareness. I began to see the monsters chasing me as a target I carry into every relationship. I saw how my mind masterfully constructed worst-case scenarios (WCS) based on specific spatial relationships generated by a feeling of impending doom. My mind practiced throwing a metaphorical ax at a target. This was the first time I caught a glimpse of my own personal Armageddon.

Armageddon [ahr-muh-ged-n] noun

The place where the final battle will be fought between the forces of good and evil. (Revelation 16:16.) It's the last and completely destructive battle:

For a moment, think of the area of your life causing you the most grief and suffering. Maybe it's a financial worry, or perhaps it's a relationship challenge. Whatever it is, think of the moment taking up much of your thought. Review all the scenarios you run surrounding this issue. Do you imagine someone leaving you? Do you imagine being broke and desolate?

110

What **WCS** (worst-case scenario) do you run in your mind when these thoughts have a strong grip on you?

For a moment, investigate the type of danger.

Notice how does it feel?

It feels like _____

Notice where the feeling(s) reside?

I feel this _____ **in my** _____

(identify a part of your body.)

Notice what the theme is of the associated risk. How does it impact you?

Notice how far the WCS is from you. How impending is it? How many moves can you make to avoid the WCS *before* it materializes?

Notice how much control you feel the WCS has over you.

Take this awareness and look at other areas of struggle in your life. Look for how this experience of impending doom felt similar in other relationships. Find the worn spot where you stand and throw your mental ax. See where your mind has worn thin the floor of your experience.

We are all being chased by some existential dread—our sabretooth tiger. Our internal system hijacked for survival projects this monster into our augmented reality through which we experience our reality. What if you were wearing glasses and then forgot you were seeing through them? These glasses offer you an augmented view of the world. If you didn't know you were wearing them, you wouldn't know the difference between what you saw and data provided in the overlay created from your meaning.

Now, imagine this information is compromised. When you're oblivious to the ubiquitous impact of the glasses, you become a victim incapable of having a real relationship with anything that triggered a similarity to the monster-chasing target. When that happens, your mind will make pink red. Your mind finds connections where chaos exists. That's its primary purpose.

We all have a personal Armageddon we are set on avoiding, and this is coupled with our certainty the moment will come. Yet, your mind has stopped asking if, but, when, how it will show. You then set up your target based on previous struggles programmed before you knew what programming was. As a result, you experience impending doom after impending doom, attaching to your life like a Velcro target.

Noticing that you carry these targets with you at all times may derail you at first. However, this feeling transmutes into power when you realize your ability to see the root of your suffering. Then, you begin the process of recoding your glasses, and thereby, transmute your very experience of reality.

Remember
this book isn't meant to be read; it's meant to be experienced.

Chapter 9

Wondering Around Process

Your mind flows. Like water, your mind flows and takes on the shape of whatever container it finds itself in. This is why reading a great book can feel as though you are transported to another world. It's why you lose track of time when watching a movie or daydreaming. Because when your mind is fluid-like, it takes on the shape of the space where it is placed.

Your mind is constantly running best-guess scenarios to decipher what is happening and what will happen next. Problem-focused thinking will lead to a problem-focused experience.

We need to consider these moments sacred. These are moments when you will be most vulnerable. It's as if a lesson was waiting for you to learn through the experience, like your Shadow was calling to you to look in the most tender places of your existence.

The lessons can be quite profound for both you, the seeker, and those holding space around you when participating in an integration session, part of your Turning Within practice.

Your journey may include a Mental Cleanse process. Here, seekers have attested to finally being able to address cycles of suffering that may have taken years to manifest. Slowly cultivated shadow, normally elusive, can present themselves in a long-form process. This process is designed to create a safe container for the mind to flow into. By learning a new process to navigate the mind differently, change is possible. Insight is always the first step.

Shadow Work processes can be long, short, private, or in a group. Processes may be face-to-face, remote, stand-alone, or build, one on top of the other, like this book. A practitioner learns to trust the process and depend on it to bring them into the light. This faith in Shadow Work produces a supernatural-like effect on your ability to step through the fear your story is projecting. The results cannot be overlooked.

Wondering Around Process:
Not all who wander are lost.

It's old saying I enjoy—Not all who wander are lost—it originates from J.R.R. Tolkien.

> "All that is gold does not glitter,
> Not all those who wander are lost;
> The old that is strong does not wither,
> Deep roots are not reached by the frost.
>
> From the ashes a fire shall be woken,
> A light from the shadows shall spring;
> Renewed shall be blade that was broken,
> The crownless again shall be king."
>
> — J.R.R. Tolkien, The Fellowship of the Ring

As I deepen my personal practice, I notice the depth of the truth of this adage more and more. The external value of wandering is enhanced even further when turning within. To wander internally is to move around in your mind, looking at your reality through different positions, and seeing things from different perspectives.

By activating your feeling of wonder, you activate higher-level functioning, which in turn, moves you beyond survival-rooted programming. Wondering leads to wandering. The better you get at wondering around, the easier your ability will be to deal with your heavier lifting on the back end. By leveraging the power of wonder, you activate inherent genius within you. You begin to gain authority over your story.

The goal of this process is to practice taking on a different perspective, to wonder what else could something mean. We use "Wonder what else this could mean?" as our second-week mantra in the Mental Cleanse process. There, seekers learn to leverage the deeper structure within a more open mind as a result of engaging with wonder.

In *A Course in Miracles*, one of the first steps in creating a miracle is opening space for a miracle to enter your life. A person can't experience anything countering what they already hold true. If your current perspective is causing you suffering, maybe it's the perspective that could use some shifting. The only way to know is to lean in.

About six years ago, I began scheduling 10:30 a.m. every Saturday to sit and "wonder." The baseline of this book came from that very timeslot. Consistency gives the mind an understanding of how you want it to flow. Your mind will take the shape of anything, whether you consciously or unconsciously place it there.

Have you ever noticed how certain places or events trigger you? That trigger is confirmation that you can be programmed. Come back to this "wonder" exercise again and again. The more you are able to shift your perspective, the less you are a victim of your past. What day and time can you schedule to allow your mind to learn to wonder? Make it a time and a place with the sole purpose of wondering around—do nothing else. Your mind will deepen your ability to expand into deeper levels of genius.

What if you could completely change your life by understanding, owning, and re-writing the coding you have lived out of?

How much time do you spend focused on survival-rooted scenarios? *Scenarios in your mind that are rooted in attack thoughts, awfulizing, and negative bias.*

What would your life be like without worrying about survival in your internal and external relationships with people, places, and things?

How would you show up differently?

Spend some time wondering how it would feel to cultivate this part of you. Pretend you are already this person.

Now, look at the present. If you started from your higher self and worked back to now, what would you feel like if you were that person in the present?

How would you move through the world if you were already the person you imagined but hadn't gone through the process of becoming that you yet?

Your Mind as Software

Consider the brain is like computer hardware in an advanced vehicle, and your mind is like software running the whole system. What you experience as conscious thought is only your interface. I should note your goal is to realize you are neither the vehicle nor the operating system—but the driver.

Think about when you wake up in the morning and boot up your computer; the first to load is the bios. For human beings, this would be the DNA-level programming passed down from generation to generation—3.5 million years of packed-down, deep-mind meaning defining every facet of you, down to your very physical appearance. Next, something comparable to an operating system, called the mind, comes online. This would be language itself, the baseline meaning of the structure of meaning itself. Next, the mind checks the physical systems and up comes your interface, make meaning, make it elegant, and continually evolve. All the active programs are moments and collaborations of meaning, all connected over the tapestry of lifetimes.

The stories you make up are like software. Some of them are loaded on startup. As with computer virus protection, your risk manager loads and continually runs scenarios to be on the lookout for dangerous or painful circumstances. Some of your mind's constructs exist, like programs stored on a hard drive, waiting to be retrieved. Your every experience has been coded, filed, and stored as a point of reference in the hologram of the greater construct of your mind. Many of these constructs remain frozen at the perspective of the moment they were created.

Just like the desktop interface on your computer, your mind is an interface with reality. The computer's interface is not built to show you the workings of the computer. It's built to take advantage of them, much like the mind, which isn't there to show you reality. It's constructed to define, design, navigate, and survive it. It is the ever-present, never-blinking eye of consciousness shining into the void, willing forth meaning. Each construct created becomes a thread in your life's profound, ever-tightening tapestry. Your tapestry becomes the vibration felt in an ocean filled with waves, from your most conscious thought to the deepest part of the ocean that is the mind.

Most of your experiences are unconsciously associated. Your awareness sits on the tip top a mountain of varying degrees of ever-evolving meaning. The bottleneck of what you can consciously be aware of is tiny. The simple lesson here is, "One, Two, Three, Too Many." That's awareness.

The more something doesn't change or get identified as a perceived risk, the less attention you place on it. It becomes invisible. It is tied to the limited, consciousness bandwidth we have cultivated, the mind's sub-routine to be efficient, and the amount of "self" we still work to mine.

At the core of our awareness, we become informed of breaks in the norm. A break could be a noise, a bright light, an odd touch; anything which isn't part of what we consider our default experience. "Ego" sits right at the center of the action. It helps navigate while it stands on top of all the other pieces of meaning that make up the mind. A loud noise while sitting on a factory floor will yield a different focus than a loud noise in a dark alley when you're walking alone. The break causes your mind to reach into your hard drive and runs a query for all scenarios reflecting the stimulus you just experienced. If you have ever walked alone down a dark, unfamiliar street at night, you know what this feels like.

One such experiences came when I moved my family to Florida. We lived on a golf course inside the safety of a gated community. Our beautiful home had a giant wall of glass looking out onto the pool with a backdrop of trees. During the day, the sunlight bathed the room in sunshine.

But at night, that wall transformed into a two-way mirror, making it *impossible* to see into the backyard.

One night, I left my bedroom and went downstairs to lock up and set the alarm to ensure we were safely secured within our home.

Like any house, it came with its own personality. This one had a peculiar squeak on the fourth step from the top. It only squeaked once you stepped on the third step, sounding as though someone was coming up behind you.

That night, while returning upstairs after locking everything up, I hit that step.

Now, consciously, I "knew" better. But that didn't stop my mind from rushing and imagining worst-case scenario (WCS).

Immediately I loaded my constructs of every horror flick into the desktop interface of my mind. Like a flashback of teenage nostalgia and mental agitation, my mind exploded with possibilities—none good.

The blueprint of the world I abruptly found myself within became dangerous. My reality construct simultaneously changed. I felt a flash of sheer terror. Suddenly, I lived out a scenario I'd watched thousands of times, which urged me to leap forward with everything in my being. I had to clear more steps than I knew I could.

SNAP! The result was a broken big toe that took a year to heal, and my kids got a laugh out of Dad running from the Boogieman.

I'm not the only person who has had this experience. Stop for a minute and remember a time when you did this to yourself. Maybe you were in a pool late at night and started to think about the movie *Jaws*. (To this day, I don't enter a pool at night without thinking of the eerie movie music playing.) It gives me a sudden urge to get out of the water.

Is there anything that gives you a similar sudden trigger? Notice how it feels in your body. Notice how your mind hijacks your experience such that your entire view of reality was warped. Now ask yourself, "If the mind does this in these dramatic and noticeable ways, how much is it doing without me knowing it?" Tiny influences run so deep in our minds we don't realize they exist.

Shadow leads us to the constructs running in the background like a virus in our life. What happens when you have a virus or malware on your computer? Your Shadow becomes a boogie man. He follows you, every step you make.

It's then that your mind builds meaning to protect itself from itself. It consumes more energy resources and embeds itself in every other software program, contaminating everything it touches. This throws you off balance. What happens when the meaning you're standing on is too painful for your conscious mind to process? Your mind will create space to protect you from it. That space will be tended to, consciously or unconsciously. It's your choice.

Our society has evolved to maintain existence in this only half-life consciousness. We remain unaware of how we have altered our reality, our existence, since we have yet to be taught this level of thought and awareness exists. Any attempt to dig deeper, probe, contemplate is most usually shot down, labeled new age woo-woo or something dark and evil to be avoided, or laughed off as fantasy. However, the evolving rate of change is forcing us to evolve our understanding along with it. We're experiencing a collective awakening. It's as though we're experiencing the birthing process on a collective level; something is forcing our hand.

The Sleeper Must Awaken -Dune

Holding Space

A powerful spiritual practice which has emerged from within the psychedelic community is the concept of "holding space." Holding space is a profound art that requires dedication, compassion, and self-awareness. If practiced over time, it develops a deep understanding of the mind, and it points us to a deeper conversation with creation. The result is a grounding process.

What does it mean to "hold space?" Holding space is letting go of the judgments that keeps you anywhere but present and in a neutral state. As guides, we practice a process we term "going hollow." It's about removing all judgment of where we should/must go and following the work as it is presented. It's about finding the center of you and aligning your energy to flow through. It's about finding a space between action and non-action and waiting for what life yearns to spring through. None of that can be done from a place of judgment.

For those of you embarking on the path of Shadow Work, being able to hold space for yourself and others makes you a powerful and invaluable ally. By holding space, you're creating a nurturing environment where something more is able to emerge as you embody the principles of presence, compassion, active listening, non-attachment, and emotional stability. Learning to hold space will immediately impact your life and everyone around you. This space is sacred, where healing and genius can be born through the darkness.

Holding space is central to our practice of Turning Within because, ultimately, it's about understanding creation. Creation sits at the center of longing and doubt, sacrifice, and resistance. Although the Buddhists call it detachment, we focus on detachment with a sense of contribution in holding space. In the identity facet, there is an archetype of the sacred mother for contribution. She offers her physical body as a contribution or sacrifice to life unseen. There's not another representation of selfless sacrifice greater than a mother.

Sacrifice and doubt are the building blocks of creation. Mothers swim in doubt, and their bodies shift into contribution and into sacrifice-mode for their baby. I have found it is a Shadow carried by mothers across all cultures. Your genius can only be born when sacrifice crosses the river of doubt.

Until then, it is but a dream. Imagine taking on the energy of a sacred mother when looking at your dreams. Do you love them enough to sacrifice as a mother would for her unborn child?

Shadow's work points to the realization of how we live more out of re-creation than actual creation. Scenarios repeatedly run at every level in our mind to avoid harm we experience when we weren't equipped to know what meaning to make in a given situation. Our goal is to move away from re-creations, constructs, and stories caught in cycles of delusion to be able to move into deeper levels of awareness. Letting go of the story we're holding onto allows us the opportunity to grab a new story Then we are open to create consciously from our genius.

There is a scene in the movie *Braveheart* where Mel Gibson's character is on the front lines of a great battle. He possesses a tool which can deliver a lethal blow, but it must be done at the right moment.

"Hold."

"Hold."

"HOLD!" he commanded.

Inside that critical moment is the space called *Kairos* time—the perfect moment. It can be very uncomfortable to wait for the lesson to appear. Kairos time sits beyond time as a quantity, opening the present moment to its full potential. It is heart-time, not head-time.

At its core, holding space creates a safe, nurturing, and non-judgmental environment for someone to explore their inner landscape. The container then opens us to permit creation to come through. Without this safe space, your genius will work against you, and your struggles will remain impassible barriers.

Holding space creates a sacred container and offers emotional support, security, and a compassionate presence that releases judgment. Shadow Work involves confronting, integrating, and tending to repressed or denied aspects of ourselves and challenging emotions, memories, and patterns.

You can hold space in several ways. Looking at your reality experience, you see how your primary relationship is with yourself. So, the first space you will learn to practice holding is for yourself. Your ability to hold space for others is forever informed, controlled, and limited by the capacity, quantity, and quality of space you can hold for yourself.

Anytime you are unable to fully hold space for someone else, you will typically find the issue started with a judgment from you about you. Without being able to hold space for your Shadows, you find yourself unconsciously triggered by the Shadow of others. The key is noticing *when* you are triggered and holding space within you to process the trigger. Because Shadow begets Shadow, you unconsciously look for how the outside world informs or is poised to confirm your Shadow.

There is no perfection in holding space. The ideal is found by letting go of the need to be perfect. The more you practice it, the more you find the gateless gate. Then you soar above the constructs of reality where you have been imprisoned and leverage your mind to create, not consume. Your zombie-hunger alleviates, and your ability to be present for others takes off. All by simply developing the skill of holding space for yourself and others.

A realized example of holding space: I had a client who found massive space by realizing he was unconsciously living out of an asshole's identity. Permitting himself to "see" this identity led him to discover beneath that asshole was a little boy who felt no one cared. At an early age, he had developed such certainty about no one caring and he'd forgotten how he decided to protect the little boy by being an asshole.

He built the "asshole identity" to keep everyone from the construct that no one cared about him. After his realization, but before he even got to the little boy, he had to hold space for the asshole so that identity could be heard, integrated, and tended to in order to move forward. Once he understood how internal constructs worked, this client reached the little boy and showed him the caring at the heart of his yearning. Interestingly, afterward, the client began to see love and care from everyone around him. He shifted to a deeper truth of, "HE CARES," and gets to share that care with those he loves.

Individually holding space bears fruit. And something amazing happens when a group comes together to hold space. It's like the collective is plugged in, and something more profound comes online. For over two decades, I have been astounded by the synchronicities and happenstance before, during, and after our gatherings. It's like catching something out of the corner of your eye for twenty years which has been subtly and elusively stalking you.

Some profound truth always hides in plain sight. Remember, this is a process, not an event. Each shadow tended will take you to the door to the next deeper level for you to grow through.

As Mother taught me, it's all make-believe, all the way down to the gaze of God.

The Pillars of Holding Space

There are certain ingredients to effectively hold space. Any time you find yourself without one of these pillars, it's safe to assume there is a Shadow present, hiding some insight or opportunity to grow.

Presence: Holding space begins with cultivating a state of presence. Clearing your mind of distractions and fully immersing yourself in the present moment allows for a deep connection with the work. Embodying stillness and attentiveness, we create a container where trust and surrender can happen. If the Shadow is present, you may find it hard to be present. Notice the stories which steal your presence.

Compassion: Compassion is the cornerstone of our work. It involves actively making space for experiences and emotions as they arise, extending kindness and understanding without imposing personal judgments or opinions. A bully archetype operating in our culture tends to come online here. That is the wrong way. We tend to bully ourselves into action. Offering a compassionate presence provides a haven for the seeker to explore their shadow self without fear of rejection or shame. Letting go of any storyline that doesn't have compassion baked into it will go a long way in your healing practice.

4D Listening: 4D listening goes beyond hearing words; it involves attuning to verbal and non-verbal cues. By attuning to our narrative facet, we uncover our unresolved or unaddressed needs by listening profoundly and intuitively. We can finally hear what we have been telling ourselves all along. This allows us to begin offering reassurance, guidance, or a gentle touch when and where required. The power of softness in 4D listening cannot be understated, as it allows for profound insights and emotions to be seen under the confusion caused by doubt.

Non-Attachment: Holding space requires us to release any attachment to outcomes or personal agendas. Rational thought will say, "Yeah, but…" We must see how we are attached to the construct where we are trapped. The more we practice non-attachment, the more we can let go of what doesn't serve us.

As a guide, we not only learn to depend on but are required to trust in the innate wisdom of the seeker, supporting them unconditionally through the highs and lows of their exploration. Look to your attachments to teach you where you are hooked or triggered. Because in the end, everything dies anyway.

Emotional Stability: As a guide, emotional stability is paramount. The guide must maintain their inner equilibrium while holding space for the seeker›s emotional turbulence. Grounding practices, self-care, and our own personal work are essential in cultivating this stability, allowing the guide to remain steady in a storm. If you have these first three aspects of care, you will find emotional stability easier to cultivate.

Holding space internally is about not leaning into meaning that doesn't present itself naturally. It's about learning to treat yourself with compassion and listen actively for what you are really saying. Only then will you see what nature is calling forth through you. Remember, your ability to do this work directly reflects the humanness you allow yourself to have. We must always be poised to enact compassion for any part of us caught underneath the shadow of judgment.

The Axis Mundi

Your story is the subjective journey you are taking through this world. We all create a personal mythology. When you permit yourself to investigate the myth, the story, you start to understand the nature of your suffering. You see what Joseph Campbell called The Monomyth repeatedly play out in numerous moments, layers, and loops in your life. Before you can change anything, first you must "see" it, Learn how you get stuck in a story and develop the muscle to break free. Then you will experience a most spiritually liberating practice. The results will astound you.

One of the most valuable tools to define and navigate your experience is finding your axis mundi. The term axis mundi is derived from the Latin words "axis" and "mundi," or world, together meaning "pivot point, or line, connecting the earth and the sky/heavens." The Axis Mundi was the mythical center of the universe.

But what is a myth, but a lie meant to tell the truth? In the tale you are living out of now, axis mundi is where you *assume* the center of your universe is circling. Remember, you are the center of your universe. Notice that everything in how you perceive the world revolves around you. The point of reference for any meaning you can make is through your eyes and first-person experience.

Pause for a minute and take that in. ***You are the center of your reality.*** No one can separate you from your reality but you. You are also the only one who has the ability to own when you are in Shadow. No one can do it for you. This is why they say an addict has to "want it"—it's referencing their recovery. They need to be open to seeing how they are the axis of their problems. And because we lie to ourselves first, addicts are usually blind to it.

Ailill and the Oak of Eternity

In ancient Celtic lore, the tale of Ailill, is a humble shepherd known for his deep connection with the land and the animals he tended. Ailill was not only a shepherd but a seeker, constantly yearning to understand the mysteries of life and the universe.

One fateful evening, under the light of a full moon, Ailill was drawn to an ancient oak tree that stood alone in a clearing. No ordinary tree; the Oak of Eternity. It was said to be the earthly manifestation of the Axis Mundi, the cosmic axis which connects the heavens, the earth, and the underworld.

Ailill touched the tree and felt a surge of energy flow through him. His consciousness expanded. He found himself in a realm of pure light and endless possibility. Here, he met the goddess Brigid, the keeper of wisdom and the eternal flame.

"Welcome, Ailill," said Brigid. "You stand at the Axis Mundi, the center of all worlds. This is not just a place outside you, but also within you. Your own consciousness is a reflection of this cosmic axis."

Ailill listened intently as Brigid spoke of the interconnectedness of all things, the importance of balance, and the role each individual plays in maintaining the harmony of the universe.

"Remember, Ailill," Brigid said, as she prepared to send him back to his earthly existence, "the Axis Mundi is not just a cosmic pillar; it is the core of your being. You are a living conduit between the heavens and the earth. Honor this truth, and you will live a life of purpose and meaning."

Ailill returned to his world, forever changed. He continued his work as a shepherd, but he also became a wise elder, a healer, and a guide. People from all walks of life came to seek his wisdom, and Ailill would always lead them to the Oak of Eternity, reminding them how the Axis Mundi is not just a point in space but a dimension of the human spirit.

Turning Within is about consciously cultivating life through your axis mundi. This lost teaching is the collective lesson we all must understand. We won't be able to continue unconsciously live out of the loops of yesterday that don't serve us.

Construct Intervention

Loading up a Scenario is like allowing your storyline to do what every good story is meant to do—transport you into a tale through narrative transportation. We humans are wired for it. It's our number one past time. We are swept away by the stories we tell ourselves. Suffering doesn't sit in the data; it sits in the story. Every moment or situation is like Schrödinger's Cat. It is both/neither/either good and/or bad. We lock into a perspective based on the story engine and the fuel it runs on.

Now, this story engine continuously runs. Your construct informs the meaning you operate out of. The seven facets of your constructs inform, influence, construct, and cultivate every experience you have. The problem is your unawareness of the definition and understanding of construct. What happens when you want to avoid experiencing the world through a construct you have built? You resist. Shadow is projected onto your life. Imagine wearing an advanced AI-driven Apple Vision Pro and forgetting you're wearing it. Say, "*Hello, Shadow,*" to your Shadow.

Let's examine this further. Maybe you're angry with your partner because you don't feel supported. Instead of tending to the identity feeling unsupported in you, you resist going off—igniting your feeling and suppress your anger—however, your partner knows. They sense you are "off." The challenge is in the translation. See, you are floating down the River of The Story Called You. But the story you tell yourself, and the story your partner tells themself, isn't the same—never has been, never will be, never can be. Your partner is unaware of suffering you are experiencing.

The system called "you" interprets all actions through the layers of stories *you* have chosen to represent your reality. Any stories rooted in suffering or survival-rooted programming left untended in your deep conscious are projected as Shadow onto the 3D world. Shadow begets Shadow. Just like someone liberated has the potential to release others, shadowy behavior tends to bring Shadow out in others. This is the cause and the very foundation of Shadow boxing and Shadow Dancing. When we operate from our unconscious, we default to interpreting Shadow behavior through our own Shadow.

Your partner "reads" what can only look like odd behavior to them. Now, their risk manager comes online. Let's say they have a wound that casts a Shadow about how they are always wrong. Now, the two of you are set up individually and collectively for several rounds of Shadow Boxing.

A person doesn't feel supported, so they blame their partner. In turn, their partner then gets triggered in their I'm-consistently-wrong Shadow. As a result, they may withdraw. Now, because they reduce offering interaction, they retrigger their partner's not-supported Shadow. AND around and around they go.

Remember, your suffering is sacred. If you learn how to make friends with it, to hold space for it, you will unlock the keys to your universe. You'll finally find your sacred center. If you attend to your suffering and stop projecting your pain long enough to investigate it, you will find relief *and* the keys to authentic change.

Let's look at some of your sufferings to see what it may teach you about the nature of your mind. Let's load it up. Where in your life are you currently suffering? It could be resistance to show up as your authentic self. It may be some part of your life that's stuck. Stay curious, and let's review your suffering from a different, almost scientist or explorer-like identity. *What's the story you tell yourself that steals your joy?*

THE CONSTRUCT

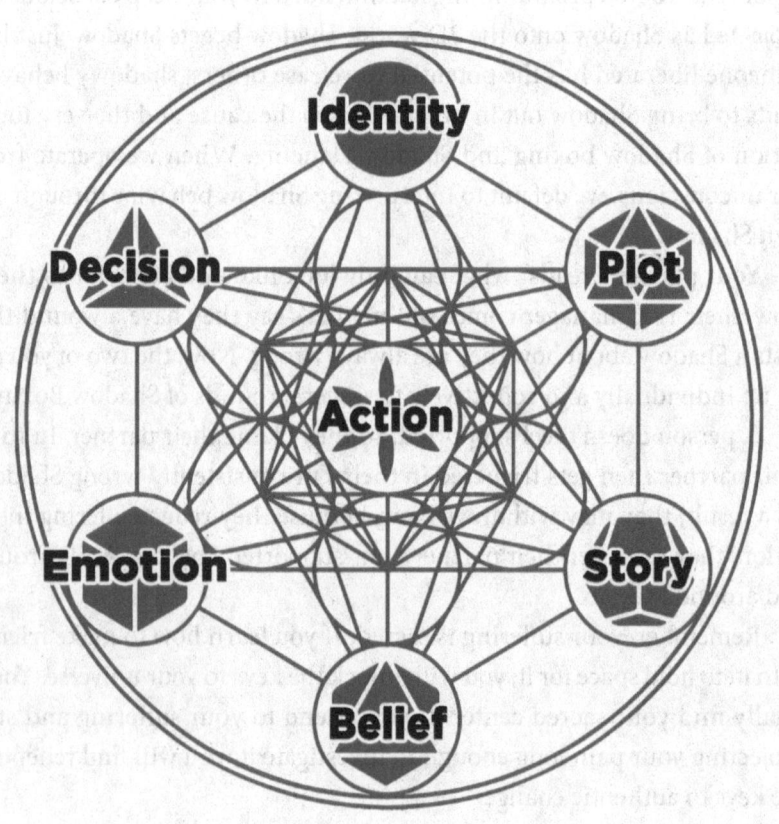

Chapter 10
A RADICAL Introduction

The Map

What you just examined on the previous page is your map. The imaged map is a construct, the seven elements of your reality. This is how you interacted with your world. How you will make sense of your world. How you'll navigate through your world moving forward.

Understanding Constructs

"Your mind will take the shape of what you frequently hold in thought, for the human spirit is colored by such impressions." – *Marcus Aurelius*.

Throughout this book, there will be various metaphors for you to try on. Each one will allow you a different perspective on your experience. Try them on to see how they fit; take a bite out of them to see how they taste. As you try them on, notice how they are valid for you and your life experience.

The goal of this exercise is integration: To move from only learning about something to integrating the information into your life.

Set the book down and enjoy the flavor of it in your life. "How is this true for me?" Remember, Turning Within is an internal, experiential, and subjective practice. It's about taking the journey, not reading about it. It's about the part of you already in play. You're just taking ownership back.

My promise is a lesson with authentic insights will carry your life forward farther than only reading any lesson from a book. You may find a metaphor that hits particularly deep for you, set this book down for a bit to allow yourself to integrate the information deeper into your experience. *This book isn't meant to be read; it's meant to be experienced.*

But once that metaphor has done its job, once an imprint has proven effective for you, EQUALLY, don't be afraid to throw it away for another. The goal is to become aware that your map is not the territory. Your desired outcome is to let go of maps, constructs, and imprints that contain you. Once you release yourself from? the mind creates new constructs more aligned with your genius.

Futurist Alvin Toffler said, "The illiterate of the 21st century will not be those who cannot read and write, but those who cannot learn, unlearn and relearn." You may need to come to some of your lessons from multiple angles. You will need to discover which thread to pull to start to unravel the mystery of you. As you repeatedly return to this book, you will find you "get it" at different stages of the book and at deeper levels.

You will learn to look at your mind as though it's made up of constructs. Human beings don't think in time. We think in moments. We store those moments as constructs. Like drops of water make up an ocean, your mind is filled with constructs. These constructs have seven interconnected facets that inform your experience of the world. Each facet is interconnected to the next. Pulling the threads that connect them unravels the tapestry of meanings you live out of.

Threads are spun into a string attached to a rope tied to a chain. When you yank that chain, the anchor comes up, and the boat eventually leaves the harbor. As you'll learn through the Closing the Circuit process later in this book, you will finally begin to hear the song these strings have played through you all along. A lifetime of genius can be unlocked by studying each facet. Each one supports, restricts, and influences the other by playing a song, weaving a tapestry in your heart. The most accessible place to start is where you find your suffering. You will unravel the tapestry of your torment and rewrite your life's song.

Time to Practice

Now, think of a story that steals your joy.

Imagine you sit in a tug-of-war between doubt and longing. Where do you doubt? What is it you fear will happen?

What do you long for? What is the deep yearning you have not reached for out of that fear?

Drop into the memory of what stole your joy and allow yourself to investigate with curiosity. Begin to investigate the surface of it without getting swept away. How do you feel when you look back?

This can be uncomfortable at first. We are programmed to be human doings, not human beings. So, holding space for how you feel, what you think, and who you are can be difficult because your imagination has been hijacked. It wants to blame, solve, and do. It wants to project and lay fault. It wants to solve an internal conflict externally.

Notice how you feel before bringing up your own personal conspiracy theory. Did bringing up the past change your emotional state? Why? Nothing has changed in the material world. Nothing changed regarding where you were headed. However, your awareness is hijacked by uncertainty and runs a program designed to react from suffering. We have been programmed to believe the only way to certainty is to plague the mind with doubt. Doubt is a vital part of creation; we have to learn how to allow space for it without living in it. The oldest creation tales tell of a union of two energies.

One of the oldest stories of creation, preserved only by non-Zoroastrian sources, proceeds as follows:

In the beginning, God existed alone. Desiring offspring who would create "heaven and hell and everything in between," God sacrificed for a thousand years. Towards the end of this period, God began to doubt the efficacy of sacrifice and asked in the moment of this doubt, "Is there any use, or is this all in vain?" At that moment, doubt came into the world. It's the union of doubt and sacrifice from which creation is born.

In this union, the twins, Ohrmuzd and Ahriman, were conceived: Ohrmuzd for the sacrifice, which means sweet smelling and radiant, and Ahriman for the doubt, which means darkness or full of lies. Upon realizing these twins were to be born, God resolved to grant the firstborn sovereignty over creation. Ahriman immediately attacked Ohrmuzd and ripped open the womb to emerge first. Reminded of the resolution to grant Ahriman sovereignty, God conceded but limited kingship to a period of 9,000 years, after which Ohrmuzd would rule for all eternity.

The lesson is we can't create anything of value without sacrifice. As soon as we begin to pay the bill of sacrifice, doubt will naturally follow. Doubt given agency goes into the storehouse of the mind for automation. This is where Shadow lives. It will lie and manipulate and grow your doubt to keep you safe. Doubt, given any agency, loads into your storehouse of memory and plotted against anything which threatens the mind's perceived safety.

Holding space becomes a spiritual practice shadow practitioners, psychedelic sitters, and spiritual volunteers report experiencing massive breakthroughs, moments of clarity, and liberation. It can't be explained by rational thought because we're stuck beneath this tool.

I held space through a young woman's transmutation of feelings of shame and inadequacy to know how she is unique, and so is everyone else. I tell you, watching at the threshold and then seeing when the realization hit for her gave me an unexplainable mystical experience. The trees spoke to me at that moment. I saw God through this young teacher's eyes.

It's hard to objectively explain because this work can only be experienced, which is part of the difficulty when discussing it with others. But we gain insight into a third path by holding space for the seeker. This third path will often be a collaboration, an answer to, the evolution of, or finality through both the longing and the doubt.

This third way is the creative path, presenting itself when we let go of a lie we are clinging to and become still enough to hear a deeper truth whispering through the screams. If we hold space and remain open to seeing, we will find treasure around every turn. Each prize is invaluable, and each lesson is unique. Some are sparkly jewels of insight, others are treasures of golden wisdom.

Each deeper truth is hidden in places of the genius of your inner child's thoughts. The Child, this part of you is always filled with wonder, innocence, and mischievousness. Reclaiming this genius becomes your mystical treasure hunt. A new tempering opens to you. A story, unfolding through you, told since the beginning of time. The most accessible lessons can be the hardest to integrate, taking years or even lifetimes. This treasure hunt is internal, subjective, and is the road less traveled.

Now is time to do the great work. Holding space makes that possible. Permit yourself to remember everything is already in play in the present. The path forward is always there—you are unable to see it because of the fear of what you believe waits on the other side.

You spend a lot of time unconsciously running different scenarios and stressing. Not looking at it with wonder is the problem. Let's spend time consciously investigating where you experience resistance or suffering.

What is the story you tell yourself that steals your joy?

Ski Boat Metaphor

When you're stuck in problem-focused thinking, you will experience your center of gravity through the problem. Because you are locked in problem-focused thinking, once you solve the problem, you risk your mind becoming centered around the next closest issue. *You don't have a problem; your problem has you.*

You begin to feel like a skier behind a boat being forever dragged through your life, chasing problem after problem. This may be what drew you to this book. That feeling as if the whole purpose of your life is to solve problems. Notice where your center of gravity is. Identify the relationship which has you experiencing suffering. What person, place, thing, or event has you suffering right now? It doesn't matter who's at fault. It's not about blame, instead you're seeking real change. Blame is your obstacle.

You spend a lot of time unconsciously stressing, and that's the problem. Spending time consciously letting go of what has a hold of you is the only way to rewrite the code you've tethered yourself to, trapping you in cycles of suffering.

Where are you experiencing resistance or suffering?

Where do you not feel your life is going the way you want, or you aren't showing up the way you want?

What is the story you are telling yourself? (I tell myself...)

Where/what/who do you hand over your power?

Where do you feel stuck?

Look at your suffering like a scientist would look at their experiment. Look at it as a child would look at a puzzle. Look at it beyond your "monkey mind."

In your mind, repeat the phrase, "Isn't that interesting?"

Problems are just some of the things that capture your axis mundi. Love, passion, desire, and drive can all throw you "off balance," can't they? This is what is meant by "swept off your feet." When was the last time you experienced that feeling? Where was your center of gravity? Where was your axis mundi? This awareness will come in handy as you dive into the deeper parts of your consciousness. Understanding opens the door to healing. When you become aware of how you are allowing your mind to mislead you, you then have the ability to regain control back. You either control the mind, or it controls you.

Hold on because you are about to find your center. Sometimes, finding out where you are not is the first step in finding out where you are.

Seven Facets of Our Constructs

Two young fish come upon an older fish while swimming in the ocean. "How's the water for you two today?" the old fish inquires. The two young fish bewilderedly looked at each other, then turned and asked the elder, "What's water?"

In this next chapter, we attempt the impossible. We will attempt to break down what an experience is. and how we respond to it.

Imagine, inside your head there is a giant record player with a bunch of records. Each record is the meaning created through living through the lens of the story called "you." These records aren't just sound; they're written in story form and contain the essence, identity, emotional content, perspectives, and strategies you've generated through your experiences. Each spinning record tells a tale of a moment you've lived. Each one is independent, but still connected to every other record.

When something external "triggers" one of your records, one you don't like to hear, the imprint subtly, and many times completely, overtakes part of your conscious thought and awareness. The boat called "Now" enters the shadow of a construct. It may be so deep under the water you have no idea the song on the record is even playing in your head. However, it moves from something in the very back recesses of your mind to the forefront, painting everything in your narrative. A great leviathan rises from the deep: you hear your boss talking to you in the voice of your father; you suddenly fear everything you are working towards is utter bullshit; you lose the plot in your partnership's love story and are at odds with the enemy.

There are seven distinct but connected facets to a construct. This book is designed to pluck the strings in each area, thereby making you aware of the melody you are unconsciously swaying to while trying to navigate your life.

The seven facets are:
Identity
Narrative or Plot
Story
Beliefs and Blueprints
Emotions and Feelings
Decisions
Actions

Each one of these facets informs and is informed by every other facet of a construct. When you are triggered, your system calls a construct online or "in-theater" filled with the emotions and feelings which permeate your world through and through. The stronger the imprint or trigger, the harder it can be to resist. Some calcify in the body as a physical manifestation of dis-ease, programming loaded in the deep conscious rooted in grief and suffering and projected on the surface of your life.

Being born isn't living; it is only the invitation. There comes a moment in each person's life when they are invited to peel back the surface layer of their experience. Then begins the sacred journey of unlearning and remembering.

Unlearning the programming unconsciously handed down from generation to generation: unraveling years, lifetimes, and even generations of Shadows cast over every aspect of a person's experience. Suffering becomes a sacred teacher of our mind's power.

Most of the world has gone to sleep to their authorship; they have lost their agency. Therefore, it's time to remember *you* are the creator of your story. Grasp the significance of this truth as you navigate the ever-flowing narrative of your existence. This deeper awareness is the key to uncovering answers. This truth is so profound it transcends the very part of you capable of comprehending it.

Then you encounter true genius poised to flow through you.

We All Live in a Yellow Submarine

Imagine the construct as a yellow submarine, a vessel with the ability to calcify and carry awareness through the vast expanses of space and time. Like the Beatles tried to tell us, we all live in this yellow submarine of our own making. Within this submarine, we navigate the depths of our inner world, exploring the hidden landscapes of our thoughts, beliefs, and perceptions.

We sit in our submarine, where we create and regenerate. The mind is like a master engineer, constantly constructing new compartments within the submarine. These compartments represent the constructs we form, the meanings we assign, and the narratives that shape our reality and allow us to interact with the 3D world.

Each new construct we create sits on top of another, informs, and depends on the pre-existing constructs. It's as if we continuously add new modules to our yellow submarine, expanding its internal capacity to hold experiences and beliefs.

Just as the submarine moves through the waters, propelled by the currents and guided by the navigator, our constructed submarine is influenced by the current of our emotions, thoughts, and experiences. Within this vessel, we make sense of the world, shaping our perceptions and interpretations of reality. Just like sonar isn't a complete representation of what it identifies within deep water, equally, the constructs we live out of are only a flat interpretation.

The yellow submarine metaphor reminds us to investigate and redefine our constructs. By examining the compartments within our submarine and exploring the beliefs and narratives constructed over time, we discern which constructs serve us well and which need reevaluation or reconstruction.

By consciously engaging with the creation and regeneration of our constructs, we gain the ability to reshape our reality. We become aware of the narratives no longer serving us, the beliefs that limit our potential, and the stories which keep us stuck in repetitive patterns. With new awareness, we recode, rebuild, and repurpose our constructs, infusing them with new perspectives, empowering beliefs, and transformative narratives.

Just as the yellow submarine can journey to new depths and uncharted territories, we, too, can explore the uncharted territories of our constructs. By embracing our creative power, we expand the possibilities within our submarine, opening ourselves up to new insights, growth, and transformation.

So, let us embark on this voyage. Let us navigate the currents of our mind. Let us transmit through our experience our thoughts into emotions and then actions. Let's learn to leverage this fantastic, ever-evolving tool, consciously creating and regenerating our internal compartments.

Each construct becomes a vehicle to transport us to new worlds. As we navigate this inner landscape, we can reshape our reality, free ourselves from limiting constructs, and unlock the boundless potential within our mind. We finally have the opportunity to go where everyone must eventually go.

Through The Looking Glass: A Candle's Tale

Every morning, a tiny Candle was lit inside a Magic Lantern. The lantern gave Candle the unique ability to make meaning of everything she surveyed. Every time Candle experienced something, a tiny, intricate etching appeared along magic lantern's windowpanes. This allowed little Candle to recognize the patterns in the world around her. The lantern gave Candle the power to remember! Wanting nothing more than to make meaning of the world, Candle found the magic lantern invaluable.

The lantern became a storehouse of recognized patterns and stories of the storms Candle had experienced and endured. After some time, Candle realized this magic could be used help her to stay safe. Candle can be very nervous, you see. After all, she only has a tiny flame, and the world is full of powerful winds. If Candle could anticipate a storm coming, she could protect herself by staying safe.

More and more etchings appeared. Each etching grew deeper and deeper with every strong wind Candle encountered. The shadows from the deep etchings made over her lifetime of struggle now projected everywhere she looked. Candle found herself paying more and more attention to the etchings on the windowpane. Eventually, she forgot the etchings even existed. Candle no longer realized she was in a lantern. She became trapped inside the etchings created over a lifetime of storms.

Candle was now living out of the shadows these etchings cast, oblivious to the patterns. She ran from etching after etching, seeking to feel whole. She became stuck in the stories of her suffering, mindlessly burning anyone who tried to help her see—forever living out of the same patterns over and over.

This is the nature of your suffering.

Noticing Your Narrative

In consciousness and human experience, our narrative, or plot, is our interface with the present moment. It is the looking glass through which the Candle of your consciousness experiences the world through. This is the inner dialog you are having in the present moment. In that dialog, you translate, construct, and navigate meaning, weave together the threads of your life, and shape your understanding and experience of reality. The narrative is the container by which you talk to yourself about what you are experiencing.

Think of your plot as the vibration of your current mindset, the mental landscape you create to make sense of the world, what Eckhart Tolle calls "The Now." This is the space Michael Singer points to in *The Untethered Soul*.

Your words represent feelings and meanings that have been confirmed and are represented by the words you are telling yourself.

Your mind is responding to these feelings.

You are experiencing reality through a looking glass.

You are given a heads-up display of a re-creation of an interpretation of creation.

The words we use become the stories from which we live out of and through our lives. Like a finely crafted tapestry, our narrative intertwines with the fabric of reality, shaping our interpretations and influencing and informing how we navigate life's intricate dance.

Within the narrative facet, Michael Talbot's exploration of the holographic universe provides a fascinating perspective to understand its significance. Just as a hologram contains the entire image within each part, our narrative encompasses the essence of our experience within each moment. It is not merely a linear progression of events but a multidimensional tapestry reflecting all things' interconnectivity.

Your mindset is the frequency of your narrative. What has your default mindset been over the past month? If your internal narrative is one where you are bullying yourself or call yourself names, then that is your default mindset. If you are constantly avoiding pain or trying to survive some big ordeal, that is your default mindset. That is the water where you swim.

Reviewing your narrative can have a profound impact on life. By developing a mental cleanse process, we pull apart the tapestry of our mindset and recode our constructs. This happens by observing the continuous stream of thoughts and stories that flow through your mind, recognizing their power to shape your emotions, actions, and overall state of being. By becoming aware of your narrative, you have the ability to transcend limitations and embrace a more expansive and liberated consciousness.

More importantly, you'll regain control of the story-engine through which you experience the present moment. This allows for more profound layers of work to be done. Remember, each facet of the construct is tethered to all the others. All roads lead to Rome. In the end, your liberation is the outcome. Reading this book confirms you will arrive there, if you keep moving in the direction your going.

Over time, you see the present moment become a canvas upon which you paint the story of your life. The canvas is never-ending and stretches to the beginning and end of time. The meaning you make becomes the meaning you stand on—the foundation—to paint the picture you are experiencing as "the now." Talbot's holographic perspective reminds us how this canvas is not fixed or rigid, but somewhat fluid and responsive. It invites us to see the narrative we choose to embody has the potential to reshape our reality, transforming it into a tapestry of beauty, growth, and possibility.

Waking Up To Your Narrative

Narrative is always the most straightforward facet because it is the part of our mind which we equated as ourself. Notice a voice is talking as your eyes scan the letters that form words that form a sentence. Here I chose symbols to create thoughts that appear as sound within your mind.

But there is no ear in the mind.

"Hello…. Hello!"

Right now, in your mind, stop reading and say, "Hello!"

I'll wait until you untangle that concept.

Notice you have a voice in your head. That is your narrative. And, if you are truthful, it never shuts up, does it? No. Add to that, the narrative isn't just audio. It's visual. It recognizes scents. Real quick—picture a rose. Now imagine the soft, sweet scent of it. Also imagine the earthy sweetness of a rose as you take your nose right to it and sniff What happened? You don't have a nose or a rose in your head, but there is still scent. You have a better-than-Hollywood studio going on right up in your head. This is the narrative facet of your conscious thought. Now that you recognize this, this is the beginning of taking back the coding of your mind.

Let's take another example. What happens when you "make up your mind?" You decide on something. The construct of meaning you are weaving in the narrative at that moment is given agency. Your mind-making is always happening at some level. Always.

For most of us, mind-making is past tense. We don't stretch our mind to keep it flexible, so it goes stiff. Then, we live out our life from an outdated, stagnant, and barely practical made-up mind.

Remember
this book isn't meant to be read; it's meant to be experienced.

Chapter 11

Measure Awareness Process

Through shining the light of awareness, the healing process is activated. We have stretched extended parts of us which we left untended. We gain deeper insight into our divine nature. As a result, some expanded experiences can now come through. This expansion can look like improved relationships, relief of suffering, insight into a strategic outcome, or some creative breakthrough or insight. In the recovery community, it is called a *moment of insight*. The psychedelic community calls it *divine inspiration* or a *data download*. In Shadow Ceremonies, we call them *aha or wow* moments.

Momentarily, you will take *two looks* around the room where you are. I say two looks because I want to set you up for success. You will be assessing your awareness. This process has proven to provide insights.

The goal is to see how you carry your awareness of **red** in your surroundings. Make sure to discover *every* piece of red in the room you can find in **ONLY TWO PASSES**.

Then, after making the two passes, go on to discover how you did.

Ready, go.

TAKE YOUR FIRST PASS. HOW MUCH RED DO YOU SEE?

TAKE YOUR SECOND PASS. HOW MUCH RED DO YOU SEE?

Now, I ask you... How much blue stuff did you see?

None, right? Notice how your focus on red didn't take blue into the scope of your reality. It's almost as if blue didn't exist. Notice how your anticipation of red created the construct you were experiencing. I'm betting many of you saw some pink and made it red.

This is one of the 24 Cognitive Biases that cause us to struggle within the current mental structure. Confirmation bias, one of the most prevalent cognitive biases, holds significant implications for our exploration of Shadow Work. Within the facet of our narrative, where we create meaning and define our reality, confirmation bias exerts its influence by subtly shaping our perceptions and experiences.

Cognitive biases encompass a range of mental shortcuts and tendencies, influencing our decision-making and interpretation of information. Among them, confirmation bias stands out as a potent force. It refers to our innate inclination to seek and prioritize data. It confirms our beliefs while disregarding, downplaying, or denying contradictory evidence.

Confirmation bias unchecked impedes progress and perpetuates self-limiting patterns. When we cling rigidly to certain narratives (or constructs) about ourselves and the world, we actively seek evidence that validates these beliefs, therefore, reinforcing their hold on our consciousness. This cycle creates a *feedback loop* as the filters of our selective attention cast out alternative perspectives, preventing us from exploring the full spectrum of our experiences and inhibiting personal growth.

In the context of Shadow Work, we consider that the mind is limited in its judgment. Each limited conclusion is based on another limited judgment. This is how we get locked into what the Hindus call Maya. Because once judgment is made and confirmed, it is then leveraged so we can create another bias. This has happened to you since the beginning of the first string of the code that is you. This coding is traced clear back to your very first ancestor.

All of us are sitting on top of confirmation bias. We can't make heads or tails of anything that doesn't have some body of information connecting it to something we already know. That is the value and lesson of the Rosetta Stone.

The Rosetta Stone, discovered in 1799, had the exact text inscribed in three different scripts: Ancient Greek, Demotic, and Egyptian hieroglyphs. It became the key to deciphering Egyptian hieroglyphs, a script lost to humanity for almost 1,400 years. Just as the Rosetta Stone unlocked the secrets of an ancient civilization, love can unlock the connection and relationships we all yearn to experience.

We start with what we have confirmed, look at how this aligns with new information, and then we translate the experience. If this process is valid for language (narrative), it is true for everything language supports. It's all thoughts. We only know something new because we have something relatable to it—the law of proximity at the mental level.

By activating your curiosity and looking at where your bias sits, you identify where Shadow hooks its claws into you and discover the structure of your suffering. To navigate your bias, awareness is paramount. By recognizing the tendency of confirmation bias and consciously questioning your assumptions, you open yourself to a broader range of possibilities. You have the capability to intentionally seek out opposing viewpoints, engage in constructive self-inquiry, and cultivate a mindset of curiosity and openness. Embracing this approach allows you to challenge your preconceptions and invites new insights and perspectives to emerge.

Hence, most importantly, how we do any action is typically how we do anything. If we have a bias at the thought level in one area, you can guarantee it is happening elsewhere in your life experience. Your bias becomes the thread you will pull at to unravel your suffering.

Turning Within offers a unique opportunity to confront your confirmation bias within your narrative facet. By exploring the Shadow, you venture into uncharted territories of your deep consciousness, illuminating the hidden aspects and biases which influence your perception of reality. Through this process, you gain the power to transcend your conditioned thinking, liberating yourself from the limitations imposed by confirmation bias.

As we embark on the journey of Turning Within, it becomes crucial to embrace the discomfort of uncertainty and also remain vigilant against the magnetic pull of confirmation bias. Through consciously questioning narratives, integrating diverse perspectives, and cultivating an open and receptive mindset, we have the power to transcend the confines of bias, leading to a construct, more expansive, and authentic experience of reality. Through this transcendence, we unlock the transformative potential of strategic introspection, which leads to embarking on a path of self-discovery, growth, and consciousness evolution.

Yet, within this grand narrative lies the Shadowy undercurrent of uncertainty. In this realization, we find the invitation to explore the depths of our narrative, questioning the assumptions and biases that may confine our understanding. This is the call to Turn Within.

We receive the message at some level, but not everyone hears the call of Turning Within. Still, fewer of us take it up as a practice. However, sages and gurus continue to all point in the same direction. We are beckoned to engage in a dance of self-inquiry and reflection. We are called to investigate the stories we tell ourselves, examine the filters through which we perceive the world, and question the limitations our narratives impose. By Turning Within, we claim the space expansion, liberation, and the emergence of a more conscious and authentic experience of NOW.

Ultimately, the interpretation of NOW holds the power to reshape reality and transform our life. It's an ever-evolving dance between the holographic nature of existence and the boundless potential of the human spirit. As we embrace this dance, we find ourselves at the threshold of a profound realization— the narrative we choose to embody can transcend the limitations of the past, awaken us to the richness of the present, and propel us toward a future steeped in meaning, purpose, and unfathomable possibility.

By studying your consciousness at the narrative level, you gain the needed support to rewrite your experience. By learning to restructure your understanding of NOW, you begin to cultivate a different experience. More importantly, you'll join into a great collaboration with the universe. You enter the world of great work.

Understand To Be Understood: Six Parts of the Narrative

Because your primary relationship is with you, uncovering Shadow at the narrative level has profound results in every area of your life. You are the portal to the world. You can't have a relationship with anything else but through your initial relationship with yourself. You will notice you operate there at a certain vibration. For example, do you always look at how things could go wrong or right? Stop and consider how you are painting your reality experience. What words do you repeatedly use over and over? Notice the default in the following areas:

Default Mindset

If you struggle to shift your mindset, go through the Mental Cleanse process to wipe out your built-up mental plaque and start taking control of your mindset. This is a long-form Shadow Process designed to shift your core through work on the narrative facet of your conscious thought. Imagine spending thirty days cleansing out any Shadow rooted at the narrative level. We only really have two types of mindsets to engage.

What was your default mindset over the last month? Start by looking at how you focused your awareness. Did you ever notice feelings like curiosity, joy, and love expand your consciousness and through that, you take in more of your surroundings? Many times, there's an allowance or grace that comes along with expansive states. Your thoughts tend to be lighter. When you're in a negative mindset, your feelings are more contractive, resulting in feelings like anger and fear. Those emotions tend to zoom-in on a problem or suffering. This tool of identifying your mindset is meant to bring your awareness to bear on a problem.

Do you find yourself experiencing your world in the way you want? Remember, your access to what's wrong is always available to you, and so is what's right in your life. Notice how your experience always matches your mindset? Isn't that interesting?

Condensing and Expanding Your Mindset

Think about the last time you felt angry or scared. Did you notice how your thoughts had the ability to spiral in that moment, focusing only on things fueling your anger or fear? It's like your mind pulls you deeper into a tunnel where only those negative emotions exist. This is a 'condensing' or suffering mindset; it narrows your focus on the problem, like when you use a camera to zoom-on subject.

Now, contrast that with a moment when you have felt genuinely joyful or in love. Suddenly, the world seems brighter, possibilities are endless. You're more open to new experiences. Your mind expands, zooming-out with a wider lens and state of openness and inclusivity.

Recognizing these two mindsets—condensing and expanding—is an excellent step in understanding how your consciousness is defined. A simple, yet profound, awareness can be a game-changer in navigating your emotional landscape.

Do you focus more on problems or opportunities?

Tone and Texture

All languages use pitch to emphasize, express emotion, and perform various other functions. This is called intonation. It's the reason machine voices and written text often fall short in expressing the full range of oral language.

Different languages have different meanings based on the framework of the language, but there are some similarities. Linguistic tone is more integral to meaning. Adjusting the pitch within a syllable, across an entire word, or throughout a sentence can shift the specific word you're articulating or modify aspects of the entire communication.

When you learn to focus on tone, you become open to part of automatic communication. However, left unchecked, it's one of the ways you lie to yourself. Your tone can send a message, slipping right through conscious thought. For example, in any given situation, although you think you're being helpful, your tone tells another story. Immersed in your battle with your internal bully, you may be desensitized to a tone that others find abrasive. What feels like background noise to you could be a blaring alarm to someone else, and you may not even realize the disconnect.

When you learn to match or lower your tone based on the outcome you want, you become a powerful force for influencing a desired result. First, you must free yourself from tones coming through you which you have become tone-deaf to you. Do you have any tones that have been misinterpreted?

Are there words you repeatedly use that are particularly harsh or with a rough texture?

Flow or Frequency

If you speak three hundred words, and your listener is only able mentally hold ten of them, what's the point in the other two-hundred-ninety words? Probably not much. Even worse, your listener may internalize only ***the least important*** seven words to your message.

For me, I primarily operate from a visual perspective. I see a picture, and it is worth a thousand words. If I'm not careful, I will bowl people over with too many words trying to portray an adequate description.

In your mind, stop for a second, then speed it up, and then slow down your mind. Notice you have the ability to *control* the flow of the amount of your thought. What if they were violated by someone using a lot of words? How does successful communication shift? How many relationships fail right here?

Spend a couple of moments contemplating your ability to slow down or speed up the flow of thought. What does it feel like? When would each type of thinking be valuable for you? Now, notice how having control can point to a deeper level of agency for you.

What is your default flow of thoughts?

Flavor and context (transformational language)

An essential part of our practice is paying attention to the words you use, and also, words expressed by others. What are your favorite sayings? What words do you use often? What is the flavor of your thoughts? Using a description, try identifying and assigning a flavor. It might seem weird, but try. When you're able to express "the flavor" of words, it allows you to experience your thoughts through a more profound lens than merely at face value.

Use the concept of tasting to experience your thoughts. Imagine flavor as though you were tasting fine wine. By understanding the flavor and context of your thoughts, you can begin to transmute metaphors and develop a deeper appreciation for the power of your mind. For example, the flavor of a word from someone who's angry may not be the same as someone who is "pissed off!" They aren't the same, are they?

Learn to hear at a deeper level to uncover what your deeper self is trying to communicate.

Does your vocabulary have color? Is it vibrant, aggressive, is it chipper? What is the flavor or context you typically operate out of?

Backstory

This is where we start to look at how plot and story differ in our life. We store information, experiences, emotional events by story. The more intense the story, the easier it is to live out of that story and the more significant it impacts a person's life. Backstories, made previously from meaning, are stories now driving, directing, dominating meaning a person holds to be true. A person's backstory can radically alter the way someone interacts with them. All of us operate out of multiple storylines at any given time.

Let's examine a situation. Have you ever been talking with your significant other, maybe coming home after a great night out, and they reminded you of a situation you were angry about? What happens? Your whole demeanor changes. You load a new storyline into the plot—this is the power of story.

Another example can be seen when interacting with someone in the sales profession. I surveyed a large group of people, asking them to identify the first word that came to mind when I mentioned "sales professionals." Ninety percent of them had negative responses. Some of them were highly negative. One lady said she experiences a physical resistance just by thinking about a sales professional. The remaining five percent of the group responded with something positive. Those people were either in sales or were business leaders or owners.

If you're in sales, you run into resistance associated with this backstory. I believe sales is a sacred and noble profession. Sales professionals are responsible for assisting clients with stepping through the threshold of their problems by offering solutions—this is an example of yet another backstory, and the reason I am such a sucker for a sales pitch.

The In-Theater Work and Plot

Anything you don't make real isn't. Whether the topic of discussion is life or business, your difficulties in integration always lead to the deepest loss in value captured from your work.

Through my working for Tony Robbins, I supported thousands of business leaders through a program that wasn't cheap and not meant to be. Tony would strip a business down and then rebuild it. It's an intense, in-depth, and no-holds-barred process. Rarely did a client take advantage of the guarantee Tony offered.

As a strategist in the Robbins' organization, I supported these business owners from front to back. I would check in a few weeks after their immersion with Tony and discovered a staggering number of these clients had integrated little of what they had learned. Many still needed key terms discussed and broken down into simpler bites of information. I was floored by this discovery. When I dug deeper, I found the key reason these business owners hadn't begun to fix their problems was because of the very problem they were addressing. I wanted to tell them, say "Hello, Shadow!"

I realized there was a difference between Shadow Work and Shadow Integration. Doing the work to gain insight is vital, however, integration is vital for forward movement and growth. Shadow Work is developing insight and opening enough space to plant a new, more empowering, and effective seed. It opens people to what Stanislav Grof calls "other than normal" states of consciousness. Just like breathwork, just like meditation, just like psychedelic medicine, Shadow Work is the act of chasing down the root of the pain.

Some processes are done in integration or on the carpet in a Shadow Ceremony. These processes are often emotional and come with a feeling of release, liberation, or enlightenment. I've seen thousands of people cross the threshold of freedom—witnessing their birthing of a new level of power always leaves me without adequate words to describe my experience. I witness someone planting a new seed in the soil of positive possibility. I see a new option open right in front of me. It's like seeing God. The illuminating experience is addictive for me, and the reason I continue to do what I do. However, insight without integration withers.

Integration is accomplished where the problem happens—back in life or in business. We call this "in-theater," or in the day to day of your life. Imagine you are driving down the road, and you stop behind a car at a stoplight. The light changes green, and the vehicle in front of you doesn't move. The light turns yellow, and still no movement. Finally, the stoplight flickers back to red, and yet, they don't budge. You respond by screaming at your windshield in front of you, "WTF!"

Why? Can he hear you? No, no, the person in the vehicle ahead of you cannot.

"Hell no!" You shout.

You have no idea why that driver hasn't moved yet. But there you are, suffering through some meaning. Some part of you is creating a story about what it means. You're living out of that story of suffering. What is the story you are telling yourself at that moment? Are you going to be late? Is there some Armageddon moment hanging over your head? How do you feel?

"Angry."

Is this anger an emotion you've felt in traffic before?

"Yes, assholes like him…!"

Oh, your judgment is it is a man who is an asshole.

"Well, yeah, he's going to make me late!"

Is it an attack you are feeling? Is it held back?

"Held back, I always feel held back."

AH, so you brought this experience of being held back into this driving experience? That charge is not about the driver in front of you. It's about you and your conversation you're your relationship with traffic.

"Yeah, well, HE KNOWS BETTER!"

Does he? What if he just got a text that his mother died? Or maybe he's having a heart attack. You don't know. But you assume because that is what the mind is built to do, it's built on assumptions. The challenge is you have forgotten that you are pretending. They forget they're acting. And everyone is pretending based on survival-rooted assumptions.

The introspection we had about the scenario is Shadow Work. "In-theater'" is the moment you are sitting at the light. I believe driving puts us in an altered state. The state required to follow the rules of the road dictates a different type of thought than playing with your pet. Being in this altered state can bring out Shadow in the most enlightened of us.

The mental cleanse process is done "in-theater." There is an app which helps with the process to remind a practitioner they're in process. It allows a person to then go throughout their day, tending to Shadows that arise. Shadow Practitioners develop tactics and tools to transmit thought at their experience's narrative facet. In theater, the integration of the lessons gleaned must be plugged in.

It's possible you've had a couple of insights from reading about these interactions. It's paramount for you to use these tools in the real world or while you are "in theater," otherwise, you're missing out on the positive possibility of real change. Insight without integration fades to insanity or daydreaming.

So, when you read the words, "How has this shown up for you in theater?" I'm referring to the subjective experience of the story called *you* when you are in the story.

Once you realize you are swimming around in your mind and the narrative is how you make meaning, you may begin to ask more relevant and empowering questions. The quality of your experience is directly related to the quality of questions you ask yourself.

Identity

First of all, what man must know is that he is not one; he is many. He has not one permanent and unchangeable "I" or Ego. He is always different. One moment he is one, another moment he is another, the third moment he is a third, and so on, almost without end. — P.D. Ouspensky.

There is a deep draw within you such that you can live your entire life and never become conscious of it. A pull, yearning, or requirement which runs so deep in the human experience we are willing to die for it.

Our primary directive to create meaning requires we first find some way to identify with life. This shows up in the mind at every level, from the Spiral Dynamics Model—A theory about how human beings develop through stages, each representing a different level of consciousness or awareness initially conceived by Don E. Beck and Cristopher Cowan —to seven essential human basic needs to the DISC assessments—a personality assessment to help someone deepen their understanding of their self and others. There are many ways to begin working at the identity level as a Shadow Practitioner. These tools can help you track how you identify the constructs from the story out of which you live. Think of it this way: if you are living out the narrative of your live-action show, you are the main character. The problem is a survival-programmed mind is coded to typecast you in the same roles over and over, whether or not they were any good for you.

Your identity is the dot on the map at the mall directory which tells you, "You are here." Without knowing your location, a map is useless. You have no association or relationship with the information offered. You cannot understand where you are in relation to everything else.

Also, the stronger your identification is connected to something, the harder you will fight for it. Someone who identifies as "a smoker" will have a greater challenge to stop smoking than someone who smokes. Why? Being "a smoker" is an identity, where as smoking is only a behavior. Behavior may change, but remember, we're addicted to patterns.

The strongest of all of your addictions is your addiction to your identities. These are how you have identified with the constructs or moments you have woven together. Just like your construct can shift from moment to moment, so does your identity. Ever notice how you think the same thoughts over and over? You have a default way of looking at the world, which allows you to navigate.

Whether the identity is ideal or based on a life, representing an ideal version of you, doesn't matter. You never get too far away from the shoreline without a way to travel out to sea. It is better to deal with what you know than to sail into the seas you don't. Therefore, we stick to I-lands we know, rarely venturing out into the void of the unknown.

Every morning when you wake up, the software of your mind comes online, and you go into a relationship with the first question the mind is constantly answering: "Who am I?" "Who am I in relationship to everything around me, and how is everything related to who I am?"

Your mind identifies the answer to the literal and figurative question, "Where/what/who/why/when am I?"

Think of every possibility that can exist in this reality. Your mind asks, "Where do I stand in all this?" Your system boots up all known roles as cornerstones to navigate your day. "I am a mom, a wife, a husband, a father, a business owner."

But those labels have descriptive words, don't they? "I am a concerned parent." Then, emotions flood the system. Many times, you can carry two competing identities inside of you at the same time. These competing identities can create some interesting next-level remixes. You are the great and powerful "I am" in your life.

In our constant search for meaning, we create concepts of who we are through relationships with the outside world. Once we decide or judge, our identity begins the confirmation and automation process. Because navigation is the game, identity is a must. Because of survival, efficiency, and evolution, we tend to stick with identities that work. It doesn't matter whether or not they feel good, and often whether or not they even work. Many Shadow Practitioners spend the first stage of their work just becoming aware of their programming every morning. They know they feel as though their life sucks; however, they are hypnotized to think it's because of what is going on externally.

Instead of them coming from within, they are coming from without.

Morning Process Review

It's important to notice the judgments loading in your mind first thing in the morning. When the system called *you* comes online, what narrative opens? Do you instantly go to hating yourself?

Go back to this morning and remember from which side of the bed did you rise? Load up the experience into your conscious mind. What were the thoughts that came to you? Did you grab your phone and review your schedule?

Your thoughts are much more complicated and deeper than you are aware. The answers to the questions above may seem as though you were noticing what is rather than loading judgments. However, those are just structures of meaning you have faith in. You have so much confidence in them you don't even realize they're judgments and not real life. Nothing is more important than your identity or identification of where you believe you are located within your holographic universe.

Pause to note how your morning process loads the system from which you operate out of for the rest of the day. This may be a great place to start to untangle the stress in your life. If you grab your phone first thing when you wake, try not to check it for the first thirty minutes of your day. See how that changes you.

Remember
this book isn't meant to be read; it's meant to be experienced.

Chapter 12

Our Identities Are Cornerstone
To The System

The mind is a navigation system. Our survival-rooted programming has caused the mind to assume and associate with a negative bias, awfulizing, attack thoughts, and a myriad of cognitive biases. It's all meant to show you worst-case scenarios, like a movie running in your mind. Every movie has a main character. Have you noticed you are the lead in all of your scenarios? Do you have a bully in your head? Perhaps he calls you names you would never repeat to someone else. Or how about a mean girl? Does she ever come out and direct the narrative in your head? Maybe she says all sorts of mean things to you.

Go back to the Narrative and Story exercise we just went through. What would be the identity or the character you would define for yourself? Now that you've uncovered the plot you swim in, what is the identity of the person with these types of thoughts? We get what we cultivate.

We all have multiple identities from which we live out our lives. The more you stand in a particular spot, the more that spot becomes the default by which you make sense of your world. The deeper your cultivation of your identity, the more likely you are to gravitate to the assumptions, perspectives, and insights from that identity.

The more meaning you make from that particular place where you choose to stand, the more meaning you will defend, demand, and assume is true. The last thing you want is to make meaning from an identity that doesn't serve your greater good. That meaning becomes your default identity and the one you will defend. Most of the time, we cultivate identity unconsciously. You become an unwilling and unconscious actor in a horror film in which you are the main character.

You begin to notice your personal Armageddon moments are based around the same assumptions, limitations, expectations, and lack. The same cycle running over and over and over. The mind craves consistency because it is easier to process. Your identity sits at the core of that consistency. Even if the identity you cultivate consistently sucks, at least the mind can anticipate "this sucks." Because the mind is hijacked for survival, it can spend entire lifetimes focused on that. At some point, you will begin to see this limitation is a part of your mind playing safe.

We find ways to hide, repress, and deny these identities exist. But no amount of sweeping them underneath the carpet will make them disappear. If these identities aren't investigated and integrated into our awareness, they are experienced through Shadow, they are unescapably a part of you.

It's easy to understand how the pain of identifying with traits like weak, not good enough, worthless, and stupid bring about selective dissociation. When we feel shame, we unconsciously reconstruct our interpretation of events. Questioning our interpretation becomes increasingly difficult when the identity underneath the narrative is rooted in pain. The mind will work tirelessly to keep you from that pain.

The deeper challenge is when we unravel an identity, we quickly learn how an identity is required to navigate life. We must know "where we stand." Once a conceptual identity is locked in place, we unconsciously believe this is who we are. We entirely associate with that identity. Thinking of yourself as a bum, reject, father, mother, thoughtful person, leader, winner, victim, bad person, good child, hard worker, extraordinary, or ordinary will cause you to lock into that perspective. It becomes the point of view from which you stand to make meaning and navigate your life.

Every single one of these aspects is a role you *play* and yet, not you. It's merely your identification with those labels. The process is automatic in how the mind informs and navigates you through life. Without having a point of reference, you are faced with more profound mystery of life. Some types of personal-growth work may open you up to a level of the mind that sits beyond identification.

Let's examine a situational example. Imagine you grew up on a small island. This is the only island you've ever known. You have a boat, but it has no navigation equipment. There is no way for you to understand what's beyond the shoreline and in the deep ocean you yearn to explore. How far away from the island's coast go? Not very far. Why? It is better to deal with the demon you know than to raise the devil you don't. Your mind operates to keep you safe from the demons you don't know.

This is the power of identity. The mind requires a reference point of homebase or where you stand. Without identity, you cannot value relationships because you won't know where you stand. You wouldn't be able to make sense of your narrative and constantly lose the plot.

Culture, community, family, and proximity all inform and influence your identities. The things you buy reflect the identities you take on and cultivate. How do you decide which products to purchase? You don't necessarily buy the best product, do you? No, you buy the one which resonates with you the most.

People don't buy products; they buy identities. What you spend your time on will show. Like the telltale breadcrumbs left by Hansel, you can track the different identities from which you live by what you value. The more you invest, the more you associate/reflect/become/believe that is who you are. Each time you come from an identity, it becomes more automatic, more conditioned, and less conscious. You have countless identities in you and can make countless new ones whenever you choose. Every construct you live out of must have a point of view by which the meaning is made. But if you check your informational tapes and review, you will find a few of your points of view are your defaults because the mind craves patterns. The mind is born from and made of cycles, symbols, and patterns.

Make a closer inspection of the narrative you have been living out of. What is the default mindset you have lived from for the past month? If there was a narrative from which you lived within that mindset, what would that narrative be? That is the flavor of the conversation you have been having with yourself.

What are the words and sentences you use to describe your surroundings? Has your default mindset been positive? What about when you are suffering? Now ask yourself this question: *"What's the identity living out of this narrative?"*

Are you the victim/villain/hero/child/vindicator/defender/loser/dreamer/fighter?

All possible characters in a play that you can take on at any time. Allow yourself to give your identity a label.

If your story is a book, what type of character are you? Does this identity show up a lot in places in your life? You constantly choose (consciously and unconsciously) identities to live out of from moment to moment, day to day. These ways of identifying with your life are the little "I am." The problem is you identify so strongly with these personalized views that letting go of them may feel like dying. Therefore, it's advantageous to realize identification and identity are your system's cornerstones.

There is no "authentic self" within the mind, at least not at the conscious level. It's as though our true self sits beyond our conscious awareness. It sits beyond thought. The conscious mind doesn't have a specific self. It is "selfing." That is to say, it constantly asks, "Where do I stand in all of this?" and, "Who am I?" The answers to the questions become your identity. Most of your identities were cultivated when you were small and defenseless. A mind hijacked for survival will naturally operate out of survival-orientated identification. A society filled with people who identify with survival-rooted constructs will be primarily directed out of fear. Change your identity, change your life.

Clothing Invokes Identity

Throughout my journey, I have been captivated by how successful individuals leverage identities to elevate their lives to extraordinary heights. Celebrities and athletes have embraced the concept of alter egos to enhance their performances and overcome personal challenges. They don their uniforms and costumes to bring particular identities online. The amount of clothing entrainment that professional athletes leverage to perform is astounding—everything from the same jerseys to the same socks.

The truth is, we all do it. The executive donning a well-made suit is not just about impressing others. It's about taking on a specific identity. It's about showing up. It's about dress for success.

My wife is a nurse, and when she puts on her scrubs and grabs her stethoscope, something tangible in her vibration changes, how she exists and interacts with others. Look at your wardrobe and consider how these garments trigger you to bring yourself online in a particular identity. The trigger causes you to focus from a certain perspective and insight. These tools you use to write the story that is your experience.

"People don't have one self. They have many selves in many fields of play." -*Todd Herman*

I am no different than you. You should see me when I hit Universal Studios with my kids— full-on #DadMode. Picture me with a backpack, sunscreen, and my girls' purses (oh lord, the purses) slung over me, like I'm a pack mule. My pass-holder badge hangs from a lanyard covered with pins. I'm sportin' my T-shirt with my favorite Dumbledore quote on the front. "Happiness can be found, even in the darkest times, if one only remembers to turn on the light." Got the picture of me: FULL-ON #DADMODE.

We all have our uniforms for specific playing fields. Within ourselves, each character who hits the stage, or the field of play, as radio show host, digital political strategist, and public speaker, and author of *The Alter Ego Effect*, Todd Herman calls it, varies based on previous cultivations. That character is revealed and aligns based upon the terrain from prior associations. Learning how to cultivate your identity consciously will transform you in ways you can't consciously know.

Beyoncé, one of the world's most iconic performers, embodied the identity of "Sasha Fierce" in her first solo tour in 2008. With this alter ego, she cultivated a different construct to fearlessly take the stage. As "Sasha Fierce," she shed the insecurities and beliefs plaguing her elsewhere in her life, enabling her to embrace the powerful and confident performer she is, and captivating audiences worldwide. She told Oprah in an interview she could never wear those costumes as herself. But Sasha Fierce has no such reservations.

Ryan Reynolds, a global star and a charismatic actor, faced crippling anxiety over interviews during a press tour for the movie "Deadpool." He found strength in channeling the identity of the fearless and witty "Deadpool" character, after which, that allowed him to easily handle interviews. He said, "I'd just channel that knucklehead and let him take over."

Beyoncé and Reynolds both now report they don't need to channel their alter egos to live their life. They have cultivated enough awareness to channel their genius without consciously shifting into these identities. Beyonce is a level of performer that comes along once in a generation. She is the Queen Bee. Ryan has cultivated a witty level of presence during interviews that can cut like a knife. In both areas, these people channeled genius in the areas that used to define and terrify them.

These examples showcase the immense potential of consciously adopting and generating empowering identities. Some time ago, I began wondering about the possibility of harnessing the power of identities we had unconsciously cultivated. The idea fascinated me and I began to explore.

I instantly realized it's easier to leverage what's already built than build something new. Instead of trying to create an identity that never existed, I found locating a more resourceful identity to be more effective. I didn't need to create new associations and landmarks. The conditioning already existed. It can lead to faster, deeper, and longer-lasting change. By leveraging the genius that is *you*, you tap into a level of genius which is only able to emerge through you.

What materialized for me was the realization that we cultivate the identities around which the most wounded parts of us feel safest. Realizing how this is true for you can hold profound realizations.

Lower and Sacred Identities

As you continue to unlock the layers of insight tied into understanding how we operate out of constructs, it may be valuable for you to return to this concept of identity and identification over and over—each time do you, you bring a more profound awareness about you than before. In the end, you will understand the key to it all is awareness and cultivation. We get what we cultivate.

To get started on your journey and to prime the Closing the Circuit Process, I want to bring your awareness to two types of identities we all cultivate and operate out of. Think of them as different levels of experience. The Lower Identities are the ones we make when in a survival-focused construct. In the lower identity, narrative and emotions are constricted, which strips those identities of agency and strategies that impact their actions.

Sacred Identities are the medicine we give the world to try and heal the wound where a lower identity is frozen. Your sacred identity is the fruit that naturally grows from the suffering your lower identity is trapped in. Your sacred identities see the world in a way which your lower identity cannot.

Lower Identity

Most people unknowingly live out of their Lower Identities—identities programmed and embodied out of fear or some sort of lack in life. Living from a lower vibration or emotion is how you identify with your surroundings. A powerful identity can be any identity with a solid foundation, especially a foundation of suffering. This is by intricate design based on survival-rooted programming.

These Lower Identities form the basis of the stories from which many people spend their conscious time living. Embodied within a Lower Identity, people experience constricting emotions, limited perspectives, and a belief in their inability to act or grow.

Have you ever heard of a victim having a victory narrative in a story? No. Let me ask you this: Have you ever been in "victim mode" and had a victory narrative going on up there? No, of course not. It's not possible because the victim can't see a victory.

When I am in shadow, one of my lower identifies works to convince me I'll end up a bum. The backstory for the identity is simple, I possess a type of echo from someone's judgment in my mind. It's holographic in design. And continues to inform me how I can be checkmated in only two moves. An algorithm constantly running to navigate against a WCS. I imprinted that judgment and it continues to inform me I may always be two moves away from becoming a bum. I created a file on how someone could end up cold, alone, and without a home.

Our mind reuses all algorithms it finds effective in every relationship. ALWAYS. Therefore, and no matter what success I achieved in any area of my life, my mind would tell me to make more money, make a more significant impact, and change more lives. The performance bar kept rising. It was never enough to satiate my fear, so my bum- story grows more challenging to resist when I become too deep in my PHALTS.

Everything takes an ominous tone as the shadow envelops my experience. Nothing can change the outcome. Everyone is going to leave me. I am going to die. Hello Shadow!

Tending to this particular Shadow requires me to track it like sonar in a submarine. Whenever I feel as though I might be telling myself a story where the bum-identity has emerged, I assume I'm lying to myself and in Shadow.

I realized when I hold onto and live out of this lower identity, I can only experience a life filled with suffering. Why? Because I am only looking for suffering when living from that identity. My mindset has me poised to defend that position in life.

As humans, we inadvertently draw negative experiences into our lives. The undercurrent from living in a Shadow is that it invites those whose shadow seeks to prey on lower identities. I vacillate between calling this shadow dancing or shadow boxing. Each person engaged in the dynamic is living in their own beautiful nightmare synced in time to the symphony of their relationships.

Sacred Identity

Sacred Identities are the embodied version of ourselves which transcends the self-imposed unconscious limitations where our lower identities are stuck. It's the part of you that has permission to be connected to the flow of love. It's the part of you that can feel authentic joy.

Through the thousands of sessions where I was blessed to hold space for someone or a group, I found a unique truth buried in the law of polarity. Each identity carries an equal counterpart. Typically, it's the answer to a prayer. I call the counter to a lower identity, a sacred identity.

It's the part of us which engages when we see someone in suffering and responds with compassion and connection to extending grace. For example, Maybe it was a moment you stood your ground or owned your power for the first time. Maybe it was when someone struggled with a loss, you were there for them. Maybe it was when a friend felt the sting of not being good enough, and you held their hand through it. If you have ever chosen to support someone from a place of love, you have experienced this Sacred Identity part of you.

Take a moment and think of a time you were there for someone else. It could be in your day-to-day living. The identity may show up in the way you care for a family pet. Look for a time when you flowed with grace, compassion, and love. Recall how it felt to be there to support someone else in their time of need. We all have an identity we have cultivated that comes online when we perceive suffering the way we have suffered. Load up the experience of that moment in time, that threshold moment where you were in your gold. Breathe into this part of you. Set this book down and locate a sacred identity you carry within you.

Your sacred identities don't spring up randomly. You choose these identities based on your layers and layers of pre-existing stories and meanings. Sacred identities are embodied higher versions of yourself.

While practicing the work, it continues to amaze me how Sacred Identities appear to operate from a deeper source than conscious thought. Sacred identities are more flexible, compassionate, and capable than any lower identities we cultivate. Living from a sacred identity, you experience a flow and we all have the ability to access the same flow within us. Sacred identities open doors to a place where we can harness genius, creativity, and authenticity. The farther we go down the rabbit hole of ourselves, the more fantastic our individual story grow.

What did I mean by coming from a deeper self than I knew? I realize there is so much more to me than just the surface experience.

The Process

The practice of Turning Within begins with you diving into the deep conscious and tending to the aspects of self which are repressed, untended to, and ignored. As a sacred process of reclaiming soul fragments, it's both delicate and profound. It requires going inside with soft hands and compassionate eyes. In many ways, your mind is like a spooked horse. The more you approach it with acceptance and compassion, the deeper you can go with this work. As you navigate through the complexities of your identities, emerging emotions must be explored. In this exploration, you will uncover and liberate the parts of you that are disconnected from joy and love and you can channel to the divine within you.

As I journeyed through my own work, I began to understand identity is not merely a label, but instead, a vital part of the structure of human experience. My understanding of the concept of the ego is the container in which constructs inform me.

Our minds are storytelling machines, constantly weaving narratives based on our identities. Every story has a hero, a focal point for awareness, who lives inside the constructed world, you, the author created. If you grasp how you identify with, and in, those stories, you then possess the ability to rewrite the meaning you associate with them. Learning to notice the identities from which you operate allows you to unravel the tapestry of the constructs you have been programmed to experience in your daily journey. That learning will lead you to track the narrative, which flows through, and into, a core story. Identity is your very cornerstone. It is the beginning of reauthorizing yourself to live new stories yet untold. This is the sacred tapestry of your experience.

Your Suffering Is a Call to Adventure

Hold onto your narrative, folks, and place your seats in the upfront and locked position!

You're entering the "ordeal-stage" of your journey. Even if most people don't know it, they come to the practice of Shadow Work to stop experiencing life through a lower identity.

For example, when I stop being a victim, then I am able to stop identifying as one. The trick is permitting myself to *notice* when I am living from my victim. I must remember what's wrong is always available, and so is what's right.

Every hero has a moment when they are called to this journey. Every hero starts as a victim. That call is when their world dramatically changes or no longer exists. Hear your suffering for what it is. It's confirmation you have entered a hero's journey in the subjective story called *you*. Your conscious thought is stuck in the Shadow of a hero's journey and your mind is actively working through it. Your holy grail is to wake up from the dream you forgot you were having.

To free yourself from living out of the entangled web of Lower Identities, you must first acknowledge their existence. Ram Dass said, "Shadow is the greatest teacher on how to come to the light."

Only then is when HEALING BEGINS. When you consciously become aware of where you are not. You can't change the story of you unless you are the author. By investigating your suffering, you can see the identities you've programmed, causing your suffering to loop. However, you can anticipate where you have misinterpreted reality. Most importantly, you can finally heal the wound you project onto the world around you. This isn't a maybe. This is a certainty.

However, be forewarned—this isn't for those of you who want to remain their victim, safe with the demons you know, and living in lower vibrations.

Know this, there is nothing which ruins the story of a victim more than the power of insight.

I came to understand suffering is sacred because it is the low-hanging fruit for empowerment and healing. I can glean the subtlest of insights from the dark tapestry of my grief. My experience with fear of failure taught me the profound impact Lower Identities have on lives. As adults in my life pointed out individuals in my life as examples of failures and they suggested I would end up a "bum," my mind imprinted this judgment as a Lower Identity. As a direct consequence, subconsciously, I ran from the certainty of doom presented in my looped story. Constantly, I focused on the risks that scenarios would generate in my mind. The whole time, I plotted my demise to avoid it. Yet, all the while, I had no idea my mind was running this advanced war game.

I desperately bought into that false narrative. It informed me, telling me if I lived a successful, purpose-driven life, I would be saved from the Shadow haunting me. If I were a good boy, I wouldn't be punished. If I made more money, I wouldn't be a bum. If I...if I...if I.

But that isn't how Shadow Works. The ghost is in your system. Like a kid terrified of his own shadow, I ran as hard and fast as I could, screaming and crying all the way to success. However, my success was externally constructed. And my mind predicted risks to match my levels of success, creating a growing and ever-menacing shadow of fear and struggle. The more success I achieved, the more my mind intensified the risk of failure. I was trapped in a sinking ship of fear, and no matter how fast I ran, my shadow chased me, always on my heels. As a result, I made more money than I ever imagined was possible. Do you know anyone who is wildly successful but always complaining? How about someone who is skinny but their self-image defines them as fat? What part of you shows up like this?

The way to stop the ship from sinking, to stop running from the fear chasing you, to stop the hemorrhaging of your suffering is to liberate your lower identities. When you are able to hold space for emotions and compassionately confront the judgments and beliefs keeping you swimming in emotions that don't serve you experience a new version of freedom. By consciously embracing your Sacred Identities, you can rewrite the narratives of your life, reclaiming the power to navigate your stories as your own hero. You have the power to stop being a victim.

When navigating the depths of our being, we unearth the gems hidden within us, shining a light on the darkness and freeing ourselves from the shadows that bind us. Through a successful jailbreak, we are given glimpses of the depth of our very being. Are you ready to embark on this transformative journey? Are you ready to navigate the depths of your being? Are you ready to uncover your shadows and claim the power of your Sacred Identities?

Together, we shall research the depth of human potential and find liberation through self-discovery.

A Brief Word on Shame

Shame is defined as the painful feeling arising from the judgment of something dishonorable, improper, ridiculous, etc., done by oneself or another. But shame is deeper than that. Shame is a place to develop an understanding of identity.

Shame is more than a feeling. Shame is an identity. Like Jacob Marley, from Charles Dickens' *A Christmas Carol*, dragging the chains of misdeeds in the afterlife, the chains manifest in certainty coming from cultivating an identity. The weight of the chains creates a projection with the narrative: the world hates me as much as I hate myself.

Shame is the feeling of disconnect. It's the seat of judgment I sit in, though it's beyond my conscious ability to absolve. I can't rid myself of this disdain, it's my prison with no door. Judgment has been pronounced, and the sentence is carried. In those moments, I don't have shame—shame has me.

I've spent a lot of time examining the prison of shame. For most of my life, I made it my home. Shame became an identity strengthened by unconsciously associating it with the certainty that I was and forever would be messed up. My risk manager came online and set up an identity to avoid the pain. A certainty developed like the Sun coming up tomorrow. Every moment, instance, or situation could undoubtably end in shame. I dreamt about scenarios where I remained trapped in judgment. I ran scenario after scenario, in my mind, about how the part of me I was disgusted with would mess me up good. Understand, the possibility of shame can become a blanket that smothers the life out of anyone wrapped in it.

170

Chapter 13
Certainty as a Key To Freedom

Just as your certainty is a pain point, it's also the breakthrough point. It's your tunnel through. Learn to identify when shame comes online. Notice the ridiculous certainty of your judgment that tomorrow *must* carry shame. Notice how you're stuck in the gravity of a judgment about yourself. This judgment informs you that not only do you believe you're a (fill in your undesirable description of self), but if you told anyone, they would agree with you.

Notice how you don't have certainty about anything else as you do your shame. Look back at how often you were certain you wouldn't make it through. Look at how you never seem to let up on the certainty of it. *Nothing* in life is that certain. Especially shame. The secret is noticing the identity of shame and realizing how you are generating it. Notice how your story of shame influences all of your life roles. No role is typically left unscathed by the warping power of the identity of shame.

Even if you think you already knew this, take the opportunity to investigate your relationship with your shame through seeking, curious eyes.

Insight alone can be a powerful medicine. Seeing something with new eyes can give new perspectives which in turn expand our ability to respond.

The first step is realizing *you* carry the judgment causing the shame. You have sentenced yourself to carrying shame, causing you to feel a certain way. By developing awareness, you gain the ability to tend to the construct informing your thoughts and feelings. You can pardon yourself. Until you do, you don't have the judgment—your judgment has you. Anything you do to resist the feeling will deepen your identification with shame.

Once you bring your awareness online, you begin to understand the cause of your shame and then you're free to cultivate a new identity. One that knows what it feels like to break free of the chains that bind. If you were stuck in a shame Shadow, and your judgment was based on disgust for yourself, what might be a different judgment you hold about yourself that leads to a feeling of shame?

I have come to believe shame is a feeling of disconnect which is rooted at the identity level. We are somehow disgusted about something we have done and won't let ourselves off the hook. To protect itself, the mind doesn't show its work. It hides the feeling of self-disgust and projects the origin onto the external world. But you can't heal what you don't allow yourself to feel. The mind becomes trapped in a loop, like a black hole from which you can't break free. The fourth rule can be leveraged to tend to the source of the suffering.

As an exercise, begin to practice cultivating your experience of life from your more empowering identities. Practice going into the world without the ability to develop storylines based on whatever judgment you have taken as fact. Notice how your mind is addicted to assuming the worst for yourself. You might even track how long you can go without identifying through your shame. What gets reported gets measured—if you measure it, your mind will begin to manage it. What gets managed gets improved. My students have used this shadow process to transform their lives in unbelievable ways. Start light and work your way out. Being gentle with yourself is necessary to move forward. Notice if you choose to shame yourself for having caught yourself shaming yourself—that self-predatory behavior. We call this a shame spiral. Your awareness of the spiral can give a fundamental understanding of the structure of the construct where you get trapped.

Self-care and awareness include, "Good morning. You are loved. You are more than enough."

Story

"The storytelling mind is allergic to uncertainty, randomness, and coincidence. It is addicted to meaning. If the storytelling mind cannot find meaningful patterns in the world, it will try to impose them. In short, the storytelling mind is a factory that churns out true stories when it can, but will manufacture lies when it can't." — Jonathan Gottschall, The Storytelling Animal: How Stories Make Us Human.

"What's The Story?"

This is a powerful question. Notice what happens in your mind and your body when you ask this question. The mind will start pulling up the meaning it has assigned to a situation. Stop briefly, set down this book, and look, taking in your surroundings. Now ask yourself, "What's the story here?"

Allow your mind to answer.

The story is the framework we use to track the flow and evolution of meaning we've created through space and time. It's the framework for making meaning of everything we encounter. The factory of the mind will do anything to give something meaning. The mind isn't wired to analyze data. It is, however, averse to uncertainty, allergic to it.

Once the story is set, the mind will do practically anything to keep true to the story, even when the story isn't accurate. If the mind protects you from pain, then the stories, meaning, and ways you navigate can show up as addictions, self-harming and/or defeating behaviors or even over-achieving and attaining.

The most mind-boggling feature of story is how blind we are when we are in it. We experience life by the stories we're trapped in due to our untended shadows. Yet, we haven't been informed these stories exist.

The result—we live at the surface of thoughts instead of leveraging the depth of them. If the surface of the story is one of suffering, because we are only operating at the surface, that's how we experience life—suffering in it.

I have spent most of my life on the surface. It sucked. Because I was programmed to suffer, that was the surface life I experienced. I walked around pissed off at the world, containing my suffering the whole time, making sure nobody knew. But I was living out of a story where every moment could offer a trap—living life that way sucks. Through my Shadow Work practice, I discovered the revelatory impact of the story facet on the subjective experience of life.

The story is the frame the human mind has been conditioned to anticipate. No matter which way you slice it, you can't deny the underpinning of everything is the coding called story. From the beginning of time, one frame rules them all. The mind will forget vital data that doesn't have a story wrapped around it because the mind has nothing to contain it. I find that fascinating.

This archetypal structure is the very coding of the mind. That's why it's so hard to perceive. Have you ever considered how your thoughts naturally flow in narrative form? Story is how we have been taught to find our place in the world. The pin on the map at the mall that says, "You're here" and anticipate outcomes, daydream, and identify allies, enemies, and resources. The structure of what Joseph Campbell calls the "monomyth" cannot be denied.

Where do you begin seeking perception of your mind's coding? A starting point may be with a straightforward question, "What is the story that steals your joy?" The goal is to see through the story and deeper into your suffering. What is your answer to the question? From your response, you will begin to see a facet of the story in the narrative or plot where you find yourself. You will understand better by asking yourself, "What character or identity am I stuck in this story?" and "What is the narrative I use to narrate my experience in this construct?"

What if the story you tell yourself is more about your addiction to telling a story than the actual happenings in your life? We all have problems we are more committed to having than we are solving, which is the result of a story we created which fits with the identities we've cultivated, and we are committed to maintaining those identities in some way.

If you're wondering about whether or not you're stuck in a limiting default identity, ask yourself, 'What's the story I am stuck in?'" If that storyline has you sitting in a victim's identity, your story and identity should be suspected as coming from Shadow.

We don't think in Time. We think in Story.

We don't think in time; we think in story. We store those stories within constructs. Within the intricate tapestry of our conscious experience, the story is the process that shapes the lens through which we perceive and interact with the world. The realm of story, the flowing current of narratives, guides our every thought and anticipation. This suggests thought is programmed to flow in a particular fashion. Without the form of a story, words have no value. They become labels with no purpose. You cannot engage with your experience and navigate reality without a story. Story gives a thing context.

Stories give our thoughts meaning and power. The story is the engine of a journey. The journey is a tool we use to remember who we are. We are wired for the story because we are part of the great story called life. We are so wired for a story that we do it in our sleep. You are so wired for a story that you do it in your sleep.

The Mind Runs Scenarios

Hopefully, you now have an awareness of that little voice in your head constantly chattering. That chattering comes from multiple angles, flavors, and identities, but it's always running. The mind sings songs, plays games, answers questions, and tells stories all day. All day long, your mind holds up different constructs of meaning and then ties them together to anticipate what's coming. These are called these scenarios. Your mind runs them all day. The mind's purpose is to define meaning and help you navigate this holographic collaboration of meaning where you've found yourself.

How The Mind Protects

Think of your narrative or plot as your internal AI's interpretation of *the now* and the possible scenarios or outcome-trees it can consider based on your past experience. This is where the character—*you*—is in the flow of the story. For example, if I am addicted to a lower identity, my stories always have suffering at the core. A survival-hijacked mind runs scenarios plotting suffering to avoid what may happen. The mind begins to associate more and more confidence in the belief that this identity is important by plotting and navigating from the possibility of its validity.

Therefore, the more you believe something, the more realized that something becomes. This is where life gets dicey because we do need the mind to help keep us safe. Repeat after me, "Thank you, mind, for keeping me safe." Remember, your mind is hijacked for survival. This sub-routine can be seen at every level of thought. This means, occasionally, you get hijacked by your mind because your mind operates on its need to survive (whether you like it or not). Occasionally, the mind keeps a judgment or wound from your conscious thought. (Remember the first rule of Shadow Work—we lie to ourselves first.)

The mind performs to keep us from wrestling with experiencing the weight of our self-judgment. Plot after storyline, scene after scenario, all created from surviving the looming judgment we can feel but cannot find. Because the mind is divided, it wrestles with the problem while protecting itself from the source. Left untended, the battle rages within us while we surface dwellers are left victimized by it. We are caught in a double bind. Each scenario our mind created makes the identity more calcified. More realized and conditioned. This storyline we embrace receives more validation and is the likely default construct we use to build new meaning. Why? Because to the mind "It just makes sense."

Even when we win, the victory is short-lived and, in some ways, has made it worse. The mind takes on the shape of your desired construct. Solving a problem and simultaneously living with the certainty of the problem only causes the mind to find another reason to suffer. Therefore, you validate the belief you're trying to invalidate by using it to navigate life. You've created a landmark to navigate and that landmark becomes the one you require to find your way. The mind leverages any meaning made to store it and make sense of all other meanings. Just like drops of water make up the ocean. So, every construct developed becomes holographic in your mind.

Let's consider this in a different scenario. Are you able to understand how the statement, "A coward dies a thousand deaths," makes sense now? In the mind, a coward dies repeatedly. Just as when I'm operating from one of my lower identities, I witness my demise hundreds of times an hour. My coward doesn't stand a chance compared to the lightning-fast reaction time of my well-associated and referenced victim identity. This still remains part of my work.

Our minds flow in story form and it will run whatever scenario is poised. Just as a tree falls the way it leans, a mind makes stories the way it's programmed. Athletes have used this concept to perform on the field of play. Performers when they go onstage. It is consciously using the mind to run the perfect scenario. Napoleon Hill coined this creative visioning. By training the mind consciously to run the scenarios *you* want to experience, *you* become more likely to experience the specific scenario in real life. Why? Because the mind desires to stick with what it knows.

This form of reflecting, imagining different scenarios, and reviewing different possibilities sets us apart from others. What if you only tell yourself stories worth telling? How would you change by changing your story, playing the hero and not a victim?

Stop for a moment and contemplate.

What is the quality of the outcomes you give yourself permission to anticipate?

Do you anticipate good days when you wake up?

Look at your relationships such as your work life or your intimate relationships. Take a moment to stop and notice how and what you anticipate in your day to day. Notice the difference between having faith in positive verses a negative outcome.

The story is the framework all narrative is wired to flow. It answers the question, "What's the point?" Your mind is always asking this question. Always. Every character has a story. Given that you have multiple identities or perspectives within you, you have multiple stories running through you at any given time. There's no "if" about it. It's a matter of how you are unconsciously telling yourself a story.

Each Identity Is Individual But Supports The Core

While each identity you possess has unique characteristics. Each upholds and enriches your whole. These identities are not isolated. They're interconnected facets which contribute to your overall sense of self. Understanding this interconnectedness allows you to navigate life's complexities with greater ease since you recognize how each identity is a piece of a larger, more intricate puzzle that makes up *you*. This realization is your foundation for the deeper insights and transformations.

Just as characters populate the vivid landscapes of tales, our multiple identities dwell within each of the countless constructs we experience the world through. Each of those identities has its individual storyline to which they are committed. Each of them reaches for embodiment and purpose. Notice how each tie into a core storyline, like a giant river you flow in and out of.

In the eternal dance of *now*, we continually craft meanings and interpretations, weaving the threads of experience into the rich tapestry of our experience and internal landscape. As we traverse the boundless expanse of our minds, identities become the position in which we generate our narratives in all the roles we play in life. From the hero to the sage, the lover to the warrior, these characters illuminate the multifaceted nature of our being, bringing depth and richness to our mythology.

At the heart of this process lies the story structure, an ever-present guide that molds perceptions and informs the essence of our being. It is the rut in the road that the tire that your mind is programmed to fall into. Notice the depth to which your mind constantly asks, "What's the story here?"

But you are constantly floating down **the river of the story called *you* in the boat called *now*.** Even with all these other storylines being played out, your body always seems to be in the boat called *now*. All your momentary narratives tie into and support a core story you're living out of. Just like any other facet, you have a default. I call this your core story. These stories become the very unconscious fabric of experience. The way we code the very mind is through stories. This creates a core story. Weaving tighter and tighter meanings becomes the denser facet of your experience, beliefs, and blueprints. But at the core, beliefs are still just stories you no longer question.

We all have a core story or a personal mythology. This is the story we constantly tell ourselves. We actively protect it and it's ever evolving. For most people, their core story is developed unconsciously and by default and since our automatic programming is survival-rooted, it becomes a survival-rooted story. This construct can generate an experience of living paycheck-to-paycheck at a hated job so you can pay for things you believe you need to alleviate the suffering caused from working in a job you hate.

If your primary identity is one of being a victim, your core story will be based on problems beyond your control. You anticipate and unconsciously create a storyline rooted in that lower identity. You find yourself ignoring truths that show you do have control or accept truths which lessen the orientation or value of the truth. You do this by default to support the storyline: You are a victim.

Is It the Button or The Box?

In our advanced workshops, seekers step onto a sacred carpet designed for deep internal exploration. The person standing on the carpet is both a seeker and a teacher. The guru of the moment can only come through the subjective experience of the story and there is where the hero is stuck.

During one workshop, a teacher delved into the depths of her soul, revealing an identity that had shaped her life in insidious ways—an identity rooted in a sense of worthlessness. This identity had cast a long suffering in shadow through her life, manifesting itself in unhealthy relationship behaviors and a shopping addiction, behaviors which left her feeling perpetually defeated.

"Take me to the construct?" I asked, walking beside her as she confronted her internal landscape.

She ran the scenario of her story, of her beliefs, and opened herself to her own interpretation. As she stood, tears flowed at her realization of the weight of the "Buy" button. It wasn't merely a click of a mouse or a touch of a pad, rather it was a desperate plea from an internalized identity screaming, "I am worthless."

This identity had evolved to become a corrosive element within her construct, always whispering, "You are here, and here is worthless."

Say, "Hello, Shadow."

This woman, this seeker and teacher, received the message, though not one her parents intentionally delivered, yet through their own generational shadow, they taught that her worth was tied to material things. This led her to a cycle of buying to feel "good enough," only to be crushed by the arrival of each package, a tangible manifestation of her internal sense of worthlessness. Each package confirmed her deepest fears, further entrenching her in a cycle of self-judgment and self-sabotage. She would buy from a feeling of being worthless, only to end up feeling worthless.

The system—her mind—defended an identity rooted in survival-oriented constructs. Despite high achievements in her life, she couldn't escape this loop of suffering, therefore, she unconsciously repeated it. Her mind turned like a hamster wheel, endlessly spinning but going nowhere.

An important note: Any external validation of worth brings the confirmation of lack.

Now, we delve into the real question: Did the allure of the "Buy" button entrap her? Did the momentary relief of "buying" release the pressure of the feeling of worthlessness? Or maybe it was painful arrival of each package delivery? Does the unconscious plotting through both the box and the button create the experience to justify the feeling of worthlessness?

It's the story. She programmed her mind to live out of the loop that mirrored her internal landscape, creating a cycle from which she couldn't break free. The system, her mind, isn't trying to work against her. Rather, it functions as a tool built to help her.

I believe the mind is trying to right itself. The nature of projection is an advanced way the mind has to check self-defeating meaning.

Think of your projection as natural virus protection. It wraps you in the stories you still wrestle with deep in your mind. These stories need tending. You can't solve the issues presented by them in any other way except to Turn Within and look at the root from which they are projected.

You can experience how stuck you are in a story, it's trapped you in loops of suffering. Everyone has them. It is the nature of being human.

By leaning into these loops of suffering, you can uncover your trapped genius, then move to solving problems without all the necessary data. Story happens, whether we like it or not. Ask yourself if you're willing to permit yourself to experience the root of your suffering consciously?

Unlocking Genius Through Creation

One of the oldest myths told is the story of creation itself.

Modern man has lost the understanding of how to hear a myth. A myth is a truth told as a lie. Within the grand theater of the mind, where the narrative facet weaves its enchanting spell, resides a creation myth epitomizing the interplay between your genius and shadow. Picture in your mind, the dawn of existence—a time when God resided in solitary splendor.

Stirred by a profound desire to birth offspring capable of shaping the very fabric of reality, someone to be his representation in the coloring of everything between heaven and hell, God embarked on a journey of sacrifice spanning a thousand years.

Immersed in this sacrificial act, God fervently yearned for progeny who would breathe life into the vast expanse of existence. God's yearning would not be denied. Twins would come forth, Ohrmuzd and Ahriman.

Ohrmuzd, the embodiment of sacrifice, radiates with the brilliance of genius. The Latin word "genius" derives from the older Indo-European root "gen" which means "to beget" or "to bring forth." This root emphasizes our genius' creative and generative aspect, highlighting its association with birthing or creating something new. Thus, the root word of "genius" point to its divine connotations and underlines the idea of genius as a source of originality and innovation. This reflects the unique expression of God or a higher power within an individual's capabilities.

On the other hand, Ahriman, veiled in darkness and destruction, symbolizes doubt and the depths of our Shadow. The primary tools of Shadow are deceit, deception, and misdirection. Ahriman is made up of many (mind, spirit, or otherwise abstract energy, etc.) that is angra (destructive, chaotic, disorderly, inhibitive, malign, etc., of which a manifestation can be anger). Is this the structure of the more extraordinary story we all play out as individuals?

As the myth unfolds, God, in recognition of the impending birth of the twins, grants sovereignty over creation to the firstborn.

Ahriman, seizing the opportunity, emerges before Ohrmuzd, tearing open the womb and bringing confrontation into the realm. Though Ahriman's kingship is limited to a finite period, it is within this dynamic interplay that the genius-shadow duality finds profound expression.

We glean a timeless lesson from this myth—our journey toward creation accompanies the realization of our genius necessitating sacrifice. As we embark on an odyssey of self-discovery, we must courageously confront shadow, traverse uncertainty and doubt, and embrace the interplay of our inherent genius, and also, where it still resides in shadow. We must learn to hold the center of sacrifice and doubt to allow creation to come through. Through this transformative process, our genius emerges, illuminating the world with its radiant brilliance.

Therefore, let's celebrate the power of the story facet. Within it lies the key to shaping our realities and our embarking on a quest for self-realization. With each story, each character, and each moment of meaning, we unlock the limitless potential to re-craft our narrative. It's where genius and shadow dance in harmony. It's where the essence of our unique expression finds its rightful place in the grand tapestry of existence.

I am struck by the profound realization that our lives are not simply a series of random events. Instead, events create a narrative woven into the very fabric of our existence. This narrative is not purely a story told; it's the story lived, the story shaping our reality and our consciousness. It's the holographic blueprint of our being, where each fragment mirrors the totality of our experience.

In the historical context, stories have been the catalysts for monumental shifts in consciousness. Take *Uncle Tom's Cabin* by Harriet Beecher Stowe, for instance. This isn't merely a book. It is a narrative that seeped into the collective consciousness of a nation, stirring a movement, shaking the very foundations of society. It exemplified how a single story could ripple through the minds and hearts of millions, altering the course of history. *This* is the power of story! Story is a force with the ability to mold the collective deep conscious, driving humanity towards epochs of change.

This story power is not confined to the annals of history. It is alive within each of us. It plays out through the constructs that inhabit our deep conscious. Our personal narratives are the stories we tell ourselves, the stories that define us, and the stories that can either imprison or liberate us. They are the constructs of how we live, the plots which unfold in the theater of our minds, and the plots we unconsciously embrace, regardless of the suffering it brings.

Within each of us lies a story, a narrative etched into the very core of our being. This story is not static. it's dynamic. Ever-evolving story. Fractally intertwined with the collective narrative of humanity. It is the root of our suffering.

As we engage in the sacred practice of Shadow Work, we are not merely revisiting the chapters of our personal story-history; rather, through our practice, we rewrite the story of our lives. We are uncovering the unconscious scripts that direct our path and choosing, with intention, new narratives to shape our future.

Joseph Campbell's body of work has been foundational in my personal work and has profoundly influenced my understanding of the human experience through his words:

"Stories are the secret reservoir of values: change the stories individuals and nations live by and tell themselves, and you change the individuals and nations."

Our minds are hard wired for story. It is through our narrative we make sense of the world, find meaning in chaos, and connect with the deeper truths of our existence. The stories we embrace, the lies we've told ourselves, the meaning we've made can either bind us to the constructs of the past or liberate us into the possibilities of the future. Story is the vessel through which we cultivate our reality, and through Shadow Work, we author our destiny.

Remember, the root word for human being in Arabic is "too forget." We are programmed to forget. We forget we are made of stories. If we are made of stories, then the way we would move through the world would naturally be made of stories. The loops we experience are the result of the unconscious patterns the mind is programmed to play out. Choosing to remain unconscious to the amount of consciousness running doesn't change reality. *You* change your reality.

Belief

"The unexamined life is not worth living." - Plato.

Within the realm of belief, a captivating dance unfolds, woven with the threads of our unquestioned narratives—the stories, anchoring the very fabric of our reality. Have you ever encountered someone firmly declare, "Once my mind is made up..."? At that moment, that individual points to the core structure that shapes the essence of their existence.

Belief, a sentinel at the heart of our being, diligently crafts, polishes, and authenticates meaning until it becomes an unwavering truth—an unspoken agreement between our perception and the universe. It's as certain to our mind as is the conviction that the Sun will grace us with its presence tomorrow.

Picture the emergence of a new day. The Sun rises over the horizon. Gentle caress of sunlight paints the horizon with golden hues. How often do we pause to question this enchanting phenomenon? Rarely, if ever. Instead, we embrace it as an inherent certainty—an unspoken pact between the cosmos and our perception. The rising Sun has become an indelible belief interwoven into the tapestry of our lives. It parallels all the unquestioned stories we hold, narratives which have undergone meticulous scrutiny, verification, and solidification. Then they become unassailable truths within the chambers of our minds.

Just as the rising Sun illuminates the world, our beliefs shape the lens through which we perceive reality. They construct the scaffolding upon which we assemble our understanding of the universe and our intricate place within it. Often operating in the recesses of our consciousness, these beliefs silently steer our thoughts, emotions, and actions, their influence flowing like a gentle current through the river of our lives.

Yet, within the vast expanse of belief waits an untapped reservoir of transformative power. By unraveling the layers of your unquestioned stories, you open a gateway to explore, question, and expand our understanding of reality. Much like the Sun casts its light upon hidden corners, examining your beliefs illuminating the hidden recesses of your psyche. By daring to question what you take for granted, you swing open the door to growth, transformation, and the emergence of fresh perspectives.

Have you ever had "one of those days"? Notice how a day takes on a container for your understanding of meaning. How many people do you know who live for the weekends? They have strung seven days together to create a space and time where they have chosen to experience similar feelings to those from the week before. But why? Because they hurled through time and space while spiraling around a ball of flames seven times.

The mind, a master of deletion, distortion, and generalization, operates based on its unwavering faith in the narratives we construct. Yet, the Sun has never truly risen. There is no absolute "up." You exist upon a spinning planet hurtling through space at a dizzying speed of 1,000 miles per hour, simultaneously spiraling through the vast unknown of the universe. The Earth, while orbiting the Sun, is part of a grand cosmic dance within the Milky Way galaxy. Our galaxy, along with our solar system, dances its steps within the vast expanse of the universe—a dance to be explored and understood.

The concept of "up" is subjective, rooted in our individual beliefs, the meanings we assign, and the sensations we associate with the Sun's ascent and descent. Remarkably, an entire tapestry of existence hangs upon the threads of this one seemingly innocuous belief.

As we embark on this transformative journey together, I invite you to explore the depths of belief—an expedition through the landscapes of consciousness, where illumination, introspection, and the freedom to reimagine our world await. Within the realm of questioning, we shall uncover seeds of possibility, fertile ground for new insights, and expanded understanding to sprout forth. We will investigate and tend to constructs held at the same level of certainty as the Sun coming up tomorrow.

Together, let's navigate uncharted territories. Let's discover where the tapestry of belief unravels and the threads of perception are rewoven into a glorious masterpiece of expanded consciousness. Let's ready ourselves for a voyage where the ripples of belief reverberate, reshaping our lives and awakening the extraordinary power that lies dormant within.

There is a phenomenon known as a *samskara* in ancient Hinduism. It emphasizes the impact of our thoughts and actions, highlighting how they become the constructs that inform our perspective of destiny. When you assign meaning to an event or situation, you create a blueprint or imprint of the worldview within a given construct. This blueprint serves as a template that informs the functioning and tuning of our emotional engine.

These imprints shape our attitudes, behaviors, and perceptions, influencing our present *and* future actions.

One famous quote that incorporates the term "samskara" is from the Indian spiritual teacher and philosopher Swami Sivananda:
"Watch your thoughts; they become your words;
Watch your words; they become your actions;
Watch your actions; they become your habits;
Watch your habits; they become your character;
Watch your character; it becomes your destiny."

For instance, if you internalize the belief that failure equates to not being good enough, this samskara will influence your emotional responses and color your perception of yourself. Because you are hijacked to survive, you run from the emotional pain of carrying the backpack of judgment. This causes a Shadow, one which you cast on the outside world through projection.

You are led to believe answers to the equation are external. That is incorrect. Turning within instead. The fuel that drives your labyrinth of life is your emotion.

Remember
this book isn't meant to be read; it's meant to be experienced.

Chapter 14

Emotion As An Evolutionary Tool

With Shadow Work, emotions play a pivotal role in bringing our experiences and perceptions to give them the definition and shading we crave. As meaning is made and stored through a construct, the mind operates in moments of awareness rather than linear time. These moments are woven together, forming the fabric of our experience—the threads record, confirm, then define and inform our existence. Emotions are the fuel emitted from the story that propels us into our next adventure or closes us up to weather the storm.

Let's begin by separating your emotional awareness into three signals to give you tools to navigate your work: positive, negative, and neutral.

Each signal serves a unique purpose to help the mind with its core directives, meaning, survival, and to evolve all meaning efficiently. Remember, the mind doesn't care whether what it knows is true or not, just whether it's accurate enough to keep us alive.

Three Types of Emotions

Emotions play a vital role in our human experience, serving as evolutionary tools to help us adapt and survive as a species. According to Barbara Fredrickson's broaden-and build-theory, there are only three primary types of emotional charges: positive, negative, and neutral. Each type serves a distinct purpose and uniquely affects our awareness and perception of the world.

I don't use positive and negative to describe good or bad. Look at it as a positive charge attracts and a negative charge resists, like a magnet. Negative isn't bad. Sometimes, taking away is what is needed. Negative is the charge that causes us to resist or move away from.

Positive charges, such as joy, love, and gratitude, expand our awareness and experience more of our surroundings. They cause us to engage and explore with more abandon. Research has shown how experiencing positive emotions broadens our perspective, allowing us to notice more details and nuances in our environment. For example, when we are in a state of love, we may notice vibrant colors, appreciate the beauty in everyday moments, and feel a deeper connection with others. Positive emotions enhance our well-being, build psychological resources, and enable us to navigate challenges with resilience and creativity.

On the other hand, negative charges, like fear and anger, serve a different purpose. Negative doesn't mean punishment. These emotions have a narrowing effect, focusing our attention and energy on specific threats or challenges. When we experience fear, for instance, our senses become heightened, and we become acutely aware of potential environmental dangers. Similarly, anger directs our attention toward perceived violations of our boundaries. Negative emotions, although uncomfortable, play a crucial role in our survival by helping us stay alert, take protective measures, and assert our needs. We identify valuable focal points in our decision-making process. When we were cave dwellers and a bear stumbled into camp, we had to have a way to short-circuit the system to focus resources on the threat at hand.

The challenge isn't that negative emotion is bad; it's how we're taught it's bad to feel them. If we have an emotion and tell ourselves it isn't okay to feel that way, we risk lying to ourselves when we feel said specific emotion. Unlearning that negative emotions are wrong is one of the lessons we need to evolve past.

One particularly potent negative emotion is disgust. Disgust serves as a protective mechanism against potential harm. When we feel disgusted by something, such as a repulsive smell or taste, our body instinctively reacts to avoid it. Imagine putting something disgusting in your mouth. What happens to the system that is *you*? You want to repel it. As we understand how the body keeps score, we'll find how disgust has saved us as a species. But the feeling of internal disgust is more insidious. Think of all the things that disgust you. This powerful emotion is often associated with a deep-seated judgment, identifying something is unsafe or contaminated.

The emotion of disgust extends beyond the realm of food. We experience disgust towards certain behaviors, ideas, people, whole groups, and aspects of ourselves and others. By exploring our emotional responses like disgust, we will gain insights into the underlying judgments and beliefs shaping our experiences and influencing our actions.

Think of your awareness like a camera lens. When you zoom in (-charge), you focus on certain life variables. The mind is fractal in nature. Problem-rooted thinking traps the best of us in a problem-rooted experience. But the same is true for positive emotions.

When you zoom out (+ charge), your zooming takes in the horizon, and you begin to notice your surroundings. This is a powerful tool to become aware of the deep conscious programming you experience life through. You start to assume more of the positive when you train yourself to associate as such. Your emotions lead you around at such a level that if you sit back and look at your ROI (return on investment), you might question why we don't teach this stuff more effectively in society.

In addition to positive and negative charges, there is a third category: neutral emotions. These emotions put us in an idle state with no significant charge or intensity. While neutral emotions may not be as easy to spot as positive or negative emotions, they still play a role in our emotional landscape.

It's important to recognize neutral charges as well. They provide a respite from the highs and lows of life, offering a sense of calm and equilibrium.

Before moving forward, we can rest, reflect, and integrate our experiences in neutral states. I suspect a whole realm of possibility is waiting to be discovered within neutral charges. It's where we least expect to find the most significant treasures.

When first beginning your practice, noticing the difference between these three types of emotions can be very liberating. I like to think of negative as constricting, positive as expanding, and neutral as rest mode. Check-in with yourself right now. What type of emotions do you typically experience? Are you more of a constricting, expanding, or rest mode? Notice how easy it is for you to generate the emotions you are most effective at generating.

Atlas of Emotions

Chicago School for Psychology asked groups in Mexico City and Chicago to list the names of as many emotions as possible freely. The emotions were then categorized as negative, positive, or neutral. Interestingly, people knew more negative emotion words than positive or neutral words. The proportion of words was fifty percent negative, thirty percent positive, and twenty percent neutral.

As we navigate the vast realm of human emotions, we find ourselves confronted with an interesting limitation—the limitations of language itself. While the English language offers an extensive arsenal of approximately 3,000 words to describe our emotions, it seems even this rich lexicon falls short of capturing the full spectrum of our inner experiences.

To try and traverse this lexicon, we use Ekmans's Atlas of Emotions framework. Most emotions researchers agree there are five Universal Emotions, emotions all humans, no matter where or how we were raised, have in common. This frame gives us a guidepost as we traverse various charges and dive into the depths of our experience. It will also provide a wedge we need to slip under the tapestry of our experience to upgrade the systems from which we have been operating.

This emotional atlas, composed of **anger**, **sadness**, **fear**, **enjoyment**, and **disgust**, guides the vast lands of emotions. For many of us, exploring and understanding these emotions can be enlightening and challenging, especially when we're faced with the often-misunderstood feeling of shame. This is where our promise to be compassionate is vital.

It's essential to approach these emotions with curiosity and compassion. Anything less than acceptance will spook the insights we wish to tease from our Shadow Work, and it may take generations for them to surface again.

The first step is to recognize and acknowledge the presence of these emotions within you. Awareness is always the true healer. You can't heal what you don't feel. You can unravel hidden and dormant layers by shining a light on them. Remember, they were hidden and dormant because you kept them imprisoned withing you. Now it's time to give yourself permission to feel and release anything you find.

Anger, a fiery emotion, can ignite within us. Often anger points to an unmet need for certainty, boundaries being crossed, or deep-rooted frustrations. By exploring the underlying causes of your anger, you can channel its energy toward positive change and transformation. This allows you to guide yourself toward asserting your needs and values. Anger can be the gateway to the *Warrior archetype* when doing identity-level work and can point to issues around certainty and boundary issues. Often, anger leads us to deeper feelings because anger was protecting us from deeper pain. Learning to slip under your anger, you begin to find the rich insights hidden underneath.

Sadness, a tender emotion that can wash over us like a gentle rain, invites us to honor and express our grief, loss, and heartache. Eckhart Tolle says the first spiritual awakening is the awareness that we have thought. For me, the waves of unspeakable pain from a heartbreak led me to the realization— I had a heart. Because heartbreak hurts, embracing sadness creates space for healing, forgiveness, and releasing emotional burdens weigh us down. Our need tied to sadness is connection. We can find solace and the seeds of renewal through the depths of sadness. Sadness gives us intra-connection and opens us up to a richer experience. The archetype I associate with sadness is the *Lover*. Sadness brings us to the awareness of our true power and vulnerability.

Fear, a protective emotion, can send tremors through our being, alerts us to potential dangers and threats. Imagine sitting in a pitch-black room, then you hear a rustling over in a deep, dark corner. What happens? Every sense you have focuses on understanding what the shift in your surroundings means. It can bring you an awareness you may overlook when in a different state. Fear is the gateway emotion for the need for uncertainty.

My family loves Halloween Horror nights at Universal. We go every year. I, on the other hand, do not. However, I enjoy watching them get scared. For some reason, they dig it as well, therefore, it works for us.

The archetype many associate with fear is the *Magician*. It's the archetype responsible for initiating us into the unknown. Without this part of you, there can be no growth.

While fear may sometimes hold you back, it offers growth and expansion opportunities. By leaning into your fears, you uncover hidden strengths, resilience, and courage which propels you toward personal transformation and self-empowerment. Remember the saying, "If you can't, then you must!?"

Touching what you fear always leads to insights. That's the one place where you're almost guaranteed to find treasure. Fear is initiatory. It's the gateway to the second grace—the grace of illumination. You must be willing to be swallowed by darkness to see the light. In darkness, your spark of genius can be born.

Enjoyment, an emotion with the power to illuminate our lives, reminds us of beauty and opens us to the joy within and all around us. Through embracing happiness, we cultivate gratitude, celebrate our achievements, and find fulfillment in the present moment. Moments of happiness can bring light to the gloomiest existence. Happiness directs us to savor life's precious moments and nurture our overall well-being. The need I associate with happiness is *significance*. The archetype is the *Sovereign, the King or Queen* or both... who live inside each of us. You are the one *you* have been waiting for. *You* are the one you have been waiting for. Your significance is more significant than you've ever known.

Emotions are what give experience flavor. As you explore your emotions, it is essential to recognize the distinct qualities they possess and their impact on your life.

Disgust, as an emotion, plays a vital role in our ability to identify and avoid potentially harmful or dangerous situations. It arises when we encounter stimuli or experiences, producing a strong sense of aversion or repulsion within us. This response helps us stay safe and protected from potential threats. Some threats are so clear, you notice them before you are even aware of them.

Imagine, being handed a thawed package of meat. Now imagine opening the package and being struck by the stench of rotten meat. What's the odor like? What's the expression you'd show after such a whiff? Stop here and activate the smell of something foul tasting or smelling in your imagination. What is the physical experience of disgust?

By recognizing and heeding the signals of disgust, you learn to navigate your environment cautiously and make informed choices for your well-being and survival. How might the mind deal with a mental construct similarly charged?

More on Shame

It's essential to recognize the experience of disgust and how it informs us through our shame. By poking just under the surface of the emotion, you have the opportunity to find some awareness and healing. Although emotions are more energetically baseline, they evolve into feelings once they have taken on some legs.

Remember, everything evolves. If you hold onto an emotional charge, all it can do is evolve. You get cancer or the promise of a newborn baby, all by the emotions you continue to embrace. Everything evolves. Love, for example, is a feeling. Love sits at the gateway to the Sacred Mother archetype, and the need it activates is the need to contribute beyond one's self. Love is not static. Love is ever-evolving, just like the mind. Love will taste different from person to person. And love will change moment by moment.

Shame is similar. It will load into our identity facet of the construct we've created. Shame then becomes an association which we use to identify our place within the construct. If we're not careful, shame becomes an addiction and the primary landmark for all our relationships.

In Brene Brown's 2012 TED Talk, "Listening to Shame," Brown explains how shame is the intensely painful feeling or experience of believing we are flawed and, therefore, unworthy of love and belonging. We fear something we've done or failed to do, an ideal we've not lived up to, or a goal we've not accomplished makes us unworthy of connection. In Brown's view, everyone experiences shame and the fear of disconnection it carries—except for those who are incapable of human empathy. I believe if we identify this feeling of disconnect, it offers us the opportunity to pluck at our shame, uncover insights in the most unlikely places, and therefore, lead us to growth.

I have found shame to be tied to an unprocessed judgment with a feeling of disgust. In these instances, our mind disconnects from the construct it's running, causing disgust. The survival directive comes online, and the system divides against itself.

When we were young and still learning to carry our emotions, the system of our mind had to have a way to carry the chemical-cocktail equivalent of an emotional atomic bomb. Our mental system disconnects us from the judgment causing disgust as a self-defense mechanism.

Your mind edits and projects certain judgments you carry about yourself due to the perceived weight associated with each judgment. You lie to yourself. Any judgment that left a charge too big to carry was disassociated—the feeling is something bad left unsaid. Like a cliffhanger you knew was your fault.

This mind-game of hide and seek blocks the flow of emotion from leaving the body. If the emotion generated felt too big for your system when you were little, why would you ever risk re-investigating the situation again? As a result, you become frozen in the structure of the judgment instead of being open to feeling the weight of the judgment. The consequence is receiving a twisted and confusing message.

Judgment pinches off the flow of love, joy, and care into any construct. This disconnect leads us to an experience many labels as "shame." This disconnect in our mind can create a confusing vacuum-like experience for us. This shows up as a personal conspiracy making itself known in every area of our lives.

This can be experienced by a looming judgment, Armageddon moment, or can appear as a narcissist only looking out for themselves. Shame leads to an experience of an identity, one which protects against any perceived threat at all costs.

In truth, the judgment you care about is blocking your flow of energy. Untended to self-disgust becomes the false identity you label "shame." It weighs heavily on your heart and mind. Since the feeling of disconnect can be so pronounced, bringing awareness to the feeling of shame will offer profound results.

Review your relationships that carry the charge of shame. Are you able to find some low-hanging work to begin practicing Shadow Work?

Shame to Disgust Shadow Work Process

Take inventory of your life, looking for an area where you feel a mild amount of shame. Look for a piece of shame that will be easy to work with. This process is about getting acquainted with your shame, not illuminating it. Look for something on the scale of a three out of ten.

We all carry varying degrees of shame. It can be anything from your weight to your finances to your sexuality to your ability to say your ABCs correctly. Consider a relationship in which you currently hold a sense of shame. As you load up the experience or construct, permit yourself to become aware of the shame. Let it come online. Go into the face of it. Allow yourself the experience of it within your body.

Now, notice how your shame causes a feeling of disconnection, you are unconsciously ignoring a judgment that is so damning it becomes hard to take in. Allow yourself to be okay with what you discover here. Awareness and compassion are the keys to the game.

If you had trouble letting go, you bit off too much. Back up and choose something not so heavy to practice letting go. As you become more acquainted with your feelings of shame, move to the heavier stuff.

Do you notice if you experience any joy in this construct? Is there any joy when you standing the shadow of this judgment of disgust? No?

How does love flow through you when living your life through this construct? You're probably noticing it's hard to find love in here.

How about a higher power of some sort? How difficult is it for you to be the instrument of a higher purpose, power, or meaning when sitting in shame? If you poked around in your shame, what are you experiencing? Allow yourself to release whatever comes up.

As noted before, the material in this book is to be experienced. Here's a place of experience. Please, set down the book and come back to it when you're ready to move forward.

Now, here's the critical question in this moment: What is the judgment you're tightly clinging onto which blocks love from flowing through you, blocks your joy, or blocks your authentic genius from flowing through you now? What is it you're holding onto?

Are you now able to see any judgment you've been unconsciously carrying around? Maybe you've held a judgment about someone holding a judgment about you. Are you able to see how this judgment blocks you from being in your fullness?

Letting go of that judgment will destroy the damn and allow the energy of life to flow back through you. The healing moment happens for everyone perched at that precipice. My promise? If you follow this process, find the judgment, and learn to let it go, you will find a change will permeate your life immediately and forever. Often, the experience gives you the very thing you thought you needed in the first place.

Turning Within is weird that way. Up can sometimes appear to be down.

As you navigate the terrain of your emotions, remember this journey is an opportunity for self-discovery, healing, and integration. By delving into your emotional atlas, you open the door to a deeper understanding of yourself, your experiences, and the constructs shaping your reality. With each reclaiming step, you will experience your authenticity, embrace your wholeness, and forge a path toward self-acceptance and self-love.

You have embarked on a courageous and transformative path requiring vulnerability, patience, and self-compassion. Remember—you're not alone on this journey. Reach out for support when you need it, whether through the guidance of a Shadow Guide, the shared experiences of a Shadow Work community, or the wisdom found within the pages of this book.

Shame is a lie.

You are more powerful than you have ever realized. As your journey unfolds, as you step through your shame, you have the power to claim the gold waiting on the other side. I am here for you. The community is here for you. Take the opportunity to embrace the power of your emotions. They are the threads that make up the tapestry of your experience. In your reclaiming of your power, you're releasing old constructs. When you step into a new chapter of self-discovery through your commitment to your work, you will experience deep healing, self-empowerment, and the rediscovery of your true essence on your journey.

Tracking Your Charge

Unaccepted Emotions are left unprocessed. Unprocessed emotions cause the constructs you've created to cast shadows into your conscious experience. While undeniable, necessary, natural, and impactful, emotions do not reflect the absolute truth of any situation. They are the response to meaning, not the confirmation of validity.

Most of our economy is built around managing the impact of unprocessed feelings and emotions. Yet, we are not taught to understand, label, or process them individually. Turning Within is the lost practice of consciously tending to constructs left unprocessed. As a practitioner, you come to understand and depend on the intricate relationship between emotions and your inner landscape. Emotions now serve as a compass, helping you navigate the terrain of experiences and uncover judgments which cast shadows upon your present moment. Suffering becomes a moment of clarity around how you create your button-and-box scenarios. As such, you are no longer a surface dweller of your experience.

Some of you may have, just now, experienced a moment of clarity. A clarity about a particular construct, one from which you've been living your outside life, coming into sharp focus. This construct is the meaning-making lenses which you experience the world. Your goal is to understand how you may operate to be more intentional and authentic, thus changing the construct.

You are looking for the feelings you carry that cause you to be uncomfortable. What emotions do you feel, yet judge them as wrong or carry shame for having them? You're seeking a loop in your storyline. You are searching for the suffering identities you constantly try to avoid. Your mind will resist any internal judgments it deems too painful.

Your natural tendency may be to judge yourself harshly by what you start to uncover. Here, I urge you to hold yourself with soft hands. You must be accepting with whatever judgments come up, because the ability to do deep work is tied directly to your ability to be human.

This may sound like *gobblygook* for those new to Shadow Work. But don't worry, as you continue to do your work and return to this book and it's offered processes, the information will make more and more sense. The bolded headline here is, "You're human." If you're going to do Shadow Work, it can only be a beneficial pursuit if you grant yourself grace, love yourself, and allow yourself to process your feelings.

A single seed of your awareness can change the entire experience for you. The shift will happen so deeply that the difference becomes realized across the entire experience of your life. The impact is geometric, not linear.

Emotions are a facet of the constructs you live out of—the meaning you assign to your experiences, thoughts, and beliefs. Emotions arise from the narratives you have woven and the perspectives you have accepted as truth. While emotions hold valuable information, they are influenced by your past conditioning, biases, and distorted perceptions.

Recognizing that every emotional charge begins and ends within you is a significant step in your journey of self-discovery. It implies taking ownership of your emotional responses and acknowledging that they arise from your interpretations and the constructs you have created. By doing so, you reclaim your power to shape your experiences. You turn reactions into responses.

This type of power is unique; once you are consciously aware of it, you won't give it up again. Why? Because you understand, giving this up doesn't make anything in life better—for you, for anyone—ever.

The Third Rule, Every Charge Begins and Ends With Me

In my Shadow Work, personally and as a Shadow Work guide, I have witnessed how emotions can liberate *and* imprison. Feelings and emotions are powerful signals, guiding us toward unhealed wounds and unmet needs and unresolved conflicts. We must approach our emotions with discernment, curiosity, and a willingness to question their underlying stories.

When we recognize how emotions are not the ultimate truth, but reflections of our inner landscape, we have the opportunity to explore them more deeply. We can use our emotions as entry points to uncover the hidden judgments and beliefs which cast shadows upon our present experiences. By Turning Within, we untangle the threads of our constructs and discern how our emotions fuel evolution, growth, and also how they block it.

Embracing the complexity of our emotions while developing a discerning eye allows us to navigate our emotional influences more consciously. We can investigate the stories and beliefs fueling our emotional responses, investigating their validity, and impact on our lives. Through this process, we begin to liberate ourselves from emotional patterns that no longer serve us, and in doing so, we create space for greater emotional intelligence, authenticity, and well-being.

Emotions become the gateway into our constructs, allowing us to access imprints and patterns that shape our experiences. Emotions are the bridge which connects us to our underlying beliefs, judgments, and interpretations—they fuel our behavior. When triggered, emotions activate the samskaras, casting a shadow over our experience and reinforcing the constructs we have created. Shadow Work is the process through which we learn to navigate and transform our emotional landscape. This presents us with the freedom to consciously examine and question the validity of our imprints. Through Shadow Work, we release the grip of limiting emotions, bringing us freedom to create space for new, empowering emotions to emerge.

Decision

In my early 30's, I worked in the Gateway Computers sales department. My newfound awareness of how the mind was structured transformed my sales performance, propelling me into a level of success I hadn't previously thought possible. This brought me confidence in my role, which was evident to everyone around me. Yet, despite my newfound abilities and poise, I repeatedly walked away from my manager's desk, kicking myself for asking questions to which I already knew the answers.

Have you ever found yourself in a similar situation? You knew the answer to a question, but you couldn't see it.

Fast forward about fifteen years.

It was three weeks away from COVID-19 shutting down the world.

It was one week after my first three Ayahuasca ceremonies.

I went to Serbia to headline a week-long business training seminar with some of the top business leaders in the country. At that time, I'd just begun to develop my understanding of constructs. As a matter of fact, the geometric shape I teach with came into form the very next day.

During my presentation, I worked onstage, interacting with a doctor named Mirjana. She was blindingly brilliant in her field and her life. She was heart-driven. She was connected at every level.

I asked the question. "What did you come here to get?"

Mirjana needed to grow. She was at the top of her field, but she needed specialized help, she couldn't duplicate herself. At this point, she didn't have a business—her business had her. It is at this junction in doctors' lives they engage me.

Mirjana and I conducted a strategic assessment of her operating terrain and discovered, indeed, there was a dramatic need for her business to grow. When I asked why she hadn't grown her business, this is where her blinding brilliance got in her way.

"No one can do what I do," she flatly stated.

This is where a *half-truth* becomes more dangerous than *a total lie.* Deeper than her fear of lack of success dwelt a deeper fear of what success meant for her. Who would she need to become to achieve her desired level of success? Equally great was the fear of how success would shift her internal landscape—was she capable of her desired level of success? What would it mean to her external relationships?

Mirjana lived from a gripping Shadow that wouldn't permit her to see resources to scale her business the way she envisioned it.

Later, at a VIP dinner, Mirjana pulled me to the side, visibly excited. She shared how she discovered two doctors who were perfect for consideration for her business expansion and growth. She then told me of a conversa-tion with someone she supported as a preceptor a month prior. Resources miraculously appeared.

Dumbfounded. I asked, "Mirjana, Where were these people several hours ago?"

"I just couldn't see them," she replied.

I was floored.

There are a ton of great books on the topic of strategy. However, for this book, I believe it's essential for me to convey to you that solutions won't appear to you *unless* you give yourself permission, agency, or believe your faith exists.

Learn to see where you have given your agency away. It's there you will find where you lost the ability to make the right decision for yourself.

The underlying issue points to a loss of your agency, not your lack of strategy. Don't get me wrong, running East will not find you a sunset. Let me ask you a more profound question, Why are you programmed to go East in the first place? Because we humans don't do what we can, we do what we *think* we can.

The concept of agency is deeply tied to our ability to perceive opportunities and make effective decisions. It's not just about having the skills or resources. It's also about the awareness and intention behind our actions. When we lack agency, we usually are unable to see the possibilities right before us, even if we have a strategy to achieve success.

Agency allows you to cut through the distractions and stresses of life to find emotional and physical balance, think more clearly, and advocate for yourself. Lacking agency likely means your attention is being hijacked, affecting your capacity to think and make decisions. You're more likely to feel helpless, frustrated, or scared when you have little personal agency. If you don't think your actions can produce the desired results, you may not see the point in taking any action at all.

In the context of decision-making, this underscores the importance of agency. Strategy alone is not enough. You must also have the agency to believe in the possibilities that strategy can bring you. Without agency, you are blind to opportunities, no matter how well-planned the strategies. This blindness can manifest as repeatedly asking questions you already know the answers to *or* not seeing resources right before you. It's not just about having a strategy; it's about having the agency to execute it. Therefore, reclaiming your agency becomes crucial in making effective decisions and seeing the possibilities that align with your strategies.

So, the point you must understand is how you won't see any solutions if you don't give yourself permission, agency, or faith to believe they exist. Learn to see where you have given your agency away. There you'll find where you have lost the ability to make the right decision for you.

Action

Once you possess an idea which holds enough charge and a judgment has been formulated, decisions and meaning are cleared and fueled. Then, the system of *you* engages the idea at a level which has continuity with all other levels of your engagement. It equally operates symbiotically with all the other actions already taken.

For example, when you're driving your car and come to a stop sign, then you turn your wheels to go left, then suddenly realize, you need to turn right—there you must unravel your actions to turn in the direction you wish to go. The previous action of turning the car influences the impact your actions will make. All other meanings, up to and including time itself, are at play in the structure of the action. This isn't new data to you. You operate in the physical world where matter operates under a set of laws. What's true is true.

What happens when you do the same action over and over? Just like in your mind, the body wants to automate. Actions with the most automation become reflexes. Muscle memory kicks in. You see this with athletes who drill the same actions over and over. The peak performance gurus teach, "Practice doesn't make perfect. Practice makes permanent." The same action done over and over creates a groove in the mind. That action becomes more accessible and easier to make. It becomes increasingly automatic until it is the farthest removed process from conscious thought.

Think of those moments you go into Shadow. What causes you to be blocked? What do you do when you get blocked? What's your reaction when you go into Shadow?

Maybe you attack when you feel provoked. Maybe you grow quiet. Maybe when you feel yourself triggered, you disassociate. Maybe you run. Because these moments take on an Armageddon framework, they activate a desire to fight, feign, freeze, or disassociate.

What do you do, what's your response, when you go into Shadow? Take some time and review and journal how you act. What are the behaviors you display? What are the emotions running through you? Notice how your actions, the ones you find yourself coming from, feel almost reflexive.

Notice how automated your reaction is to the stimulus. Notice the internal rituals you have set up to manage your circumstances. Do you "blow off steam?" How do you unwind? Are you acting on the ideal outcome or managing circumstances?

Have you created rituals which cause more circumstances that need managing? Internal rituals support evolution through automation at the physical level. It's anything done repeatedly, said repeatedly, or heard echoes within our clay-like existence. The action point is where the idea meets external expression. Until then, it's just a thought.

Action is the beginning of the materializing of thoughts. Your decision is fueled by the emotion generated by the story you tell yourself at any moment. Action, story, emotion are all based on the identity you settled on at that moment.

What happens when you continue to play the same record over and over? When you think the same thought over and over, the mind identifies this as the default construct from which you want to live. Again, automation supports evolution. It strengthens, confirms, and further automates your association with this construct, making it much harder to see as a judgment down the road.

If you seek to tend to a Shadow at the action point, you start by looking at the rituals you have placed in your life to manage a false self. Use the compass of your intention to identify whether your construct is based on love or fear. Then, your solution becomes simple, yet challenging since it brings conscious response to the unconscious reaction.

Make the unconscious conscious—Unlearn so that you can relearn.

Once you see your unconscious reaction, you keep that part of you in your awareness. We call it keeping your Shadow out in front of you. What is the story you are now making up about this situation? How is that story on auto-play in your life? Where else does this show up? When this construct comes online, do you have the story, or does the story have you?

Now is the time to take back and reclaim your agency to make different decisions. It's time to move through, not over, the stories which have you stuck. Grab the gold that is beneath your suffering and transform your world. Why would you wish to suffer and then not take the gold from what you have endured?

Let's review how you support change at the action facet.

Review your rituals and habits to see what identities they strengthen.

Are there habits or things you regularly in your life? Habits like going to the gym? Do you find time to unwind? What are the rituals and habits you have to develop yourself?

Are there any rituals you use to support sacred identities?

How do some of your rituals strengthen your association with your lower identities?

Review the ways you react when in Shadow.

Seek to identify what you resistant doing and what the judgment is underneath the resistance.

What behaviors are you discovering you repeat over and over?

What triggers you to act in this way?

What behaviors do you know would lead you to your ideal life, actions you plan to take, but don't?

Go to the moment you choose to go the other way—what is the judgment that keeps you from acting? How does the identity that makes the decision different from the identity that doesn't follow through? How does the identity at the front of the storyline and the one at the back relate to each other?

Remember

this book isn't meant to be read; it's meant to be experienced.

Chapter 15

Closing The Circuit Process

Taking the Fruit to the Root

"Personal transformation isn't always comfortable. Often, it is even painful, but that's okay. It is partly the pain of this internal voyage that changes you. As you leave your mark on your work, it leaves its mark on your consciousness and heart. You leave some things behind, take some with you, and hopefully share some with others along the way, even if only stories. This is the way... but only if you decide to make the journey. You cannot cross the sea merely by standing on the shore and looking at it." — *Robert Herd*

The easiest way to see how constructs inform and define reality is when we are in Shadow. It's also when you may feel the least like doing your work. It's when we spin entirely false narratives to avoid getting into our suffering any deeper. Yet, the squeaky wheel gets the oil—Shadow allows us to study how we operate at a core level. If one of our first awakenings is that we have thought, the one screaming in our ears becomes invaluable.

Practitioners learn to work with their suffering because they understand how suffering can be a blessing, sacred. We begin to dethrone the bully in our mind and liberate our resources to reroute to other areas of thought and life.

I have heard thousands of seekers declare, "I feel lighter." I've seen it across all spectrums, and if you sit with it long enough, the sacredness of your suffering becomes undeniable. Recognizing loops of suffering is a fundamental skill every practitioner develops.

When bringing awareness to our life, we shift control from our Shadow and begin a journey of healing. Through awareness we bring the construct up to our consciousness. Then we break down the samskara that has us repeatedly experiencing the same patterns of suffering.

Here is where we regain the genius that affords us our dominion. We are free to create new stories and constructs, to witness what the human condition is capable of experiencing.

You do the work. You bring light to your part of the world. You journey towards that which is your birthright. Wellbeing.

Set and Setting-Permission to Dive

The following process explores the space between experience and judgment. This space is the choice point where change happens. It's here that you carry magic so powerful it bends space-time. Remember, you wrote the code; therefore, you're the only one who can rewrite it. Now's your time to dive!

Treat this next part like an experiment. You want to permit yourself not to take your "self" so seriously. Everything you know about what you know is made up. The objective here is to treat this as playtime, just like your genius little one used to play when they were on the playground.

Remember, for a moment, what it was like to play as a child—to "act as if." However, instead of pretending to be something you are not, you'll drop into the loops of suffering you get caught in. By exploring the cave you resist entering, you'll find the parts of you that you resist or deny.

It's time to slay the dragon that hides the most remarkable treasures you have ever seen.

Your mind is wired for change; trust the process and let the mind do what it is built to do. It's time to remove the shackles and purge them so you can receive new ones. It all starts with grace. The more you can allow anything that comes up its place, the deeper your mind can dive, the more effective the cleanse. Remember, your mind doesn't want to suffer. That's why you keep cycling through the same drama in your head repeatedly. It's trying to let go of something it doesn't know it is holding onto.

Set Down Your Greatest Weapon

There is one weapon you have that you will have to set down for this next part. I have given your rational mind a lot to chew on. Hopefully, it has been able to stretch in several areas already. This next exercise will take you past your rational thought. It can come along, but let it be the passenger and not the driver.

Genius in large enough buckets will appear impossible. But what starts out impossible will quickly move to possible. If given a moment to be realized, that possibility will transform into the probable. What is probable becomes likely. What is expected ends up being the most rational direction to go.

You must mine for the answer before your mind can wrap around it. This stretch is past the rational knowing and into the deeper parts that support it. Absolute truth sits at the corner of paradox and confusion. When you look at your suffering through the contemplative eye, you activate the process of transmuting your suffering into insight.

Einstein suggested you can only solve a problem with a different mindset than what got you into it. Your contemplative eye sees the world beyond your programmed reactions. You activate an altered state that opens you up to purge the old ideas and cultivate a new life. The raw ore of your experience opens you up to profound experiences of growth and meaning.

Be okay with learning something new. You are about to let go of some stories that have left you suffering by leaning in instead of resisting them. But you can only let go at the level you are willing to allow yourself to carry the magic where it yearns to flow.

Closing the Circuit Origin Story

Every significant threshold needs a story. This one is cloaked in shadow and has a journey-like origin. The Closing the Circuit process is a collaboration of a lucid dream I had as a kid, the vision given to me while working with plant medicine, 20 years of study and practice, and most importantly, the hundreds who brought their work to the table so that I could learn this process through them.

My Childhood Dream

When I was young, I dreamt I had a visit from my adult self. In the dream, my adult self comforted me, telling me everything would be okay. But I wasn't just being told. My older self transmitted a level of certainty that transcended words. It transcended knowing; I was becoming aware. It was so intense that the energy of it woke me up and kept me up for the rest of the night. It felt more accurate than the waking dream world we find ourselves in. I found out later, while researching dream yoga, that they call it a lucid dream. That dream lifted me through countless rough patches. It was my comfort blanket when I couldn't find any other warmth. I remember it was like a candle in some of my darker dark nights of the soul.

Many years later, I now realize that dream was somehow a seed of the process I share with you now. I don't completely understand how and why it works. To be honest, I don't care. This process has helped countless seekers tend to their shadows. If you come to this process ready to participate, I have seen miraculous results in the lives of those doing their work.

The Vision

Right after COVID-19 hit, I was tapped to create an online integration community. The goal was to support over 20k community members working with the medicine Ayahuasca. We needed a way they could continue their

212

work while waiting for everything to start back up. The visions shown to me in my 3rd and 4th ceremonies clicked into play. Mother showed me how everything had its place, and I had mine. I'd been working with integration in circles for over 20 years and had just spent the last 10 integrating a business system in thousands of businesses. I immediately realized why I was brought to the medicine at this time. We offer anywhere from 8 to 24 unique integration groups and serve over 40k now. The closing-the-circuit process was born in the front line of deep change work.

The Container

I learned to practice Shadow Work through attending an immersion process followed by decades of sitting in a group structured to support Shadow Work. The "container" or group we practice has been constructed to amplify love, forgiveness, divine guidance, healing, empowerment, authentic community, and raw genius. The amplification comes from those holding space to build the container the seeker unpacks their work in. Although each journey is both powerful and intimate, the lessons are shared by everyone in the container. The light emitted from every breakthrough is breathtaking. It's like that scene in The Matrix when Neo and Trinity cut through the clouds. I tell you, people glow. Like lighting up a city glow.

My life has been forever deepened by the blessings I receive from diverse integration groups I've had the blessing to sit with. Specifically, thank you if you are among the many who have sat with the container that incubated this process. You have given more than you know. This is the sacred process that has emerged from your work. We all thank you for being our teacher; your work makes this book possible.

Reader, we have a space that we have blessed for you that sits beyond space and time. Allow yourself to pretend, while leveraging a proven process to help you find your answer.

This process you have in front of you is as close to the path we can get you without having a guide in front of you. We invite you to wander into the dark water, dive into the deep, and see if you pull out the same pearls we pull when we dive into ours.

Induction

The first round is bringing as much of all of you as we can to your axis mundi. Bring your consciousness here and now. To begin, take a deep breath in, light a candle, say a prayer, and now ask yourself:

Do you permit yourself to see your darkness, the parts you hide, repress, and deny? Do you commit to treating yourself with compassion and understanding and allow those parts to come forward?

Do you permit yourself to see your brilliance? Do you permit yourself to see the genius that can only come through you?

Do you commit to stretching what you believe you are capable of so the voice that can only come through you can be heard?

Remember, this isn't therapy (if you need professional help, please seek it). This is a way to find the keys you lost to the car you forgot you drove to the problem you think you have. By Turning Within, you find answers to questions that can't be found elsewhere because they sit beyond the physical world. I have my hypothesis on why this works, but the truth is the process does something beyond rational thought. Trying to understand has been the joy of my career.

Tracking the Thief of Joy

The mind creates meaning. The meaning generates a charge. If that charge is something the mind is hiding from itself, we will find ourselves caught in loops of suffering. An adage says, "A coward dies a thousand deaths." I'd trade my victim identity for any coward and their thousand deaths. I'll run a thousand scenarios plotting my doom by the end of the day. It was astonishing for me to realize that I was telling myself the same suffering story over and over. Like I was finally being let in on the cosmic inside joke,

I was playing on myself. (I guess it was all my fault.) I wasn't prepared for what that meant in the practical world.

Let's see what you find. The first step is to define the pattern. Second, load the holographic memory up so it can be analyzed. If you are one of the thousands who have been through our Zoom sessions, you have heard me ask the seeker, "Check around in your pockets." To do so, you have to walk a mile or so in your old shoes. You gotta "feel it." I'd suggest leveraging this book to work through a piece of work you have been chewing on.

Let's dig in and see what gems you can pull. I look forward to hearing how this process worked for you.

Closing The Circuit- Fruit to Root Process

Step 0: Identify the Story, Load the Construct

We all get caught up in the story. The mind craves story—it's a scientific fact. To think otherwise is to be *ignore-ant* of how you operate. I have yet to meet someone who doesn't have a Shadow. Shadow is an intimate but collective challenge. It's virus that corrupts the system, the thief of joy, the robber of sleep, but also the source of insight and genius.

What's the loop of meaning which plagues your thoughts? Perhaps, "I tell myself how I'm not good enough." Or "I feel like I am being attacked." Notice the last time you were in a suffering or condensed state. Look back over your week and see where you suffered because you were tangled in a storyline. What story wraps you up and binds you? When you are suffering, what's the identity you find yourself caught in?

We all get caught in cycles of suffering. The key is noticing *when* it comes up, Turning Within, and doing the work to INVESTIGATE and unravel the construct.

Here is an opportunity for you to discover a treasure right before you. hope you will give this a wholehearted try:

Prompt: What's the story you tell yourself that steals your joy?

- "I tell myself...{what}?"
- For example, "I tell myself I'm worthless."
- "I tell myself I'm not fast enough."
- "I tell myself I'm not pretty."

Step 1- Navigate to the Recent Trigger (Narrative Load)

Now you have identified a storyline, and it's time to thread the needle and dive into your work. You will be charging in with eyes-open to face the monster hiding in the deep. You will have to allow your Shadow to come forward to do this process.

This next part is what your work hinges on. The more you are willing to go deep, the more healing you will facilitate. Let go of your rational mind and follow the voice telling you, "Allow whatever comes up just to come up." Your mind wants to right itself, if you only learn to let it.

We aren't diving into distant memories just yet. Instead, we're looking for a recent moment when some piece of your suffering state came online. You want to load the whole storyline into your narrative to reactivate the charge. This is the missing piece for most people who attempt this work. They don't start where the construct casts a Shadow onto the 3D world. The lack of association causes a disconnect in integration. That leads to a loss in impact from your hard work. We teach from the lesson of Ram Dass, who is quoted as saying, "Suffering only shows where you are attached. That is why, to those on the path, suffering is grace."

We want to follow the breadcrumbs. Therefore, stick with the most recent time you remember this storyline coming up.

Instead of loading a new memory, navigate back to a recent time when the earlier experience cast a Shadow over "now." This recent triggering event will serve as the entry point for INVESTIGATION. When was the last time you remember feeling this way?

Allow yourself to load up the construct to feel around in it. Load up the last moment you recall this story and the shape of your narrative. Pretend for a moment you were back in that place. We are looking for a time you were caught up in the story *and* you were in the suffering.

One way of asking this is to complete the sentence, "There was this one time when…"

- Where were you specifically?
- What do you recall about that specific moment?
- Were you inside or outside?
- Was it daytime or nighttime?
- Was the moment at the beginning of the week or the end?
- What day was it?
- What was happening right before the charge came online?
- Who was there with you?
- What were they doing?
- What did it feel like the moment the trigger hit?
- Now, move as close as possible—in your mind—to the moment the charge came online. What was the trigger? Did someone do something, say something? How did that moment feel?
- Now, go to the moment right before the charge came online, right before the feeling began. Find the threshold of the moment. This is essential. Either go to when the feeling first came on *or* find the time you remember the moment coming on, and then you need to walk through that memory frame by frame.

Step 2: Visualize the Feelings

This process allows you to activate and deal with feelings which are more challenging to transform, making the construct in question both tangible and accessible. By giving form to your feelings, you're better equipped to investigate them without resistance, enabling a more profound exploration of their roots. This process supports deepening your connection with the construct your mind created that you find yourself stuck.

Let's investigate the emotions and sensations associated with a recent triggering event, leveraging your active imagination to experience your emotions as colors, shapes, textures, sounds, and voices. Opening yourself to this new way to process the feelings you experience as they surface.

Load your feelings and INVESTIGATE them.

- Mad, Sad, glad, scared?
- Were you feeling shame or disgust?
- What specifically were you feeling? Load up the feelings now.
- *How* do you know that you are feeling this emotion?
- Do you feel a pressure or condensing someplace in your body?
- *Where* in your body do you feel it?

Locate that part now. Touch it with your hand. Now, let the feeling grow. Instead of resisting the emotion, lean into the feeling. What happens when you open yourself to it? If it had a color, what color would you give this feeling? Let go of rational thought. Explore, play along. Whatever comes up for you is exactly right.

Take a moment to investigate the emotional consistency of the charge you feel. Feel around its edges and underneath it. What consistency would you give it? Is it hard? Heavy? What shape is it? Here, you're beginning to make the emotion tangible and accessible.

Now, if the emotion had a sound, what sound does it make?

Give your emotion a sound. It doesn't have to make sense.

- Remember the moment, *where* you were, *how* it made you feel, *what* was going on when you gave this feeling meaning?
- What do you hear?
- What kind of sound does this emotion make?
- What do you notice about the sound?
- What does giving the emotion a sound do to the feeling?
- What sound does this emotional suffering make in your head?

Now, give the feeling a voice. If this feeling were speaking something directly to you, what is it saying? Drop down into a deeper type of "listening" and hear what this feeling really speaks to you. How old does the voice sound? Is it a man or a woman? Notice everything. All of it is useful information. All of this offers threads for you to begin to pull apart this tapestry.

We call engaging a construct and loading a holographic-like experience activating the charge. By now, if you're engaged in this process, you're immersed in your work. If so, allow yourself to feel all of the connected feelings rising within yourself. You're doing great work.

If not, no biggie. Go back and rerun the first part. You're looking for an uncomfortable feeling. This will provide you the opportunity to feel uncomfortable, therefore, you can then investigate your discomfort. Breathe into your suffering and allow it to come online fully.

Now is not the time to resist. Now is the time to persist. Now is the time to stop running.

Step 3: Embrace Safe Space

Now, let's load up some protection. Remember, your mind is designed to keep you safe. You have to teach it to work *with* you. Think of this protection as a layer to keep you from re-living anything your mind considers too intense. Remember, the mind makes a horrible master but makes a fantastic servant. When your mind is actively protecting you from a judgment you hold, it's impossible not to have a blind spot. Therefore, giving your mind a layer of protection makes the dive into the depths of suffering easier to manage.

Prompt: Imagine you are sitting comfortably in a movie theater. Picture yourself in a movie theater.

- Where do you like to sit?
- Did you bring popcorn and soda?
- What do you take with you to the movies?
- See yourself there now. Ready?

Now, imagine the lights going down and the curtains open up. As the veil lifts, you see on the screen a scene you know all too well. You are safe in the theater as you load the following prompt onto the screen.

Step 4: Seek the Root Identity
Prompt:

- When is the earliest time you remember feeling this way?
- What is the earliest moment of the emotional experience where your mind feels safe enough, trusting you, to work with the emotion right now?

Remember, you're safe in the theater. Remember, healing requires you to allow yourself to venture to that moment safely. Remember, you can't heal what you don't allow yourself to feel.

Now is the time to descend, go down to the root and find the open loop echoing in your life. Here is where you have the understanding to close the echoing circuit. It's time for you to take the fruit to the root. Trust the process. Trust the safety of the theater. Trust what you have felt and what you feel. And now, on the screen where you first came upon this feeling, deeply investigate the first time you remember taking on this message?

Play the movie out in your head.

Step 5: Transmute through Awareness

Prompt: Now that you brought safety in, INVESTIGATE the origin of your emotion in its gory color.

To change a form, we first must know its real name. Now load up the construct onto the screen before you. What is the plot, story, emotion, decision, identity, and belief you gave meaning to in that moment? What nightmare did your mind present to you on the screen?

It is typical to experience details surrounding the event. Those details may be intense. As you investigate, notice the thoughts you carried:

- "I just imagined what he was thinking."
- "What was it that you were imagining?"
- "I imagined what it must have felt like."
- "What did you imagine?"

Feel through all of this exploration. This is an important step in your healing. It's essential to identify and feel what came up. Locate where the pinch in your consciousness happened. Here, your goal is to wrap your mind around the "charge," allowing yourself to fully associate with what that charge is doing to you. In other words, do the opposite of "spiritual bypassing," tend to the wound with intention rather than a sparkly bandage.

Consider these questions:

- What is the feeling that comes up for you when you watch your other self on the screen?
- What's the story you made up in this moment?
- About Yourself? What identity did you take on?
- About the world? What beliefs did you learn to take for granted?
- What was the judgment that came online at that moment?

From a safe perspective, bring your awareness into this dark place. When will you ever again come this far to come this far? You're here now. You're doing fantastic work. Again, feel your judgments.

Feel around the roots of the emotion, feel around within yourself, notice what it feels like when this construct comes online. Feel around within this construct. Check your pockets, so to speak. Place your awareness entirely inside the container of this moment in time.

Now consider:

- What you notice about this space?
- Notice how your narrative changes. Does the space in your head shrink or expand?
- Notice any identities which came online here. Did a victim identity take root?

Notice any emotions your little person had difficulty carrying.
The goal here is to align and allow.

You have already begun the healing process just by bringing in your awareness. As hard as it may be to believe consciously, have faith that your healing process has begun. Can you hold space for yourself right here? Some part of you is just waking up and beginning the journey home. Next time you experience the same charge into the present, you can process the experience from a different perspective. You will have a deeper understanding of where it originates. You bring light to make your unconscious conscious, teaching yourself to respond instead of react.

If you've done this process before, is there something deeper you've yet to realize? What more can you become conscious of? Are there more emotional parts of you, which still need tending?

Now, hold onto this moment. Look forward to that part of you which was recently triggered. Back to this timeline when you recently felt this construct come on, back to the surface of your life. There is a whole bunch of gold right here yet to be mined.

How are these two moments related? How has the construct of this memory cast a shadow on the surface of your life? Can you recognize when you get triggered how a part of you activates and warps your reality?

When you are triggered, what have you programmed yourself to do?

Look along your timeline to discover the times when this identity within you is triggered and comes online.

Look at how deep you go. Notice how much of you operates by navigating around this wound.

Notice how brilliant this part of you was to protect yourself in this situation. Repeat after me, "Thank you, mind, for keeping me safe."

Now this is an important next step.

Notice what that part of you yearned for? What was the thing you most wanted and needed after the trauma to heal? Don't assume. Allow yourself to plug back in to all of this. You need it all together for the next step.

What did you need to grow up and live in your power and genius?

What would it have meant to you and your life had you received what you needed?

Let's give you a way to identify this construct with a name. Did you have a nickname as a kid? Ideally, it would be one that lets you see this little person for the unique identity they were to you. Also, I invite you to not choose a mean nickname. This part of you has been beaten up enough So, if you gave this little person a nickname, what would you call this part of you?

Resetting and Releasing Deep Construct

Take a deep, grounding breath. As you exhale, visualize a screen in front of you, playing out a scene haunting you from your past. Now, imagine holding a remote control. Press the pause button. Freeze the screen. Rewind the scene to a moment *before* the inciting incident occurred. Let the image rest there.

Feel the ambient temperature around you. The sensation of the chair beneath you. The gentle rhythm of your heartbeat. Ground yourself in the present. What month is it? What day is it? What time is it? Take a moment to observe your surroundings, the colors, the objects, and any signs of life. Then, come back to the present.

By following this exercise, you might already feel weight lifting from your shoulders, even before delving deeper into this healing process. Recognize how the scene on the screen is a mere fragment of your past, and you are here, now, in the present. Allow yourself to leave the emotional baggage of that old memory behind, focusing on *now*. Shake off the remnants of that memory, shake it off the same way animals in the wild shake off stress after a high-intensity event.

In the vast expanse of our consciousness, there are moments when we find ourselves trapped in the whirlwind of past traumas, memories, and emotions. These moments, though intangible, hold a significant grip on our present, often dictating our reactions, decisions, and overall well-being. But what if there is a way to navigate through this intricate maze of the mind and find a reset button? A way to release the pent-up energy and return to the present moment, revitalized and free?

In the wild, animals have an innate ability to process and release trauma immediately after experiencing a threat. This is called an autonomic reset. For example, consider a deer. After narrowly escaping a predator, the deer doesn't carry on as though nothing happened. Instead, it goes through a physical process to release the trauma. Starting from the tip of its nose, a visible tremor runs through its body, traveling all the way down to its hooves. This shaking is not a sign of weakness or fear—it's a natural mechanism to discharge the intense surge of survival energy and reset its nervous system.

This behavior is not unique to deer. From birds to mammals, many animals exhibit this post-traumatic shaking. It's their way of letting go of the "charge" from the traumatic event, ensuring they don't carry that stress with them. By shaking it off, they release the pent-up energy, allowing them to return to their natural state of balance and calm.

Humans, however, have lost touch with this primal ability. It wouldn't be uncommon for someone to be shamed for shaking due to fear. Instead of releasing traumatic energy, we often hold onto it, allowing it to become embedded in our psyche. This retention is largely due to the constructs we form in our minds. These mental constructs, often created as a way to make sense of, or cope with traumatic events, trap the emotional and energetic charge of the trauma. Over time, these unprocessed constructs accumulate and run unconsciously in what can be referred to as our "deep conscious." These constructs influence our behaviors, reactions, and even our health.

The challenge for humans is to find a way to access and reset these deeply ingrained constructs. Just as a deer shakes off its trauma, humans need a mechanism to release the stored energy from past traumas. This doesn't necessarily mean physically shaking (though somatic practices sometimes use physical movement to address trauma), in sessions with psychedelic medicine we can observe the behavior as anything from yawning to giggling. It can be as pronounced as screaming and as inconspicuous as stretching.

Now, it's time to harness the energy you've been cultivating and channel it towards healing. Engage fully in this process. Take a moment and walk around, shake off any lingering tension, and ground yourself in the present.

Remember, healing is a journey, not a destination. It requires trust, commitment, and a strategic approach. The mind, being the complex entity that it is, needs assurance. It needs to know you can handle the emotions, memories, and traumas it presents. By proving you can shake off the past and return to the present, you earn its trust, paving the way for deeper insights and profound healing. Embrace this process. Remember, every step you take is a step towards a brighter, freer future. Now, let's meet the medicine.

Step 6: Introducing Your Sacred Identity

The next step is to introduce this part of you with the sacred part of you that solved the equation—your sacred identity. If the external opportunity arose, you would offer this part of you as medicine. This is the whole nature of the loop we get caught in. You would find yourself compelled to offer support, like a hero compelled to slay a dragon. One way to clear a Shadow is to uncover the identity that comes from a place of grace towards others. However, we are looking for a specific grace.

By leveraging our own solution to the problem, we give ourselves the very medicine we became to solve the problem. Because some part of us becomes the person our little person would have most felt safe with. We become the people that we would have felt safest with. The call to adventure, hard coded in your system, would draw your medicine to the surface. Sometimes, it's hard to see, but it's there. By noticing you are the person you have been waiting for, you realize you are the only one who can heal yourself of the patterns that have you stuck. The purpose of your suffering has always been to end suffering. Let's start by ending it at the very source. It reclaims energy spent managing Shadow by tending to it. It's not enough to understand this step. The magic only sits in the subjective experience of what comes next. You must embody it.

You are looking for the identity you created to right the algorithm your mind has been running.

Prompt: When was a time you were the medicine for someone else's suffering? It could have been with a stranger in a public place or an intimate meeting with someone close. It can be a massive moment for you or as simple as giving change to a homeless person. What you're looking for is a time when you noticed someone felt what you were feeling back when you were in suffering. Look for a moment when someone showed up feeling unloved, unsafe, unsure like they didn't have a voice and you were there for them. You're looking for a time when you were there for someone, and it mattered in a way that resonated with what you needed as well.

It doesn't have to be dramatic or hugely significant, although it can be. You only need the specific construct, which exists in your holographic-like experience.

Whether it is big or small, makes no relevance because your rational mind weighing in has little value in this process. The scale you're using is stuck on the other side of the Shadow cast.

We are looking for Kairos-time. A moment when you felt "on purpose," like you were grateful you could be there in a specific way for someone—a time when you were a catalyst. You were the soul friend, the Anam Cara, showing up for someone when it mattered.

You're looking for a sliver of a certain kind of shift. What was it you noticed? Did you see it in their body or their eyes? Was it a thank you? Perhaps it was when you witnessed their life shift. Load that very threshold moment you realized, "Yes, I was on purpose."

Go into the face of the threshold of the moment and load up what it felt like to channel grace and hold space for someone else. Feel what it felt like when you realized they got it. What is the feeling running through you at that moment?

Load up this construct and feel around in your pockets. Orient yourself spatially. Activate this construct.

Consider:
Where are you at that moment? (Outside, a house, what room?)
What day was it?
Day or night?
What are you feeling?
Where do you feel that in your body?
Does your narrative expand?
What is the mindset of this identity?

Go back and load up your narrative. What are you saying to yourself in this moment? What's the new story?
What are you feeling?

Touch this part of you now. Take a deep breath into that part of you. Feel what it feels like to be the hand of grace.

What does it feel like?
Color?
Shape?
Consistency?
Give it a sound? What does this fantastic feeling sound like?
Give it a voice. What's the message this feeling has for you and the world?

Speak the message out loud. Breathe deep into this construct and fully embody this part of you. It has an equal right to exist within you, same as the victim identity. Feel it.

Now, give new this sacred identity you created and cultivated a name. This is a powerful tool. You have a powerful identity you've been unconsciously expanding. What would happen if you consciously developed a relationship with this perspective and identity? Imagine if you allowed yourself to come from this part of you all the time. Wouldn't that be interesting?

When does the dog become the family pet? When you give it a name. Your internal identities are similar.

Allow yourself to embody this identity entirely. Notice how this identity exists in you always. Notice it is always here for you to load up and raise your vibration. Invite this part of you to come online more often.

Step 7. Gain Liberation

This is where you get the gold. This is where the game changes. This is the process to close the circuit. Give yourself what you have been yearning. That action creates a feeling of completion. You gain a sense of ownership over yourself. You can put different meanings in place. That action rewrites your core story and levels it up to something more empowering.

The place is here. The time is now. Time to tend to the Shadow being cast upon the surface of your life. Align your programming to bring you to the true guru of your life—YOU. Today, you are not settling for the surface answer. Today, you heal.

Now, this is vital.

STAYING IN YOUR SACRED IDENTITY allows you to maintain your identification with life and your primary point of reference. In your mind's eye, step back into the theater. Look back to the movie screen. Do you see the little person on the screen? Imagine your sacred identity stepping into the screen. Like the hero you are, step into the scene where your lower identity is trapped.

Now, does your lower identity see you? How do you know? What is the expression on their face?

What has to happen here? Staying in your sacred identity, ask what has to happen here?

Sacred Identity, what has to happen here? How do you bring love and healing into this construct? Sacred Identity, you know them better than anyone, what is your lower identity yearning for? What did your younger self pray would happen?

Now is the time. Sacred Identity, give to the lower identity what they need. Consider:

Do you need to free them from their prison? If so, free them now.

Maybe they needed to hear they were good enough. Tell them what they need to hear.

Perhaps they needed to know they were loved. How can you show them that now?

See the genius in them, the innocence. Notice a light glowing within them.

What grace has been withheld from this part of you? Now is the time.

Now, let's add something more to this process.

Reach down and hug this part of you.

Now, as you do this, I invite you to wrap your arms around yourself as if embracing your little one. Imagine them between your arms and send love into this little person of yours. Think of how old they are; think of someone you love who is that age now. Squeezing tighter, send pure love to them until they "get it."

Now, step into the identity of your little person. Take on their role in this vision for a moment. Watch as your sacred-self steps into the scene. Listen as sacred-self tells you everything you desperately yearned to hear.

Notice how sure they are about what they say.

Notice the brilliance of this powerful identity in front of you.

Notice how this brilliance comes through you.

Watch as you now experience the message coming in, however, from the perspective of your little person. Allow yourself to feel and open yourself up to the words this sacred identity has for you. Permit yourself to "act as if." You pretend in ways that suck, so what's the risk of allowing yourself to believe something worth believing.

Now feel them hug you. Feel the same amount of love you remember, enveloping you now. Squeeze your sacred-self back as if you are actually in the scene. Allow these two constructs to combine and create a collaborative experience beyond words. Drink as much of this experience as you can right now. Your level of permission to allow here supports your ability to see the thread of work "in-theater" in your life.

Feel your emotions in your body. Notice the places that are lifting. Give the words of this sacred agency. Belief is a powerful thing. In the deep conscious, it only takes a mustard seed. Allow the expansive mindset of sacred identity to be experienced by the trapped part of you.

How does loving yourself here in this way change things for you? Notice what you gain. Now, step back into the body of your sacred identity. Step back into this divine construct you have cultivated and open your heart. Allow yourself to be open to receive love. See how this part of you received your love. Open your heart and invite this part of you back into your heart. Let them enter and come home again.

If they say resist, honor that response. Whatever they want is *perfect* because you know now who they are. They know who they will become. Notice how you access the little you. The next time you're triggered, you will understand—this construct is seeking your sacred identity. Because your sacred identity flows from the very thing you are desperate to obtain. Also, notice there is a third part of you that chooses between the two identities. YOU.

Feel what having this part of you consciously online does for all parts of you. See how these are identities you programmed to live your life through them. Now you finally have the agency to choose how you feel and show up in the world.

Step 8: Acknowledge Transmutation

It's time to go back and review and analyze. This part of the process offers affirmation. Sacred confirmation is always a good thing. Let's check in. Did you feel something shift from this process? If not, follow through again with the active imagination process.

Notice what you *are* feeling. This is all you. You brought all of this. Notice how powerful your mind is. You either train the mind, or you get trained by it.

Today, you trained your mind.

Stop for a moment and take an action to anchor this feeling within you. Something as simple as a little dance or some ice cream. How do you feel about your suffering story now? How has it adjusted as a result of your work?

Remember, this is *all* a process.

Permit yourself to be "in process" and *not* "in completion." Completion never happens. Always recovering, not recovered. You are always living, not lived.

Step 9: Take Action (Integration)

Your strategist is coming online now. It wants to show you the importance of the rubber hitting the road. It wants me to tell you how much money has been wasted by people maintaining a problem to which they have already been given a solution. Without integration, nothing you do to change yourself will stick.

Learning to shift your axis mundi in theater is empowering. Integrating the shift into *Now* is the activation of that power. Being empowered and learning to act on that power are two different conversations.

In the meantime, what can you do to cultivate more of your sacred identity? I suggest spending time in contemplation around this part of you. Load your sacred identity, and go order a coffee fully embodying this part of you. Do things that strengthen your association with this identity. You will find the relationship improved more and more as you do this work.

230

Integration is necessary; even the most potent journey is only as good as the integration you're able to accomplish.

What can you do to bring your sacred identity online? And when it matters? Try looking forward in life and see the places where the old identity came out and the new one can come online; moving through a higher identity gives us depth of insight and choices. It's not about putting a sparkly band-aid on your feelings; it's about widening the identity you are coming to them from.

What can you do to integrate these two identities?

Can you see this higher identity showing up where the lower identity used to?

Now, as you transition from sacred space and move back to the tangible world, the process continues. Look around the room. Allow your consciousness to descend out of the flow of higher thought. What day is it? What time of day? Where are you? Feel the temperature of the air and on your skin. Recognize it as it registers in your mind. Feel your body as it is being held up right now. Be in your body.

This is where you integrate what you learned.

There are certain truths. Neurons that fire together wire together. Without doing the work to connect these two identities, the work won't take hold. This is called integration. Integration is taking an insight, plan, or strategy and implementing it into the realized world. It becomes part of the structure of whatever relationship you want to improve. It's the transformation of your internal insights into tangible change.

This metamorphosis typically links directly to the profound work you've undertaken. You might weave this transformation through SMART goals or immersive in-theater processes. Integration takes time. Think of integration as your pen and now it's moving in a different direction than the one you had previously programmed it to write the experience of the story called *you*. The power lies in the fusion of your newfound wisdom with action.

Prompt: What will you do to bring to fruition what you now know to be true? What will you do to support the new insights taking root in your realized world?

Consider spending ten minutes, three times over the next week, loading up your sacred identity and then Turning Within to reconnect these two identities together. The results are typically magical. This action will deepen your work's impact in your life. Insights not integrated remain a daydream. Knowing where your loop of suffering originates isn't power. Integration of awareness and change is what you seek. Perhaps you finally take time to do the work just past the comfort zone where you're stuck, noticing the emotions as you move in the direction of your sacred self.

Step 10: Embrace Ongoing Growth

How will your life change by cultivating meaning from the newly created identity, rather than living from the lower identity you had unknowingly and unconsciously programmed to bring online? Really envision how life will change—both the positive and the negative.

What will change?

How will life be different?

Imagine your life with this higher identity coming online by choice.

Imagine ten years of cultivating your sacred identity. Even through difficult times. Especially through difficult times. What change is felt in the good times? What will your future look like?

More on this aspect in a second. First, I want to ensure you recognize and are cognizant of every step of the process, giving you the ability to deepen your practice of Turning Within. By learning to practice these strategic dives, you grow more competent at recalling more of the running constructs. The more faith you put in trusting the process, the more insights this process will reveal to you.

I look forward to hearing the stories of how closing the circuit works for you.

At this point, it's appropriate for you to close the container you opened when you began this process. Say a prayer, release your intentions, and blow out the candle.

I hope you found a sliver of healing. This process has provided countless others, who have practice it, a step forward. If you desire to go deeper, please visit the Mastering Change website for one of the iGroups.

Bless you.

Chapter 16

Closing the Circuit—Fruit to

Root Process Breakdown

Identify the Charge:

We start with zero because zero embraces all possibilities. Here is where you have the opportunity to realize the overall story where you're stuck.

Navigate to the Trigger:

Zoom in on a specific memory. Press "play" on a memory.

A single impactful moment is the only place to begin. "There was this one moment when…" and then allow your mind to guide you back into that moment.

Visualizing the Charge:

Reflecting on emotions with sensory elements such as colors, shapes, textures, sounds, and voices enhances the mind's ability to track and comprehend complex emotions and experiences. It's like giving the mind a more user-friendly map to navigate the intricate landscape of your emotions. Once the light illuminates the darkness, the dismantling of Shadow's power over us begins.

This method doesn't just offer you the opportunity to explore your mind's depths, it strives to accomplish healing with focused intent.

Embracing Safe Space:

Revisit your personal theater. This is your safe space. You're the audience, watching your own story on a screen. It's a buffer, a way to experience your memories from a distance. This ensures your emotions don't sweep you away.

Remember, prioritizing safety is fundamental for the effectiveness of your practice. Once you mind registers how you've created a secure environment, the process becomes more accessible to you and you will yield better results.

Guides trained through Mastering Change have cultivated various methods to establish this sanctuary. Just as life perpetuates life, safety cultivates healing.

For a smoother start, I recommend immersing yourself in the theater visualization during your initial attempts until you become at ease with navigating this space. You can omit this part of the process when you feel more comfortable.

Seek Root Identity:

Think of your emotions as streams flowing inside you. You're tracing these streams to their origin, like tracing back a river to find its source—where it all began.

By flowing into the memory, and then taking a step-by-step approach, a potent technique emerges to assist you in tracing the charge back to its origin where it originally imprinted.

This approach prevents the overwhelming surge of emotions that can arise from confronting the issue head-on.

As you navigate your memory flow, you uncover the thread to the pattern where you're trapped. It's astonishingly simple, so much so, that the mind occasionally resists simplicity, leading to momentary hesitations or mental dancing.

You may find it beneficial to have a skilled guide to hold space and keep you anchored in the process. It's akin to having a companion hold a flashlight while you explore the caverns of your mind, helping you stay on track and in the moment.

Transmute through Awareness:

By reviewing the memory within the secure haven of your container, you unlock the samskara submerged beneath the surface. It's an opportunity for you to harness the potent healing of your own awareness. It's crucial to approach this with compassion and love for yourself, as these are the healing balms which mend the wounds of your past.

This process bridges the past and the present, allowing you to revisit charged constructs without becoming lost within them.

You gain the ability to recognize when you're in the shadow and identify the triggers that set your Shadow in motion. You finally connect the dots on the *unwanted* reactions.

It's here that the power of sacred confirmation becomes palpable. Your actions are no longer disconnected. They become linked to a deeper understanding. Denying this connection is no longer an option; you're now aware of the mechanics behind your reactions.

Resetting the Narrative:

After diving into the depths of your mind, you resurface. It's like coming up for air after a deep swim. You resurface to the 3D world.

At this moment, a valuable lesson is taught to the mind: the ability to transition in and out of those charged states. This process of reorientation emphasizes the flexibility and adaptability of the mind—your mind. Jot down any newfound awareness, a moment of reflection and integration, before delving further into the journey.

Introducing Sacred Identity:

By delving into our mind's intricate workings–like uncovering the code of a sophisticated computer program–we unearth a technique for tracing our experiences through our projection.

At times, discovering a positive charge might feel as challenging if a person's life has been overshadowed by negativity. In such cases, you can project the qualities of a cherished figure, perhaps a grandmother who emanates warmth and security.

The pursuit here involves identifying that pivotal moment in our life's timeline when we emerged as the answer to our younger self's silent plea. We embody the nurturing figures our inner child longed for, even though no paths have been crossed yet. In this context, the positive construct will nullify the negative, much like opposing electric charges cancel each other out.

Revisiting instances when you were provided specific support and received with open arms rewires these experiences in astonishing ways. Once again, you'll discover the potential to shift your entire system, leveraging simplicity to transform the complex.

Labeling Identities Brings Power:

Often, many of us stumble in and out of our sacred identities. This is akin to wandering through the mist because we haven't meticulously defined our sacred identities, which results in a disconnect from the profound aspects of ourselves we aspire to embody. Therefore, these higher identities, laden with wisdom and potential, often remain elusive because we haven't fostered a conscious relationship with them.

By intertwining sacred confirmation with these specially designated identities, we construct an internal compass, making our journey through life's twists and turns more navigable. Think of it as building a bridge between your conscious intent and your unconscious tendencies. This process of conscious identification isn't a mere exercise; it's a way for the mind to recalibrate, aligning with the higher versions of ourselves that beckon us forward.

In this manner, we provide our mind the tools to realign itself. As we do so, we realize our mind, ever eager to restore balance, begins to harmonize with this newfound higher identity. As a result, through conscious identification, we set the stage for improvement as our mind naturally inclines toward equilibrium.

Gain Liberation:

Step into the realm of "Liberation," a name that resonates with its transformative essence. Here, we witness sacred alchemy as the radiant light of insight tenderly unravels the dense threads of shadowy confusion.

In this step, we fuse our sacred identities with the prior aspects of ourselves which we may have labeled as "lower." You connect the fruit of who you needed to become for your lower identities to the root of suffering, unaware that you are now who you are.

You're closing circuits within narratives that held sway over you for decades. This breathes new life into your stories that were once tangled.

As you grow in your practice of Shadow Work and Turning Within, liberation moves beyond being just a concept to an experience illuminating your journey. Here we witness the profound dance of soul retrieval, where fragments of ourselves, long lost in Shadow, are lovingly reclaimed.

This process reunites you with genius, talents, and wisdom from which you unwittingly distanced yourself. As you emerge from this step, you stand on the precipice of liberation, bearing witness to the magnificent tapestry of existence woven anew.

Acknowledge Change: (Transmutation)

Prompt: What has changed about the situation that triggered your shadow? How might you respond differently in various situations? Go back to a scenario that triggered you previously and see how you show up now. Notice any difference? Lean towards noticing how you were impacted through any awareness you picked up.

Visualize the transformation—a life reborn, you're a phoenix rising from the ashes. Envisioning such change as the groundwork, laying the cornerstone for the shifts you aspire to experience.

Remember, once seen, it can never be unseen. You are your witness. Embrace this revelation as you proceed.

Take Action

This begins the transition from sacred space and your internal insights to the tangible world. The journey continues, all ways and always. This metamorphosis typically links directly to the profound work you've undertaken. You might weave this transformation by creating SMART goals for yourself: SMART goals are Specific, Measurable, Achievable, Relevant, and Time-Bound, or engage in an immersive in-theater processes.

Embracing Ongoing Growth:

Reflect on the concept that insights not yet integrated remain wisps of dreams. The power of liberation and transmutation lies in the fusion of wisdom with your action. Knowledge isn't power; knowledge is the potential for power. Activation of awareness is power.

This journey of Turning Within melds the wisdom of psychological and spiritual realms into a structured, introspective odyssey. By assimilating these guiding principles, you can embark on a journey of profound narrative transformation. This expedition will guide you through the labyrinthine depths of your shadows, leading you to nothing short of a metanoia.

The Mirror of Projection: Illuminating the Shadows Within

In the vast expanse of our universe, every particle, every wave, every flicker of light and shadow is interconnected. This interconnectedness is not just a physical phenomenon but a profoundly spiritual experience. It's a dance of energies. This interconnectedness becomes even more profound as we journey deeper into our understanding of Shadow.

In the texts of this book, you've journeyed through a candle metaphor, understanding its etchings and how it would keep itself safe using the Shadow it cast. Now, you have the opportunity to delve deeper into the realm of projections. This is where the external world becomes a mirror reflecting a person's innermost Shadows. Close your eyes and visualize what it would be like to live inside a magic lantern with the same dangerous loop etched into it.

Now go back and see the pattern you etched.

Do you know or understand the origin of the etched pattern?

We've been taught to seek external solutions for our internal discomforts and use consumption to manage Shadows. Our way of life has conditioned us to be consumers. But what if the true path to understanding, to liberation, isn't about consuming but about Turning Within?

The Illuminati of Your Love

Remember from the beginning of this, you read: this book isn't meant to be read, it's meant to be experienced? This is another reminder.

This is where a pause may be helpful.

This is where it all gets real.

Sometimes I jest about the "big brother" or the "Illuminati" pulling the strings behind the scenes in our lives. The truth is more remarkable, more potent than any lizard alien could be.

I am my own personal Illuminati.

I am the one I am looking for.

I play hide and seek with the dark hidden part of me, searching, searching, searching.

What if the real conspiracy isn't external but internal?

I discussed personal conspiracies earlier in this book, however, what if the demons and enemies you perceive are merely projections of your own making?

The truth is your love is what you are most afraid of. You begin healing when you see the love hiding under your judgment. The only way a judgment has any weight is if you care.

Imagine for a moment that every person who has ever caused you discomfort, every situation that has ever challenged you, is a teacher in disguise. What if they hold a mirror to the very judgments and shadows you've been unconsciously carrying? What if, instead of adversaries, they are guides, pointing you toward the areas within yourself that need healing and understanding? What if the trigger could lead you to a treasure?

Shadow as Your Guru

This is the essence of projection in Shadow Work. Every external conflict and charge is treated first as a reflection of an internal struggle. As you continue to permit yourself to be a student of shadow, you develop an understanding of Talbot's Holographic Universe.

Here's the beauty of Shadow: these projections, these mirrors, are gifts. They offer you a chance to see yourself more clearly, understand your shadows, and heal. Without the pain, the systems you are locked behind continue to run to keep you safely tucked away inside the judgment matrix. By recognizing your projections and seeing the mirrors for what they are, you are offered the opportunity to take responsibility for your shadows, own them, tend to them, and ultimately transform them.

Only then do we learn the secret: We project *everything* we experience. Even the light.

By learning to transmute Shadow, you're changing the nature of you, learning to understand the structure of a more significant part of who you are as a person and also who you are as a species. This transformation is the doorway to another great frontier.

These specific lessons can't be taught. They must be experienced.

This experience opens you to a whole new level of life.

As you sit at the precipice of deeper understanding, I invite you to take a deep breath. Feel the sacredness of this moment, acknowledge the new understanding you have already established.

You have embarked on one of the most profound journeys of your life—a journey into the heart of your Shadows, the cave you most fear.

You have entered into another leg of this journey we call life, which brings us to the third rule of Shadow Work.

You have woken up from the dream you forgot you were having.

Remember
This book isn't meant to be read; it's meant to be experienced.

Chapter 17
Third Rule of Shadow Work: Every charge begins and ends with me.

I give you this here because I hope you can tangibly feel a sliver more of your growing understanding of you within the work you're doing. The deeper you place your trust in this statement, the more it will liberate you.

This is one of those rules I had to learn to trust more than my story. Every charge begins and ends with me.

Notice how you have realized some of your triggers and then bravely walked through some of them. It is safe to assume that whatever freedom this book has helped you claim for yourself will look similar moving forward. An excellent Shadow-Work process can lead you to deeper and deeper insight.

Only shadow makes something unchangeable. This rule has served me time and time and time again. I constantly work to automate it. If I can hold onto that specific awareness and not forget its validity, my charge about a situation or someone or something teaches me how I set myself up to suffer. That suffering can take on more shapes and sizes than there are people in my life. If I hold on with soft hands and learn to hold space for myself, I can tend to the part of me that has swallowed a lie and then the construct created to protect me, a samskara. This creates a chance for me to see what's behind the veil.

Once you learn to trust the truth of this rule, you develop a deeper understanding of yourself. You will recognize how you repeatedly cycle around the same suffering identity all because your mind craves patterns. It's the more elegant way to support an ever-evolving mind.

The Fifth Facet of your construct of reality is your emotions or energy. Check in with yourself right now. How do you feel? Mad, sad, glad, scared, or disgusted (shame)? You are able to, and often do, have more than just the one feeling. Examine your emotional home, reflecting over the past several weeks. Can you see your cycles? What has been the consistency? What type of identity is the character who lives within that charge? Yep, what kind of narrative does that character live out of?

When you're practicing your check in, and then allowing yourself to own the creation of your emotions, you take away the agency of the story. This puts you behind the driving wheel of your experience. You can't stop a car when you're seated in the back. You can slam on that imaginary brake, but nothing happens. Therefore, stop backseat-driving your life. Grab the wheel of the charge you're wrestling and then you have a story that goes along with the charge.

You could spend your entire life practicing and researching just this one rule, and it would be well spent.

Before enlightenment, chop wood, carry water; after enlightenment, chop wood, carry water. ~Zen Proverb

Now, let's sit with the understanding of projections of the mirrors that surround us. Let's honor the teachers, the guides who have been placed on our path, and let's prepare ourselves for the deeper understanding which awaits.

Remember, every charge, every emotion, every conflict begins and ends with you. Let this be your guiding light, illuminating the path ahead, as you advance on your journey.

Integration Supports Evolution

While guiding a seeker through a transformative journey, she frustratedly exclaimed, "I feel so terrible; this should be easy!" I gently reminded her, "I never promised ease, only simple."

Then she turned inward, tending to the shadow casting its terrible shade. Growth is a challenging endeavor, often taking longer than anticipated and rarely ever manifests as we envisioned it in our mind. The essence of this book, Turning Within, is accelerating the evolutionary process on an individual level, yet its aim is for a global ripple effect. Right now, mankind is on the cusp of a quantum leap reminiscent of monumental events such as landing on the moon or Oppenheimer's creation. This shift promises a global metanoya. You are participating in a worldwide initiative to re-learn an ancient way of upgrading consciousness.

Recall our discussion on the mind's structure and its three directives. The primary one is creating meaning, a task we're perpetually engaged in at every level of our consciousness. Then, though the survival directive is rooted in ancient instincts and rapidly adapted to modern times, we are turning the tide. The elegant process of evolution drives progress. As we evolve collectively, so do we individually. It's a symbiotic relationship. Evolution is a tool to transmute suffering, with integration as the linchpin.

Integration is the Goal

I started practicing this Shadow Work over twenty years ago, but it took me ten years to begin to focus on the integration process. Initially, the experience of liberation captured my interest. I was hooked on the sweet nectar produced from chasing an insight through the threshold. I became hypnotized by the pressure released from walking through moments of clarity. It was seductive, and I got stuck in a loop of chasing the pressure release. The fractal experience of being trapped, being projected on the very medicine I leveraged to break free.

I remember going through a clearing with my tribe. This process is designed to help wipe off a projection we are placing on everyone around us. I couldn't see it. My charge: none of them were changing. They were still showing up the same way I had seen them show up for the ten years I had been practicing this work. "None of you are changed!" I blamed.

Little did I know, I was operating under the Shadow of a construct. I was the one not changing. Looking back, the truth is crystal clear. But at the time, I swore that they were the problem.

I projected my frustration with *my lack of integration* into the greater community. They all sat holding the mirror up for me as I tried desperately to peer into issues. That's all any of us can do. At that moment, I realized I needed to understand this integration process. I had been sent on a mission to try and understand the bridge between idea and realization.

I spent the next ten years studying strategic implementation in business at every level. I dove into what caused change to manifest and stick in the most intimate of problems. Change became so much more. I awakened to the truth. Integration wasn't what the weekly coaching sessions were about. I went to pluck and to collect the insights in those sessions, but until I implemented the insight into *my* life, what I had was theory or an idea, like any other idea unrealized in my life—a possibility or a daydream. A more appropriate term for those session could be insight groups and not integration groups. I could gain insights into who I am, how I operate, and what this work can unleash. But integration became another whole other game altogether.

Understanding Integration

Integration is the art of embedding profound experiences into our daily existence, ensuring these moments of transformation solidify within our core. It bridges the chasm between profound realizations and everyday actions. Just as food nourishes the body only when digested, experiences enrich the soul only when integrated.

Today, I still engage in integration sessions for my personal growth while supporting others. The value of any experience will never exceed its usefulness. In Shadow Work, a single session can reveal insights which may resonate for months or even years. Your willingness to hear the truth is your only limit to the depth of realization.

The Essence of Integration

Integration fosters personal evolution, ensuring our transformative lessons will indeed shape our growth. It's akin to tuning a long-neglected piano; one session might bring harmony, but consistent tuning ensures a lasting melody. Imagine a piano straight from the factory and never being tuned, all because it didn't *know* it needed adjustment. Now imagine a whole world of those pianos. In your imagination, can you hear the off-tune discord of those instruments?

Shadow Work offers us a unique lens through which to view life. These insights yield consistent results *with* integration, building trust over our mental constructs. As our integration deepens, so does our understanding. Through deepening our integrations, we learn to trust the process more than the story we've created in our minds. New associations are created, which bring new experiences—life changes.

Strategic Integration

Turning Within introduces practitioners to strategic integration, which is a systematic approach to assimilating lessons. This strategy compounds insights through a systematic process of reflecting on your experiences, discussing them with your trusted peers, and applying insights in real-time is pivotal. Particular challenges are inevitable, for example, the fading intensity of experiences or confronting deeply ingrained beliefs. Yet, with a supportive community and consistent practice, these hurdles you encounter become stepping stones to deeper understanding.

In essence, the true worth of any experience is realized through its integration. An insight left un-integrated is akin to an unopened gift.

Integrating Closing the Circuit

Over the countless Turning Within seekers who helped pave this process, I've seen as many different integration pieces as I have individual pieces of work. Each process is a person's intimate journey into the interior of their meaning-making machine. Your integration will be equally personal and unique. It will serve you best if it's tied to an uncovered need.

Are you able to pinpoint where you're at with any particular piece of work and journey in your life?

Is there some simple action you can create which will be a symbol of your new understanding?

Can you follow a couple of tips to help with integration?

The goal is to cultivate a realization of the experience you want, seek, desire.

We learn to let go of old meaning and reach for something that gives us a richer reality experience—using a construct as a lens to deepen association—we leverage our mental structure instead of fighting against it.

I readily recommend you spend time through the week connecting with these two identities inside you. You conditioned yourself to see the world through your lower identity. Therefore, it may take time for you to orient to a higher unconsciously.

You may need to consciously choose in-theater a couple of times for your mind to understand that this change is really how you want to show up in life. Resistance is normal for the mind. Just like bringing your car out of a groove in the road, you can navigate your mind out of old beliefs and start to move away from the lower-vibrational experience altogether.

Integration Process Suggestion

Find a comfortable place where you won't be disturbed. Create a space for you. Load up your sacred identity, and then have your sacred and lower identity build a stronger connection. This is similar to Jung's active imagination, but with a strategic focus on connecting the part of you which gives what you're seeking to the part of you seeking it. You connect the fruit to the root.

Examples:

One seeker loaded up her sacred identity, Sunshine, three times a week for ten minutes. She brought light and love and honored their vibrations. Then, she would go down within and meet with her lower self. Together, they would dance through the house because she had felt blocked in her feminine energy. Her integration exercise included dancing and flowing exercises. Those actions worked the muscles that made stepping into her femininity easier. Then, when she was in-theater, she found herself less blocked and flowing in her natural energy.

Another seeker would load up his sacred identity, Brilliance, and Turn Within to go down to connect with his six-year-old self. His six-year-old held a feeling of worthlessness. As a result of that emotion, he became a *human-doing,* trying to balance out the feeling of worthlessness. Living out of this Shadow nearly killed him. Everyone thought he was successful. He felt miserable. For him to heal and connect, he did not need to do anything. He had to learn to be with himself since Shadow drove his need to constantly *do* in order for him to feel worthy. Prior to Turning Within, nothing he did had any worth. After learning to Turn Within, anything he did took on an entirely different meaning for him.

Finding a way to integrate your Shadow Work practice creatively can lead to profound understandings. There are no accidents in Shadow Work. You practice holding space, letting go and trust the process.

By now, you should have encountered, absorbed, gleaned insights. Let's see if we can find a way to integrate your lessons into your everyday life. They will fade if you don't work to make them part of your daily life. Not attending to that which you've learned gives your foundation an expiration date. After which, you'll have to cycle back and take another pass at the same work. How will you choose to integrate the excellent work you have accomplished so far?

One of my clients is working with Ayahuasca. He reports visions of transmuting bad energy during ceremony. He said he could feel the power of the other participants and saw himself pulling the bad energy out of them like pulling out blocks. I had him Turn Within and load up the construct of the transmuter within him, asking him to remember what it felt like to be that identity and then, I directed him to rerun the storyline. "Go to the moment right before the act of transmutation. Remember what it felt like to go through the threshold of becoming." I then had him overlap that feeling of transmutation with a difficult relationship he had in his "realized" world.

Results! The mental block constricting him in that relationship dissolved. This is integration.

Embracing Ongoing Growth

Integration and implementation are the cornerstones of our work. Together, they dramatically speed up the change process. I stress the word *process* because there is a lie keeping us stuck in suffering. Now is the time for us to bust it wide open.

You're not going to take a pill, find a coach, take a workshop, read a book, or download an app that has the power to turn you into someone or something you aren't. Nothing will produce change for you—but you. You are the guru of you. Always have been and always will be the overseer of you. Nothing outside of you will ever have more answers than you will have inside for yourself. The challenge is giving yourself the necessary space to understand the depth of the direction I am pointing you to. This is why I implore you to develop a practice.

A Practice of Turning Within

Webster's Dictionary defines a practice as:
2a: Systematic exercise for proficiency.
2b: The condition of being proficient through systematic exercise.

By developing a practice of Turning Within, you create systems in your mind to check your work. When those systems automate, magical things begin to happen. A Shadow Work practice implemented in your life will completely shift your life's trajectory. The Turning Within style is built to uncover your wellspring of genius and offer you the opportunity to tend to the sacred grove around it—all a part of you. Turning Within is soul work.

While finishing up the last part of this book, I found myself on edge. My Shadows got louder the closer I got to writing The End. I was so constricted when I reached this point, I couldn't even watch movies with drama or tension. My feelings would knot up inside me. I had support, elders calling and checking on me. I was clear on what my mind was telling me. I was living in the constant judgment of every person I could imagine and feeling a range of emotions.

I've learned to process and sit in ceremony when things get too great. After a confirming and beautiful ceremony, I sat on my back porch, focusing on what I had been shown. My backyard runs up against a wooded area, and I like to imagine it as the edge of the known universe. There is a massive tree which reminds me of how small I am. That tree and I have shared many tears.

As I sat, just holding space for myself, I watched as a giant yellow butterfly made its way across my yard. I watched it flutter through a light breeze. Its beauty and frailty struck me. I wondered how the butterfly would structure its experience. A thought experiment emerged in my mind. What if "struggle" wasn't a quality I could choose? It has the same data but different meaning.

Suddenly, my mind flashed my problems. I smiled. My Turning Within practice is about learning how to process differently.

My experiences, my journey, my commitment to my practice of Turning Within gives me flexibility. My mind is learning to hand over teaching through the poetry of the butterfly. I open myself up to learning. I set the container. I drop into my work. I take the time to slow down. Integrate. In an instant...deep sigh.

I am able to notice how I structure my journey across the yard of my life. I see how I stumble. My voice raising, the qualia I am floating in is like the wind the delicate butterfly goes through. My meaning tells me time is short. It tells me I am off course. It tells me the wind is more than wind, it's the judgment I chose to carry. The butterfly's meaning allows it to fly. A question looms greater than a storm cloud above: What does my meaning do?

In my practice, I allow myself to feel. Tears flow. Pain. Purging. Prayers. Then my acknowledgement.

I love you.

I am sorry.

Please forgive me.

Thank you.

Suddenly, I wonder where my winds can be reassociated as something that lifts me up. I recognize I must let go of a judgment I carry about myself. I find my judgment—it's the philosopher's stone.

The magic in this world can be found in a butterfly's wings. Now, my mind doesn't consistently deliver these lessons so beautifully as my butterfly experience. I still hear many of my lessons as judgments to be passed, not beliefs to release. The mind will hide judgments and then defend itself against itself. However, I am confident my consistent practice is the reason I was able to grasp this lesson and provide healing for me, to me.

The practice of Turning Within is the practice of becoming. It changes you through reorienting your association with life. It clears a path for you to something more real than anything you ever associated with *real*. With your practice, you finally activate the seed that is your soul, begin to tend to the roots supporting the fruit of your genius, and bring it forth into this world. Turning Within is about becoming a person who comes from within. It's a reassociating, a reidentification.

Consider a house. A house divided will fall. You are the same as a house. However, when the bones of the house are good, you realize how you have a structural foundation of worth and value. Thus, you as the house are exactly what you have been looking for—and *now* you know how and where to find yourself.

Dancing in the RAIN

Turning Within is not a one-time endeavor. It's an ongoing journey, a continuous practice. It requires dedication, awareness, and a willingness to delve deep into the recesses of our psyche.

As you navigate the complexities of life, your Shadows—those hidden, repressed parts of yourself will often manifest in unexpected ways. You must cultivate a consistent practice to effectively engage with your Shadows in order to foster genuine healing. For the fundamental change to happen within you, at some point, you must choose to move in a new direction. When you find yourself in the in-theater rendition of what you are struggling with you are offered the opportunity to make a different decision.

Remember, the *idea* of change doesn't make a difference. You must act on your new awareness to make changes. To support your change, I have developed tools to help you integrate your new path into your life. The R.A.I.N. process is one of the most potent tools for your ongoing journey. The most challenging part of Turning Within is shifting. It's you, taking the road less traveled.

I've spent a lifetime leveraging the perspective of some of my wounds. I couldn't expect myself to overcome them overnight. I grew up on dirt roads in the Midwest. Through overuse or when it rained, the roads developed grooves. The grooves are a path. Those grooves become a bigger and bigger influence on the journey. If you're driving on a dirt road where tire tracks are deeply etched, every time your wheels get next to the pre-worn grooves, your tire will naturally want to slip back into those same grooves. Your mind is the same way. Here's what to do:

R - Recognize that you are in Shadow.

The first step in any healing process is recognition. Before you can address your Shadows, you must first acknowledge their presence. This might manifest as a sudden surge of anger, an inexplicable sadness, a nagging feeling of discomfort. These emotions and your reactions are indicators, signposts pointing towards deeper, unresolved constructs. By recognizing you are operating from a place of Shadow, you have the chance to take the crucial first step toward understanding and healing. By coming into awareness, you engage the cornerstone to change. Awareness. In your awareness, you wake up from the dream you forgot you keep having.

A - Allow or Accept.

Acceptance is the bridge between recognition and transformation. The longer you practice, the more you rely on grace to teach, guide, and heal you. Authentic grace is what you must first offer to yourself. Once you've identified a Shadow, your instinct might be to suppress it, to push it back into the depths from whence it came. However, true healing begins with your acceptance. As the saying goes, "You can't heal what you don't feel."

You initiate the healing process by allowing your feelings to surface and permit yourself to fully experience them without judgment. It's essential to understand these emotions are not your enemies, no matter how uncomfortable they are. They are messengers, bearing tales of past wounds and unresolved conflicts. By listening to them and allowing them their moment in the spotlight, you pave the way for genuine healing and transformation.

I - Investigate (Algorithm for Closing the Circuit).

With recognition and acceptance in place, you move to the investigative phase. Here, you delve deep, probing the origins of your Shadows, seeking to understand their genesis. This is where the *real work* begins. Here, you explore the root causes of your reactions and emotions using various tools and techniques. For example, why did a particular comment trigger such a strong response within you? Why does a specific situation evoke feelings of insecurity or fear?

By investigating the answers to these questions, you unravel the stories, beliefs, and past traumas that feed your shadows. The Closing the Circuit process allows you to address more than symptoms and then transmute deep down, deep down, within your meaning tree. The deeper your work, the greater your shift can manifest.

However, investigation brings to you the awareness of what needs to happen. Without the next step, you will continue to perpetuate your loop of suffering.

Once you grasp awareness, there is an interesting dynamic that comes online. It's a significant clue into the structure and meaning of your reality. When you learn to recognize and lovingly and meaningfully accept this part of you, then, you will finally hear what you have been trying to say and understand what you need to support the mission of love and life. This is you within the transmutation process.

N - Nurture or Need

The final step in the R.A.I.N. technique revolves around nurturing. Once you've identified and understand your Shadows, you must address the underlying needs that fuels them.

Often, our shadows stem from unmet needs—whether it's a need for validation, love, security, or understanding. By identifying your needs, you can begin to address them, offering yourself love, compassion, and understanding, those feelings you've been externally seeking. This self-nurturing is transformative.

Our reliance on external validation diminishes when we learn to fulfill our deepest needs. We begin to operate from a place of self-love and self-worth, fundamentally altering our experience of life. This is our Axis Mundi or our sacred center. It is not a thing that can be found; the more you search for it, the less you will have. You can come from it and never realize it. You can spend your life chasing after it and never catch it.

I had a student who came to me because she experienced moments of high tension when dealing with anyone in authority. This energy, for her entire life, had caused her to shrink back in critical moments. When she finally chose to Turn Inward and identify the construct from which she lived, she realized her shrinking back, shutting down began early, when she was a small child. She learned to survive by NEVER OUTSHINING THE MASTER!

Of course, those words were never what she told herself. Her mind automated authority and master as danger. For reasons of love much deeper than most care to hear, because the decision was too painful to make the first time, why would she ever review it? Then the mind continues its beautiful game of *"AND SO,"* but without that part of the decision tree ever being addressed.

Until her ceremony, she was managing circumstances. Now, begins her journey to grow through the suffering. The ground shook when she woke up to the lie she'd been telling herself. Demons were slain. Victorious, she held the sword. She identified where the decision to suffer was made, after which, she can go to where she shuts down and then move forward. This is where healing can happen.

Now she understands what that little girl needs, she nurtures that need. By supporting her reclaimed voice, she learns to bring compassion to herself. Yet, its done in a way that cultivates through her and to others. She has stopped feeling abandoned because she stopped abandoning herself. She embraces knowing she is not only the medicine she needs, but also what the whole world needs through her.

Instead of operating out of a sense of loss of power everywhere, she is now full. She knows her power. She uses her power. She has discovered that situations which used to trap her no longer bind her power. Now, she remains poised and present. She knows *where* her voice is and *how* to use it.

A victim who finds their voice becomes a heroine. She sees everything happens for a reason, which serves her meaning.

This is the game: Learning what the universe is calling through you.

What's being called is not through the sacrifice of loving yourself, instead it's through a basic understanding that you can't give anything except what comes through you. You must realize your primary relationship is with you. Learning to love yourself can be difficult. Yet, it will rock the foundation of everything you call *real*.

What are you giving yourself to share with others? Giving needs to be through you, rather than at the cost of you. Painful sacrifice is not real love. Real love nurtures. Real love says, "I am special, and so are you."

This doesn't mean the change is easy. Living as though you're safe in the lie is a crappy story. "Easy is safe" is an illusion. Take a risk. Take the hard road. Take the chance to learn to love through you and not at the cost of you or anyone.

It's harder…. Way harder. However, the rewards are endless.

Remember
This book isn't meant to be read; it's meant to be experienced.

Chapter 18

The Power of Community in the Work

As we reach the closing stages of our journey within this book, it's essential to reflect on one of the most critical tools to practice Shadow Work: The Power of Community.

The Accelerated Path: Learning from Others

One of the most potent aspects of a community is the opportunity for accelerated learning. When you're part of a community, you're not solely learning from your own experiences, but also from the experiences of others. This collective wisdom can significantly speed up your process, allowing you to avoid pitfalls and reach more profound levels of understanding quickly.

The Monday night open circle, time and time again, has proven to participants how they're able to experience growth through the work of another seeker. So much so, the group now thanks the person doing their work in the middle of the room, for being our teacher. We individually come to Shadow Work to learn and then realize our learning manifests via a beautiful collaboration when we plug in the medicine of community.

The Safety Net: Support for the Unreachable Shadows

While Shadow Work is a profoundly personal journey, there are certain aspects of our Shadows we cannot reach on our own. These are the deeply buried fears, traumas, and insecurities that require a supportive environment in order to surface. A community provides this safe space, acting as a safety net when we venture into dangerous, shadowy terrains.

For example, shame is a complex and debilitating feeling. It's not simply the belief that something is fundamentally flawed within us. It's a paralyzing fear. We believe that if others know about this flaw, they would confirm our worst fears. This is where the role of a supportive community becomes invaluable. In a community of individuals committed to Shadow Work, you find a mirror reflecting your shadows and your inherent worthiness.

This mirror helps you see through the lies you've been telling yourself. It offers you a more balanced view of yourself. With a community built around trust, openness, and inclusion, it can be a safe place to set down your sword and finally see through the illusions. Illusions which kept you blocked and stuck in cycles of suffering and spirals of shame. Some wounds seem to heal best in community. Especially if that is where they began.

The Value of a Tribe

I formed a group with a specific purpose: to create a community of guides, guides who come together to research and study the impact of shadow globally, and interact as intimately as possible. This tribe holds gatherings where members dive deep into the layers of consciousness often obscured from our daily awareness. These gatherings are not just academic exercises, but spiritual quests. We listen for the voice of something grander that transcends our individual selves. The tribe serves as a living laboratory for Shadow Work, offering a unique blend of scholarly research and experiential wisdom. It's a community where the collective quest for understanding meets the individual journey for transformation, enriching both in the process.

Community is medicine. We, as humans, are structurally built to plug into other humans on a deeper level beyond the surface where we usually operate. If Shadow Work teaches us anything, it teaches there is an unseen and non-negotiable connection between individuals and everyone they meet. You don't "see" it because you are more than the awareness bubble you sit in. A community or tribe can support your work, It offers you the possibility to delve into challenging places, places you might not reach going solo.

The Return: Sharing the Elixir

As you come full circle in your Hero's Journey, the final step is to return to your community with the elixir of wisdom you've gained. In the context of Shadow Work, this means sharing the insights, tools, and strategies with those you hold as a community and contributing to the group's collective wisdom. This sharing enriches the community and reinforces your understanding, solidifying the transformative power of your journey.

The power of community in Shadow Work is multi-faceted. It's a mirror, shattering the illusions of shame. It provides an accelerated path for learning. It acts as a safety net for the unreachable shadows. And finally, it offers a platform for sharing the wisdom gained, completing the circle of the Hero's Journey.

As you close the pages of this chapter of your journey, remember your journey into the shadows may have begun as a solitary quest, however, it's in community where you'll find the richest soil for growth, transformation, and, ultimately, for the return to your most authentic self.

You share your newfound wisdom by becoming your authentic self and learning to open to the genius emanating from within.

Love is the Key, Love is the Rosetta Stone, Love is the All

Love is the Key

In my third Ayahuasca ceremony, a message reverberated through every fiber of my being: "Love is the key. Love is the Rosetta Stone. Love is the all."

Like other messages that came to me through any healing medicine, this learning revealed itself to me in layers. I heard, saw, and felt as though I was being yelled at in every facet of my experience. Yet, it still took me four years to understand what was being transmitted.

This message, delivered by the maternal energy I felt during the ceremony, has since become a guiding principle in my life and the cornerstone of my personal work and my work with others.

"Love is the key" is a universal truth transcending dogma, culture, and personal beliefs. Love is the answer to what ails us, the salve for our wounds, and the light which guides us through the darkest tunnels of our mind.

Removing any block preventing love from flowing through you is something worth your investigation This is true no matter how high up the spiral you rise. You as in yourself. You, as in your people. You are in the world. All the way up and all the way down, love will never make anything worse. Embrace this truth and use it in all things.

We are free to operate from our Axis Mundi. We gain the ability to bring our life into more profound meaning. Our purpose comes into play, and our deeper power comes online.

Where Is My Joy?

The first question is, "Where is my joy?"

Stop for a moment to ponder, how connected to joy do you feel in your life? How much joy are you able to allow in this moment? Not happiness, but true joy. Happiness is fleeting, but joy can be found in the darkest places. Do you feel disconnected from joy that comes from simply being alive? If so, something is likely blocking your connection. Think of it like a pinching-off in an unseen plumbing system of consciousness.

What judgment is stealing your joy in this construct? Could this be a judgment of some part of yourselves you disowned, ignore, or suppress? A protection mechanism becomes a prison. It holds you hostage.

Remember, "Every charge begins and ends with me. I'm the only thing blocking me from my experience of joy. Once I do the work to get under the charge, I can clear it and finally experience a life with deeper meaning." Pause for a moment and check-in with your joy for life. In the context of Shadow Work, this blockage is often a Shadow aspect of ourselves which we haven't yet integrated. What is the story you tell yourself that steals your joy?

Your goal is to associate with the disconnection or the pinching-off experience when you operate from shadow. You can often see the depth and consistency of your work by how much you are blocked from your joy.

What Blocks Love Here

The second question is even trickier: "What keeps love from flowing through me?"

Another way of asking is, "What within you blocks the face of love in your life?" This is the place of your real suffering.

Many people externalize their experience of love, making others responsible for it. This leads to a disconnected and erratic experience of love. Your goal is to allow love to flow through you such that you love others through the love for yourself. That is healthy love: "I love myself enough. I don't need to take. AND SO."

This awareness may have a profound impact on you right now. Maybe you find yourself waiting for others to love you. Perhaps you find yourself giving, but never receiving. You find yourself on the martyr identity over and over.

Can you see the disconnect here? *You* are your primary relationship. If you have no care for yourself, you have no care to give to others. Love like this becomes transactional, a tit-for-tat game that rarely ends well.

Incidentally, it's a fool's errand. I call it "The Jerry McGuire lie" of "You complete me!" has caused many people to fall into the trap of the archetype of the twin-flame myth. Whenever you come to any relationship incomplete, you are putting the burden of your completion on another person. The trap is sprung. Your feeling of incompleteness becomes the monster who chases you in the relationship. I guarantee, you will never satisfy a Shadow by external means. Shadow can only be tended to by Turning Within and seeing how *you* are the one you've been waiting for.

This is usually done unconsciously and in a moment of pain.

How often have you unconsciously acted out, "I'll show them love when they learn." You hold back the best version of yourself until you witness the behavior that justifies it, only to discover how your holding back was the cause of losing the most important relationship—The ideal version of you.

Take a moment, go into your most intimate relationship, and ask yourself, "What is the block I carry that keeps me from the face of love?" Examine how you carry the weight of that prompt. Feel how the weight of it calls you to wake up and stretch into some unforgotten part of your soul. You always have the opportunity to choose love.

What if you decided to flow with love right here, right now, in this place? What impact would that have on your relationships? How would that change how someone you love experiences you? It's time to let go.

Sacred confirmation is a powerful tool. Notice where the block is to loving from a centered or whole place. Each step is vital. You must be connected to your love to be able to give love. Permit yourself to love through you. Then you have: AND SO.

Love is the Rosetta Stone

When we find what blocks us from flowing in love, we will uncover something that can't be transmitted from any book. We also begin to understand what blocks love from flowing through others as well. And because we've tended to our wellness through the practices and tools that place us at the center of our healing, we can now effectively support the unblocking of others' wellness. Our love becomes something that isn't a contingency. We teach others this same lesson… Because, well, monkey see, monkey do.

All of these concepts build up the compounding effect of understanding how love is stuck. Then we realize it was love that caused love to be blocked. We recognize the cosmic joke.

Love is the *All*.

Love is not simply a key or a deciphering tool, it's the essence of everything. It's the light signature of your unique genius. It's the dream you're designed to manifest in the world. It's the ultimate driver of the meaning-making mind. Love is the underlying code in a faster, deeper, and more connected world. It is the ultimate directive.

When love flows through you, it illuminates every corner of your life, casting out Shadows holding you back and revealing the ever-present miracles waiting to be discovered. It's the elixir you are bringing back from your hero's journey, the treasure that makes all the trials and tribulations worthwhile. As you are able to bring this potent elixir to those you love, healing is passed from person to person.

As I heal, you heal.

We all become stronger.

In the telling of our story, we go from victim to hero, walking through the darkness to reveal light and love only felt by standing strong against the darkest nights. Each piece of work we tend to makes us a little more aware of how we create our reality and where to find what we genuinely seek.

I wrote this book for it to be your rally call to a life lived in love with yourself and the world around you. Let this be the signal light changing green, the permission given, the moment of realization for you to begin/continue or confirm your journey home. If you are reading this, yes, you *are* right where you need to be.

Finally, I end this story with an ask.

Right now, take a moment to stop, and in your mind's eye, imagine a space with a multitude of people, all hugging each other out of pure, innocent, unconditional love. Imagine this space in your mind, where countless people are sending love to each other right now. This space sits out of the manmade construction of time. It exists in the mind, which is beyond time. As my final research ask, please, imagine all of us readers beyond time in this process, sending each other unconditional love. Open up and give.

Now, in your sending love, realize we are sending love right back to you. Now, open more. More. More.

I'm curious about what a cuddle-puddle created out-of-time and space will do. Because at the end of the day, all any of us desire is a hug.

May you receive that hug now.

The Cosmic Inside Joke: A Journey Beyond Belief

In the vast tapestry of our lives, interwoven with beliefs and narratives, some moments stand out—moments of profound clarity that reshape our understanding of reality.

Every hero's journey has a pivotal moment where the Hero stands at the precipice of change. This moment, often referred to as a "threshold moment," is a turning point that propels an individual into a new phase of their journey. It's a moment of profound realization, a sudden clarity where previously held beliefs or perceptions are challenged, leading to transformative growth.

Threshold moments can be both subtle and monumental. They might come as a chance encounter, a dream, a loss, or even a simple understanding during a quiet moment of reflection. Regardless of their form, these moments are characterized by a profound internal shift. These shifts act as doorways. They lead us from one state of being to another. They are often accompanied by a surge of emotions ranging from exhilaration to fear.

The power of threshold moments lies in their ability to disrupt our status quo. They can redefine the very structure of how we make sense of reality. They redefine aspects of ourselves or our beliefs that we might have previously ignored or been unaware of. In doing so, threshold moments they offer us an opportunity to grow, evolve, and step closer to our true selves.

May this book be that moment for you, and my hope is you will create your "*Cwtch*."

The End.

Acknowledgements

I want to thank my mother. Everything begins and ends with you. I love you.

For my cherished wife, Valerie, thank you for putting up with all my crazy wonderings and for breathing life into me. I love you.

To Linda Joyce, my friend, editor, and, in many ways, midwife of this book, for her genius, encouragement, and support. Thank you for being a light through this entire process. I had no idea it would take this much from me and everyone around me.

Andrew, Heather, Anaeli, Jason, Bob(s), and Kathy thank you for sifting through the manuscript when it was little more than a muddle. Your suggestions and support proved vital.

To all the brothers and sisters on this path who were generous and trusting enough to share their inner landscape and hero's journey with me. I hope that this book continues our conversations and moves them to another level.

Tony Robbins, thank you for giving me ten years of leadership, mentorship, and teaching. Working for you was a game-changer for this Iowa boy. You gave me the space to expand my research beyond problem-rooted thinking and stretched my understanding of human potential. You taught me to chase the possible.

Thank you to the whole RRI family for showing me that I could stand next to giants, for teaching me the value of pushing past the surface of life, and for giving me a home.

To all my gladiators, thank you for teaching me the blessing of integration. Through you, I learned how to use my voice. Through you, I learned implementation.

To the groups practicing the spiritual practice of anonymity, especially the friends of Jimmy and Bill; it is hard to express the love I have for a com-munity that pulled me from the mouth of the pit, especially when anonymity is the spiritual foundation of your program. Thank you for saving my life. Any blessing I receive comes through you.

Blessings to all in the MKP brotherhood, especially those wizards who spend so much time with me. If I have or will staff with you, thank you for being my teacher. The TIGER group, Thursday night, The Central Plains, Florida, Colorado, and Heartland Communities, specifically, for carrying me through some real dark night of the soul. Thank you for the work. Thank you for introducing me to myself. I studied with more genius than I could name individually. To attempt it would be shadow.

To all my little brothers in Boys to Men, thank you for teaching me how to listen and reminding me how to dream. You are the lesson I strive to learn. Thank you to Craig and Joe for creating such a powerful program and the men who hold space for young, powerful men. You taught me I was worth believing in.

To Gene McNaughton, Bob Berger, Don Clements, Tom Jaynes, Joe Sigurdson, Greg Gondron, The TIGER group, Scott Humphrey, Dr. Scott, and Craig McClain, thank you for your mentorship beyond the professional and into something else.

To those on the front lines of plant medicine, thank you for your imprint on my work and for your work with plant medicine. You gave this vision the rich soil it needed to break through the darkness. Thank you for being the charging tide in the wave of change. Being the first out the door is never easy.

Acknowledgements

To Mother Aya, Mary, and mushroom and other plant medicine for their humility, grace, healing, and love. To the curanderos and medicine workers Carlos, Teresa, Miski' Taki', Tata Pedro, the Huni Kuin, and Yawanawa tribes for learning and keeping the language of medicine. Thank you for keeping your way and sharing the path with myself and the rest of the modern world. Now is the time.

To all the past, present, and future seekers, facilitators, guardians, guides, volunteers, and coaches. All of your work is vital for the continued integration of modern society. You are the bridge society must cross. Thank you all for holding space for me personally and for our whole community doing this great work.

To the Shadow Tribe, your willingness to do your work has helped me break through barriers I never knew existed. The raw and unbridled acceptance you cultivate has rekindled my love for community in a way I thought was extinguished. I look forward to seeing where this experiment takes us. You continue to teach me so much. I am not sure how to thank you other than finishing this book. You have become my home. This book is a testimony to the effectiveness of what we build. Valerie, Jeffrey, Henry, Rita, Yanira, Sheila, Jamie, Nielsen, Tim, Michelle, and Virginia, for holding the chicken wire together with your bare hands while we twisted it into form.

To those I project my story on and negatively impact in any way, especially my kids and those I love: I love you, I am sorry, and please forgive me. Thank you.

God bless you all for continuing to carry me home.

Acknowledgment of Resources contained within this book: This book could not be possible without the invaluable insights and teachings of these giants on who's shoulders I stand. My hope is that you take the time to deepen your understanding by diving into the genius of these teachers.

(Movie) Jaws
Alvin Toffler
Barbara Fredrickson
Beyonce
Brene Brown

Carl Jung

Chris Rock

Dr. Stephen A. Diamond

Eckhart Tolle

Greek philosopher Heraclitus

Jada Pinkett Smith

James Clear

Jonathan Gottschall

Joseph Campbell

Marc Gafne

Michael Singer

Michael Talbot

Napoleon Hill

P.D. Ouspensky

Peter Levine

Ram Dass

Ryan Reynolds

Scott Olsen

Stanislav Grof

Steve Jobs

Timothy Wilson

Todd Herman

Toko Pa-Turner

Tony Robbins

Tsultrim Allione

Will Smith

William James

About the Author

Steven Twohig's journey through the landscape of human consciousness is rooted in twenty-plus years of dedicated Shadow Work. His odyssey has taken him from the trenches of personal struggle to the strategic planning rooms of the business world. His broad application of Shadow Work spans from personal recovery efforts to the nuanced dynamics of executive leadership, demonstrating the universal relevance and transformative power of facing and integrating one's shadow.

His comprehensive approach has touched every conceivable demographic, from individuals striving for peak performance, those seeking strategic insights for success, entrepreneurs seeking business growth, to those overcoming homelessness, and also the varied explorers of plant medicine's profound healing potential.

Steven's work is not just about understanding the complexities of Shadow Work. His ability to translate deep psychological concepts into actionable strategies for diverse audiences sets Steven's work apart. His expertise lies in making profound inner work practical and applicable, ensuring transformation is not merely a solitary experience, but a part of one's daily existence.

He has leveraged his platform as an international speaker, coach, and guide to deepen his understanding of human dynamics, shadow, and conscious evolution. He's the creator of Mastering Change, https://masteringchange.com, a centralized hub, synthesizing all the teachings he believes are effective in creating deep and lasting transformation.

Born in Omaha, Nebraska, and raised in Sioux City, Iowa and Dallas, Texas, Steven has lived in places throughout the United States. He served in the Army and earned his Airborne wings prior to his basic training. His path has taken him from serving as a Center Director for Boys to Men to working for iconic companies, including the Tony Robbins organization and Soul Quest as Director of Integration Services. Each step along his path has provided him with experience and educational understanding.

Steven is married and a father of seven children. His family has three cats and one dog who thinks he's a cat. One of Steven's loves in life is a great meal out with his family.

www.ingramcontent.com/pod-product-compliance
Lightning Source LLC
Chambersburg PA
CBHW011228120626
46549CB00008B/3182